Speed! Understanding and Installing Home Networks

Mike Wolf

SAMS

201 West 103rd St., Indianapolis, Indiana, 46290 USA

Speed! Understanding and Installing Home Networks

Copyright © 2002 by Sams Publishing

International Standard Book Number: 0-672-32186-6

Library of Congress Catalog Card Number: 2001089506

Printed in the United States of America

First Printing: October 2001

04   03   02   01   4   3   2   1

Trademarks

Warning and Disclaimer

ASSOCIATE PUBLISHER
Jeff Koch

EXECUTIVE EDITOR
Terry Neal

DEVELOPMENT EDITOR
Steve Rowe

MANAGING EDITOR
Matt Purcell

PROJECT EDITOR
Andy Beaster

COPY EDITOR
Cheri Clark

INDEXER
Tim Tate

PROOFREADER
Plan-It Publishing

TECHNICAL EDITOR
James Turner

TEAM COORDINATOR
Chris Feather

INTERIOR DESIGNER
Anne Jones

COVER DESIGNER
Aren Howell

Contents at a Glance

Table of Contents

PART VII Creating a True Digital Domicile

21 Smart Home: Home Automation Networks 351

22 The Coming Digital Domicile 367

About the Author

Mike Wolf is a world-renowned writer of research reports and technical books that have enchanted generations of people across the globe, and is the future writer of the great American novel. He has a fancy business degree from some school in Arizona and plans to someday make the Seattle Mariners roster as a left-handed middle reliever with his deceptively fast 40-mile-per-hour heater. He also dabbles in puppetry and lawncare. He can be reached at homenetmike@yahoo.com.

Dedication

To Tiffany

Acknowledgments

Writing thanks to all those who have helped me in one way or another to bring this book together is a daunting task. The list is long and I'm bound to forget someone, so if I do, I apologize.

I'd like to thank the team at Sams Publishing who helped me take what was a good concept and turn it into a great book. Without the unwavering support of my Executive Editor, Terry Neal, this book wouldn't have gotten off the ground. I'd also like to thank my Development Editor, Steve Rowe, and Technical Editor, John Gosney, for their insightful direction to steer this book where it needed to go. Thanks as well to the help of Andrew Beaster, James Turner, Cheri Clark, Katie Robinson, and all the other great folks at Sams.

I'd also like to thank the many companies who helped provide the information necessary to get this book completed. While this list is by no means complete, I'd like to thank Karen Sohl at Linksys, Bradley Morse at D-Link, Paula Brici and CT Wu at SOHOware, Patrick Lo at Netgear, Dan Sweeney at Intel, and the good people at SonicBlue's RIO division. Also, I'd like to thank the folks at Waggoner Edstrom for helping me get information on Windows XP before the public release.

Thanks to my family and friends for their support during this process, including Shannon Pleasant, who has been a great editor and a better friend, Cameron "Corky" McClurg for his technical prowess, and my parents for their constant support and unbridled enthusiasm. It's because of them I didn't (thankfully) go into the mime arts. Lastly, I'd like to thank my wife and best friend, Tiffany McClurg. We've been through hell (otherwise called the Arizona desert) together, and some pretty good times as well. She has been a constant beam of light in my life ever since I met that long-haired girl almost 10(!) years ago, and now she's the mother of our new baby boy. I love you, Tiff, and here's to the rest of our life!

Tell Us What You Think!

As the reader of this book, *you* are our most important critic and commentator. We value your opinion and want to know what we're doing right, what we could do better, what areas you'd like to see us publish in, and any other words of wisdom you're willing to pass our way.

As an Associate Publisher for Sams, I welcome your comments. You can fax, e-mail, or write me directly to let me know what you did or didn't like about this book—as well as what we can do to make our books stronger.

Please note that I cannot help you with technical problems related to the topic of this book, and that due to the high volume of mail I receive, I might not be able to reply to every message.

When you write, please be sure to include this book's title and author, as well as your name and phone or fax number. I will carefully review your comments and share them with the author and editors who worked on the book.

Fax: 317-581-4770

E-mail: feedback@samspublishing.com

Mail: Jeff, Koch, Associate Publisher
            Sams Publishing
            201 West 103rd Street
            Indianapolis, IN 46290 USA

Introduction

Here's the first and most important thing you will learn from this book: Home networking is easy. With the options available today for consumers, you can connect two or more computers to do such tasks as Internet sharing, multiplayer gaming, digital music distribution, and file and printer sharing, all with a basic understanding you will gain through spending a little time with this book.

How Is This Book Different from the Other Home Networking Books Out There?

Most other home networking books were written as if home networks were just small office networks, where we could simply take the same equipment and build a network similar to what we see at work. The problem with this approach is that the home is a very different environment than the office, where people not only want to work a little (or not at all), but also want to make their lives better through entertainment, communication, and the other potential applications of a home network.

This book starts with the home user in mind, understanding that you will want to have all the options available to create your Digital Domicile, from new wireless technology that allows you to connect computers without any cabling, to phoneline or powerline networking technology that takes advantage of existing home wiring. We also look in-depth at whole-home wiring systems, for those who might want to create a cutting-edge distribution platform for data, voice, and entertainment in the home.

Home Networks Are Not Just Hardware

Not only do we explore and explain how to install the wide variety of home networking equipment, but we also take an in-depth look at how to *use* your home network. We examine home network applications such as these:

- Sharing a dial-up or broadband Internet connection
- Distributing music or video around your home
- Playing video games head-to-head with others on your home network
- Whole-home communication such as home network intercoms and instant messaging
- Controlling your home systems and appliances in a true Smart Home
- Creating a secure home network, using the latest in Internet security technologies to protect your personal information

What Types of Computers Does This Book Support?

This book allows users of different operating systems—including Windows 95, 98, ME, and XP, as well as those using Macs—to create a home network using the latest technologies.

Who Should Buy This Book?

This book is targeted toward the beginner who has never picked up a piece of networking equipment, as well as those who understand basic networking but want to explore how to create a better home network and how to use the technologies to make their lives better.

So Let's Get Started!

If you're just contemplating buying this book, or if you've bought it and are still thinking about how you can possibly ever build a home network, it's time to stop hesitating and get started. This book was developed for those who want to build a home network and enjoy the benefits, not spend all their time tuning and tinkering with electronic gizmos. So stop procrastinating and let's get started building your home network!

Getting Going: Networking Overview and Planning

IN THIS PART

It's a Networked World

IN THIS CHAPTER

The Internet. The World Wide Web. E-mail. Ethernet. Wireless Communications. DSL. Cable modems. Buzzwords we've all heard and things many of us use every day. Although it might not be apparent from their names, these things have one thing in common: They are part of or related to a network.

Network? What's a Network?

So what is a network, you ask? No, its not the multilevel marketing business your neighbor Brad told you about last weekend at his barbecue (okay, so that might be a network, but not the kind we'll be talking about in this book). Think of a network as the connection between two or more devices. Don't run off; the word *device* does not mean a neuro-photonic asynchronous reassemblator—well, at least in most cases. It mostly means computers, from the kind in your den, to the slightly more powerful ones that might handle your e-mail at work, to those huge suckers that are doing the heavy lifting behind your favorite Web sites such as Yahoo or Amazon.com.

As defined previously, the network is composed not only of these computers, but also of special equipment designed specifically for helping all these devices to communicate. Remember the definition above: A network is the connection of two of more devices. What's doing the *connecting* is a special type of communications equipment. We won't go into detail this early in the book, but it is important to know that the things hooking up all these different devices have their own names and a whole industry of different companies (do Cisco and 3Com sound familiar?) that make their money making these pieces of equipment. Must be important, eh? Well, considering that without this equipment most businesses today couldn't operate nor could you surf the Internet for the latest Backstreet Boys interview (we won't get into why you would want to do such a thing), networks *are* important.

Many types of networks and communications equipment make up these different networks. Words like *Ethernet*, *Internet*, *DSL*, *Cable modems*—they all contribute something to one of these networks. (Or, if you're talking about the Internet, this is a network itself. In fact, as you'll find out later, the Internet is the *king of all networks*.) By the end of this book, you'll be able to impress your neighbors (including Brad) with your knowledge of these words. Oh yeah, you'll also be able to brag about your cool home network. This'll really get Brad to shut up.

Networks Are Everywhere

Most of us have heard of the Internet, and even the least technical of us had some sneaking suspicion that the Internet is some kind of network. But, as you just read, there are many other kinds of networks, some that interconnect with the Internet itself and some that just keep to themselves. Some examples of different kinds of networks follow.

Office Networks

A large percentage of the population work in office environments today. Besides keeping many of us from getting a decent tan, this type of daily activity exposes us to the networks many businesses employ today. Office networks work behind the scenes for those of us who use PCs to send e-mail, surf the Internet (get back to work!), and check the company's human resources or finance database.

Wireless Phone Networks

Many of us have a wireless phone that we carry with us almost everywhere. Some of us even have more than one. (Then there are those really annoying people who talk really loud on these phones in the movies. We won't talk about those people except to say that many of them are named Brad.) You might not know this, but the wireless phone that you find so handy is part of a large network. Large wireless carriers (or phone companies, to use an old-fashioned term) spend billions of dollars for you to be able to communicate on that wireless phone just about anywhere in the country (and for that matter, the world). Increasingly, the wireless network is intersecting with the Internet, with millions of people surfing the Web on their wireless phones daily.

The Good Old Phone Network

That phone that sits in the kitchen is part of what is the oldest network of all: Ma Bell's network. Yep, the phone system, while having changed quite a bit in the past few years due to advances in technology, is basically a communications network that allows you to shoot phone calls to Grandpa Nick in Florida from your house in Walla Walla, Washington. This phone network also communicates with the Internet, as you probably have done when using your dial-up modem to send an e-mail or surf the Internet. That weird squeaky sound you hear when you first connect is the sound of your modem translating computer speak (bits and bytes) into a language that can hop onto those old phone lines and then out onto the Internet. The sound you hear is an analog sound, which basically means nondigital.

> **NOTE**
>
> The world of computers and other electronic communication is a *digital* one. This means that the information that is processed is made up of essentially 1's and 0's. Don't worry, we won't ask you to learn how to transform the world of analog (everything that is not digital) into these numerals—just remember that this is how computers think.

Your PC is a digital creature. When it has to communicate over phone lines on a dial-up modem, it has to use the modem to translate its 1's and 0's to analog while it uses the phone lines; then when the information gets to your telephone company's local phone building (called a central office), it is received by another modem, translated into a digital signal, and zapped onto the Internet.

Powerline Networks

Believe it or not, the powerlines into our neighborhoods and homes not only transfer electricity, but also can be used as a network. And why not; powerlines connect to nearly every home, making this network even more widespread than the phone network. Industrial businesses use powerlines to let heavy machines transfer data about the work they are doing, and technology exists today that allows you to connect your PCs over in-home power wiring.

All this is well and good, you say, but what about my home network? Well, I'm glad you asked....

How Does My Home Network Compare to Other Networks?

So what about home networks? Those big industrial-strength networks that businesses operate on aren't the same as what you want in your home, are they? Well, they are different in that they handle much more information than any network in your home could handle, and they are much more widespread; the Internet spans all seven continents and has literally tens of millions of computers connected to it. The ordinary home network has two or three computers. And the Internet is not a single network like your home network, but instead is a large collection of individual networks that are all interlinked.

Home networks and the Internet are similar in that they use the same language to connect and send information. This language, or protocol, is called IP, which is short for Internet Protocol.

Note

Internet Protocol is the lingua franca, or language, of Internet communications. When you surf the Web or send an e-mail, this communication is translated into what are called IP packets, which are chunks of information that make their way across the network to their end destination, or IP address. Just think of an IP address as something akin to a mail-office address, because it serves a similar function in helping the information get to where it needs to go.

One key difference is that your home network, and many office networks, are what's called a local area network, or LAN. The Internet and large business networks that help people send information over long distances are called wide area networks, or WANs. In most cases throughout this book we'll be talking about LANs, but because it's likely that you will want to hook your home network up to the Internet, we'll also talk a little about WANs. But don't worry, we'll make it clear what is what. Take a look at Table 1.1. Here you will find some explanations and examples of important terms we will be using throughout our home networking journey!

TABLE 1.1 Network Terms and What They Mean

Term	What It Means	Example
local area network	A network in which communication between devices is a short distance	A network in your office or home
wide area network	A network in which communication between devices covers much longer distances	A nationwide network used by a large Fortune 500 company
the Internet	The world's largest network, which is a "network of networks"	You build a Web page and anyone can view it if they have the "Internet (or IP) Address"

One of the cool things about home networks is that they come in many shapes and sizes. In fact, whereas some might resemble the network used in your office (and might even use the same equipment), many use equipment designed specifically for home networks. Think about it: Your home is very different from your work, and is worlds different from the big computer centers that Yahoo uses to run its business. And what you do at home is very different from what happens in these other environments. This book describes the types of networks available for the home and how you can purchase, install, and operate these different networks. Talk about useful (you can see your investment in this book already paying off, can't you?).

How Does the Internet Compare to My Home Network?

In most cases, local area networks such as a home network will connect to the Internet through some form of Internet connection, such as a dial-up modem or a high-speed connection using DSL or cable modems.

NOTE

DSL is short for *digital subscriber line*. DSL is a high-speed, digital communication technology that allows you to connect to the Internet at speeds much higher than a regular dial-up modem using the same phone wiring you make telephone calls over. And even better, DSL can be used simultaneously with normal phone calls. Cable modems are also much faster than dial-up modems, but they communicate over the same wiring you receive your cable TV connection through. We will discuss both technologies in depth later in the book.

Figure 1.1 shows a chart that shows how a typical home network connects to the wide area network, or Internet. When the home network is connected to the Internet like this, it's possible to shoot information from your home to your computers at work in seconds, or even, if the Internet is not too congested, in less than a few seconds. We will spend a considerable part of this book talking about the ways you can connect to and share an Internet connection over your home network.

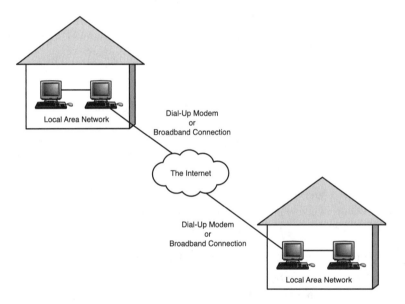

FIGURE 1.1
How typical home networks connect to the Internet.

So You Want a Home Network

At first it might not be apparent to the typical person why on earth they would need a home network. The conventional wisdom is that networks are complex and expensive and only guys with pocket protectors would ever consider one in their home. Let's assume, because you are reading this book, that you have asked someone you know about whether they think it's a good idea to have a home network. The responses likely were similar to one of the following:

- "A home network? What, are you crazy? Networks are incredibly expensive, way beyond the budget of anyone except Bill Gates. And even he had to sell a few shares of stock to pay for his."

- "A home network? You must be insane. They are complex and only qualified technicians would ever consider having the tangle of wires snaking through their house to all those huge humming boxes. Word is Bill Gates spent weeks installing his."

- "A home network? What on earth would you need one of those things for?"

- "A home network? I am glad you've discovered the secret to a happy and healthy life. How do you think Bill Gates became what he is today?"

So maybe the last one is a slight exaggeration (we can only assume). But nonetheless, it is safe to say that the likely response was one of the first three. Well, you'll be glad to know that you are not as crazy as these people would have you believe, that in fact you are an absolute genius for having the foresight to consider installing a home network—kind of like Bill Gates.

As you will see in part II, "Digital Plumbing: Network Wiring and Hardware Options," a basic home network is extremely affordable. A kit of basic networking equipment with all you need to hook up two computers can be purchased for less than $100 at your local computer or electronics store. Although not everyone has $100 sitting around, you will find that a small home network will produce big returns for your investment.

And as for complexity, we can only say that this isn't your daddy's network. In fact, Microsoft Windows and other operating systems have incorporated easily accessible networking capabilities that can make configuring a network extremely simple. Other operating systems such as Linux and those used on Apple computers also have built-in networking capabilities. Networking equipment and PC companies have realized that most people don't want to hire Larry the network manager to live in that extra room in the basement, so these companies have worked very hard to make things easy for people like us. Much of the networking equipment you purchase today is what they call "Plug and Play." You simply install the card in the appropriate slot in your computer and the computer will automatically recognize the card and install the appropriate software components, called drivers, that make the equipment work properly with your PC.

And what about that unimaginative person who seemed to think there couldn't possibly be anything you would need a home network for? Boy was he wrong.

Reasons to Own a Home Network

So, besides increased wealth, a slimmer figure, and being the envy of all your friends, why would you want a home network? Next, you will investigate reasons why almost anyone would want to install a home network in his or her home.

Sharing an Internet Connection

About 50% of the households in the United States have access to the Internet, and that number is growing every day. Of that group of 50 million or so homes, almost half have more than one PC. You add all this up with the fact that often different people in the same house want to use the Internet for research, paying bills, or plain old surfing at the same time, and you might develop a good, old-fashioned logjam. Although many of these PCs have their own modem and could conceivably connect to the Internet through their own ISP account and through a separate phone line, it doesn't have to be that way. With a home network, different users can access the Internet using the same ISP account. Figure 1.2 shows how a home network can be used to share an Internet connection.

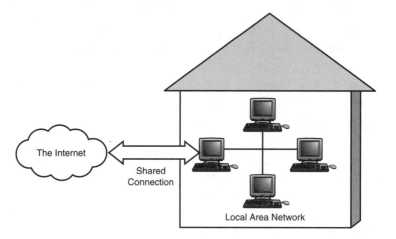

FIGURE 1.2

Share that Internet connection.

A high-speed connection such as a DSL or cable modem line (we'll explain the differences between the high-speed Internet choices in Chapter 14, "Internet Sharing on a Home Network") provides an even better experience because there is plenty of bandwidth to go around.

What's This About Bandwidth?

Bandwidth is a term you have probably heard. Bandwidth refers to the total amount of information you can put over a communication line or system in a given time frame. When people talk about DSL or cable modem, you have possibly heard terms like "1 to 2 megabits per second." Megabits per second, or Mbps, is a commonly used measuring stick for bandwidth, and you'll also hear it applied to different home networking equipment. One to two Mbps is plenty fast for an Internet connection when you consider that most of us are using a 56Kbps, or 56 kilobits per second, modem. One megabit is 1,000 times a kilobit. A 1Mbps cable modem connection is about 20 times as fast as a 56Kbps connection. Although all this might be somewhat confusing, think of it this way: A music file, such as a song by your favorite artist, might take up to 30 minutes to receive over a dial-up modem operating at 56Kbps. With a broadband modem, the same file might take only a minute.

Those who do have a high-speed Internet connection know that getting information from the Internet, sending large files to one of your coworkers, and loading Web pages all go much faster with a high-speed connection. Chances are if one of the PCs in the home has a high-speed connection, this is the most frequently used machine in the house. Why not spread the wealth with a home network?

And not only do you spread the wealth, but you save a little of your own as well. Cable and DSL connections are generally more expensive than dial-up, so using a home network to share this connection allows you to get more out of your monthly subscription fee to your Internet service provider, or ISP. Sharing the broadband connection also means you will need only one cable or DSL modem in the home. Without a home network, a second connection to your broadband connection would require an investment in another broadband modem, which would set you back as much as $200 to $300.

Sharing Files

In the dark ages (about 10 years ago), most people using PCs at home, and many at work, would share files using what was called Sneakernet. Sneakernet is the highly complex network that is built using floppy disks and an old pair of sneakers. If someone wanted to, for example, look at the family finances file from the PC upstairs on his other PC in the basement, he would have to employ his Sneakernet by trudging upstairs, putting a floppy into the hard drive, copying the file, and then walking downstairs and popping the floppy into the other PC. The bandwidth on this network was, suffice it to say, not breaking any land speed records. But with a home network, all this changes. Someone can access the family finance files, or any files for that matter, through a home network by simply clicking on the appropriate networked drives and folders (Chapter 11, "Sharing Files and Printers on a Home Network," will show you how to share files and drives).

What's that—some of you might actually enjoy shuffling around the house with floppies in hand? It's how you get your daily exercise? Well, eliminating Sneakernet is not the only benefit associated with the file-sharing capabilities of a home network.

Perhaps the most important benefit is that a home network allows you and the other users of the home network to access the same file on the network, ensuring that there are no redundant, outdated copies of files. Consider the possibility that your wife has an important PowerPoint presentation that she's asked you to look over and add some formatting to and then send it to her at work through your e-mail account. You dutifully pull up the file on the den computer, where you saw your wife working on her presentation this weekend. You make a few suggestions, add a few effects, correct more than a couple of spelling errors (you always were a better speller), and shoot it off to her with 10 minutes to spare before her big presentation. You're so happy with yourself that you take the rest of the day off and go golfing. Halfway through the second hole you get a frantic call from your wife, demanding to know why you didn't include the second half of the presentation. You patiently explain to her you sent her what she left on the PC in the den. "The den!" she says. "I've worked on the presentation on my laptop for the past few days!" You rub your head at this point and start planning for your home network.

Because with a home network you can have a shared file folder called Jane Presentations and access this folder from anywhere on the network. Although not every family shares PowerPoint files, in your case it might be the most up-to-date finances, the family photos, the home networking book you're working on, or whatever files more than one member of the family has to access (my wife is a great proofreader when it comes to home networking books).

Sharing Storage/PC Resources

It seems to be the case that the PCs are getting bigger and faster, nearly doubling in capabilities every year. That is certainly true of your PC's hard drive. I remember in college that my first PC had a 30 megabyte (30MB) hard drive. Today, many program files are multiples of that size, and if you're using Windows, chances are your operating system alone is taking up gigabytes (GB) of hard drive space alone (1GB is equal to 1,000MB). Although someday we might be telling our giggly grandchildren about the day we only had 10 or 20GB hard drives, today that is *plenty* of space for most things. However, unless all your PCs are less than a year or two old, chances are you might own only one PC in your home that has plenty of hard drive space to spare. With a home network you can designate this powerful machine as the home server, allowing you to share the wealth with the other users.

And it might not be just your hard drive. Many people are now taking advantage of CD-ROM read/write drives (CDRW) that allow you to write onto CD-ROMs. The low cost of these drives, which now come standard on many new PCs, has helped put a powerful new tool in the hands of many users. With a CDRW drive, you can create your own music CDs, copy large amounts of data (over 650MB, compared with 1.44MB on a floppy), and even use your CDs as an alternative method for backing up files.

The capability to back up files, whether on your hard drive, a CD-ROM, or some other alternative storage device such as a ZIP drive, is very important, and a network provides a quick and easy method for ensuring that more than one copy exists. With a home network, you can simply save a backup copy on a drive other than the one on which you are working on, and you have made your life potentially much easier. Many people who have worked with computers know that it is possible to lose an important document due to your PC rebooting at the wrong time or a power outage, or for a number of other reasons (the temperamental computer has become the modern-day equivalent of the "dog eating my homework"). With a home network, you have a quick and easy way to back up important files.

The Home Network as a Communication Tool

Almost everyone has used e-mail in some form or another to communicate with friends, family, or coworkers. In fact, e-mail is by far the most popular use of the Internet today, even more popular than surfing the Web for Backstreet Boys' pictures (although the lead is rapidly shrinking). Well you don't have to send e-mail over the Internet, you can actually send it to different members of your household by using one of your PCs as an e-mail server. You can use the built-in capabilities of Windows or some of the publicly available shareware e-mail server programs.

Besides using your network as a virtual post office to send e-mail, you can also stay in touch with family members through instant messaging. The capability to send quick messages to tell someone it's time to eat is one of the benefits of the real-time nature of a home network. You can also leave messages for people to get later, essentially creating virtual sticky notes.

Another neat communication application of a home network is an electronic intercom. Intel's Anypoint home network comes with software to create an intercom over the home network, allowing one user to tell the person whose butt they just kicked in Doom that they are the ruler of the universe. The capability to transmit voice over the home network is a real benefit and what I would call true multimedia!

Sharing a Printer

Although some might feel that in today's world of $100 or less bubblejet printers there is no reason to share a printer, consider that if you put that $100 into a home network kit (or a savings bond if you already have a network), you can take advantage of the capability to share that printer and all the other things a home network allows you to do. Figure 1.3 illustrates how a printer can be shared on a home network.

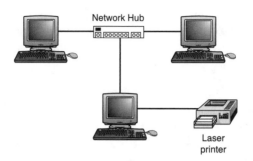

FIGURE 1.3
Sharing a printer on a home network.

You can also utilize a home network to share a printer when one printer in the home is clearly better than any other printer. Some homes have invested in a laser printer, which can cost anywhere from $500 to $1,000, and using a network to share the "nice" printer is the way to go.

Shoot Your Brother or Roommate (Virtually, of Course)

Okay, so we don't really recommend shooting your roommate, at least not in a real sense. But if you happen to blow away his character in a networked multiplayer game, then more power to you. Many of today's popular games come in versions that allow for multiplayer gaming, and with a home network, two or more players can be in different rooms on their PCs while racing or blasting away.

Consider the way it used to be, in the prenetwork home. You'd be racing down the track or dodging bullets from one of the big green monsters coming at you, and your brother or sister would be behind you, wisecracking about how he or she could have easily made that corner or walloped Mr. Slime while you, you are just a little slow. With a network, it's "GO TIME"—no more empty threats. Tell Mr. Joystick to go over to the other room because you're going to kick his...

Well, you get the picture. The fact is many games today support multiplayer gaming over a network, and over the Internet as well. If you don't want to shoot your brother in the next room, you can choose to shoot your friend miles away through an online game. You don't necessarily need a home network to play a multiplayer game over the Internet, but we think it's a little more satisfying to hear the groans of your opponent in the next room as you emerge triumphant.

Some games that support multiplayer gaming are

- The shoot-em-ups such as Quake, Doom, Diablo, and Heretic
- Racing games such as Re-Volt
- War games such as Warcraft

Play Your Digital Music Anywhere

One of the most popular uses for computers over the past few years has been to play music. The widespread availability of CD-ROM recorders and writers, and a new music format called MP3, has created an incredible change from the world we knew only a few years ago in which most people were happy to play all their music from $20 CDs on their stereos in their living room. With the capability to record CDs to a PC or download music from the Internet, many people have started to change the way they listen to music. And now some companies are beginning to create products that allow you to network your PC to your stereo so that you can listen to your music from your PC through your stereo system. For those people who have nicer speakers on their stereo system than on their PCs, which is likely most of us, this can be quite an attractive reason to use networking technology.

Video Distribution and Monitoring

Many of today's PCs have a DVD player on them. You can play movies on your PC as you would in your living room. Or, with a home network, you can play a movie from your DVD player on your PC to be viewed on your TV in your living room. The capability to transfer digital video signals over a network to an entertainment device such as a PC is possible and within reach of almost everyone today.

It might not be just a DVD. You might want to take advantage of your network and your high-speed Internet connection to enjoy streaming video, such as that based on Real Networks, Microsoft, or Apple's Quicktime.

What is MP3?

Chances are you have heard of MP3, as the ability to share music over the Internet has been very popular the last few years, and the predominant technology used for this has been MP3.

What is an MP3 file? It's a music format, similar to the way VHS or DVD is a format for video. The impressive thing about MP3 is that it is very efficient; it takes music files, such as those on a regular CD, and compresses them to approximately one tenth of their previous size, all without losing any noticeable sound quality. Considering that many people download MP3 files over the Internet, the compact size of MP3 files are very attractive for those who do not have ultra high-speed connections to the Internet. And even for those lucky enough to have DSL or cable, an MP3 file can take only a minute to download versus 10 minutes for an uncompressed CD song.

And it's not just such things as watching movies or video clips from the Web. You can place a small lightweight video camera in different areas in the home and watch what is happening on your PC. If you're a new parent and you want to monitor your child, why not place a small camera on the wall next to the crib and check on your little critter every few minutes while you're finishing that work project on your PC? There is even technology that will allow you to monitor the camera over the Internet while you are working. If you are working and someone rings your doorbell, wouldn't it be nice to be able to get an alert and see who this person is through the camera? This is what you can do when you combine the video monitoring capabilities of a home network with some basic smart home technology. Speaking of which...

Smart Home

The first true home networks besides your good old phone system were those installed by the home automation folks. Back in the early 1980s a technology called X-10 started showing up in people's homes, turning their lights on and off at certain hours and brewing coffee at the time they instructed their X-10 controller to turn it on in the morning.

This technology advanced and soon enabled people to manage their home systems from their PCs. They could create instructions through a software program on their PC that instructed their different home systems to perform different tasks. And it wasn't just X-10 (although X-10 technology is by far the most widely used home automation technology). Other technologies with names such as CEBus and Lonworks came on the market.

Some of the things you can do with a home automation system include these:

- Control lights automatically, having them turn on and off at predefined times.
- Monitor and control your heating and cooling system, having your PC or home automation controller implement a routine defined by you to optimize these resources to make you more comfortable when you are home and to save you money when you aren't.
- Control and gain access to your home through electronic key pads, automated driveway gates, and door locks.
- Place sensors throughout the home that are aware of changes in the environment and can alert you to these changes. Some of the different environmental changes you can monitor using smart home technology are changes in temperature, moisture (you can be alerted to such things as flooding in your basement), movement (get alerts when a door opens that shouldn't be opening), and noises (such as glass breaking).

You're probably thinking that these types of smart home systems are expensive and out of the reach of anyone who doesn't run a large software company, but that's not the case. This book discusses the different systems available from companies such as X-10.com and Xanboo that use wireless or power-line technology that can allow you to have a really "smart home" for only a couple hundred dollars. That's not to say that there aren't more elaborate home automation systems that require installation of new wiring, call for an installation technician, and costs thousands of dollars. We'll look at those too, if you want, Mr./Ms. Moneybags.

Wrap It Up

So home networks will not help you drop weight and rejuvenate your marriage (unless you and your spouse find network gaming romantically stimulating). However, there are real advantages to having a home network, for both your pocketbook and your peace of mind.

In summary, home networks allow you to

- Save costs of having separate Internet subscription fees
- Share resources on the network such as files, printers, and disc and CD-ROM drives
- Create a whole home entertainment system by sending music or video files over your network to different PCs, your stereo, or your TV
- Play multiplayer games across the home network or over the Internet
- Create home communications systems such as a home intranet, e-mail, instant messaging, and intercom systems

Home Network Building Blocks: What Makes Your Network Tick

IN THIS CHAPTER

Have you ever known anyone with a home network? In years past, chances were that this person worked in a technical type of job or industry, talked about bits and bytes, and had a different color pocket protector for every day of the week.

Things have changed quite a bit over the past couple of years. The number of people with home networks has started to grow and is expected to surge in the next few years (I know, predicting these kinds of things is what I do for my day job). If you're into reading bar charts (which makes you as much of a nerd as Mr. Pocket Protector), you'll see in Figure 2.1 how this number will just keep defying gravity.

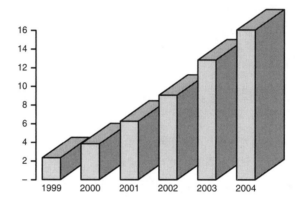

FIGURE 2.1

Home networks in the United States (millions).

Why is this expected to happen? Well, aside from a secret plan by Mr. Pocket Protector and his like to take over the world (this has the makings of a bad made-for-TV movie), there are other reasons:

- High-speed Internet connections provide users with enough bandwidth to share (compare a cable modem line at 1.5Mbps with a 56Kbps modem).

- Many homes now own more than one PC. With PC prices falling below $1,000 and many times being closer to $500, it makes sense that some families would have different PCs for different members of the family.

- Networking equipment companies are beginning to make easy-to-use products geared specifically toward the home user. These products are easier to use and more affordable than their office networking big brothers.

- Microsoft and other companies that make software for your PCs are continuously making it easier to network different devices.

- A thing called convergence is beginning to change the way different products look and interact. It used to be that a PC was a PC and a TV was a TV. Now each is starting to act like the other.

Tell Me More About Convergence

Convergence is basically the word to describe how the different technology products in our homes are starting to morph to take on new capabilities. One example of this is how it is now possible to access the Internet on your wireless phone. How far will this go? At this point there doesn't appear to be any stopping point, because the chips that go into all these devices are getting smaller and more powerful, allowing everything that has an electronic pulse around us to get smarter and communicate with each other. Believe it or not, some people are now talking about having your refrigerator talk to your PC, which will then talk to your front door. Kind of scary, isn't it?

2

HOME NETWORK BUILDING BLOCKS

Make a Choice: Do I Move to the Hills or Learn About Home Networks?

With the inevitable trend toward networked homes, I would suggest that instead of avoiding it, you embrace the trend and learn about home networks. As I told you in Chapter 1, "It's a Networked World," you'll see all types of benefits in your life, not the least of which is increased intelligence and a better golf stroke.

What's the first step in becoming a home network owner? Well, before you run out and buy a bunch of cables and network cards, let's go over the basics of what a network comprises. This chapter discusses the different building blocks you will need to consider when looking to create a home network.

What Makes Up a Home Network?

The home network can include a multitude of different pieces, each of which we will discuss in this chapter. We will start very slowly, avoiding any real nitty-gritty about how you will actually go about hooking up these different pieces so not to give you a headache. Don't worry, you'll get plenty of handy info later about how these pieces come together to form a home network.

The traditional home network is much like the kind you might see in your office network. These types of networks are called local area networks, or LANs.

This is where we will start, discussing the fundamental concepts involved in the home network. Of course, as I explained at the beginning of the chapter, convergence is creating a world where different types of devices are beginning to act like one another, and it is hard to tell what types of equipment will end up on the network in the future, other than to say that more things will be networked than not. But to start, we'll stick to the basics; in later chapters we'll go into detail about some of the neat newer products you might consider putting on your network.

As you can see in Figure 2.2, the typical home network is composed of a few PCs, some network cabling, and devices that allow for the communication of these PCs over the network cabling. The network hub, or "hub" for short, is the central station on your home network, where all the different communication signals get sent on their way to the other PCs. Also included in the network are network interface cards, or NICs, which are inserted into your PCs to connect them to the network. Because they are installed inside your PC, you can't see them. Don't worry, NICs are not as complicated as they sound, and we'll show you how to install them in later chapters. And in case the idea of installing an NIC still has you a little intimidated, I'll talk about some NICs you can simply plug in to a connection on the back of your PC and be ready to go.

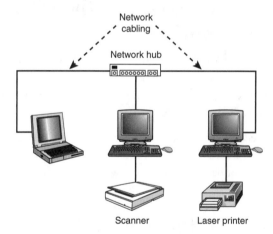

FIGURE 2.2

A typical home network.

But the network is made not just of things you can actually touch and feel, but also of some more elusive things such as software. Although you can't actually touch network software, it is something you can get your arms around in a figurative sense, especially after I explain what composes the basic networking software.

Home Network Building Blocks

Okay, we've discussed the different pieces that make up a home network, or what can be called the *home network building blocks*. The term *building block* might remind you of Legos, which are, in reality, not all that different. You might remember that when you played with Legos as a child (or for those of you who still do play with Legos), you imagined what you wanted to build with your Legos and then you'd pick up the appropriate size piece that would do the job and snap it in. With networks it's the same thing: you find the appropriate Lego or building block and plug it "in" to your network. Although this might seem overly simplified, eventually you really will be able to just snap the building block in and be ready to go.

What are these building blocks? Glad you asked:

- Network interface cards, or NICs
- Hubs (or other more advanced network "central stations," such as switches)
- Network cabling
- An Internet access/sharing device
- Networking software

As you'll see, the network is not just made of physical boxes and cables you can touch. It also uses a term you are probably already familiar with: software. This primarily means a *network operating system*, but it also includes some software that allows your PC to work with your networking equipment, called *drivers*.

Now we are going to go over each of the building blocks in a little more detail so that you'll have a better foundation for when you actually go out and buy and install these different networking building blocks yourself.

The Network Interface Card

Poor old NIC. In the big world of corporate networks and the Internet, the NIC is not seen as the most exciting or crucial building block. In fact, if you read about companies that provide networking building blocks, you usually read about big industrial-strength hardware such as routers, servers, and switches. Although each of these is equally important, and in some cases might even have a place to play in a home network, perhaps no piece of equipment is as important to your home network as the NIC. A NIC, or network card, is probably the one piece of equipment, aside from a PC, that will be in the home network. Although we've discussed the hub as the central station on the home network, it is possible to build a home network without a hub. It is also possible to build a home network without cabling, such as in a wireless or phoneline network. But most networks use some form of NIC.

Figure 2.3 shows a typical NIC you would install in to a PC to help you communicate with a network. The card itself is nothing impressive, just some chips (or what a techno-geek like me would call a semiconductor) on a small card that plugs in to your PC.

FIGURE 2.3

A desktop PC network interface card (NIC).

There's also a connector for the network cable, a little metal strip that helps the NIC fit in to the back of your PC, and some indicator lights (called LED lights) to indicate how fast your NIC is communicating after it is installed.

NOTE

LED stands for light-emitting diode. LEDs are little lights present on all types of networking equipment, such as NICs and hubs. LEDs basically give you an indication of how busy your piece of network equipment is. Depending on the equipment type and the design specifics of the equipment manufacturer, the LED light can also be an indicator of potential problems on your network.

As you can see from Figure 2.4, the NICs are the closest piece of equipment to your PC. In fact, in most cases, they actually reside in your PC. Certain types of NICs can plug directly in to an external connection on your PC, such as a USB-based NIC, which we will discuss in Part II, "Digital Plumbing: Network Wiring and Hardware Options."

> **NOTE**
>
> *USB*, or *Universal Serial Bus*, is a type of connection on your PC that allows you to hook up new gadgets or network cards. Most new PCs come with USB "ports," and you can equip even older PCs with USB connections by buying USB cards to fit inside your PC.

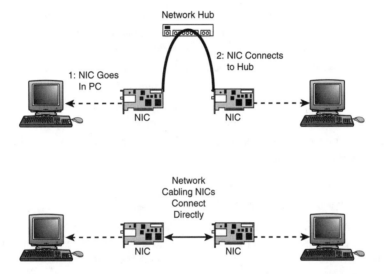

FIGURE 2.4
How the NIC goes in to the PC and then connects to a network.

The Network Hub

The network hub is the central meeting place for your network cabling and the information that passes over the cabling. The typical hub has anywhere from 4 to 16 connections for incoming cables (these connections are called ports by network professionals), and the traffic passes through these ports onto another port and to their final destination.

In the preceding section about NICs, you read about how the poor NIC was oftentimes considered a necessary but unexciting part of the network. Well, the NIC has it good compared to the hub, which has a reputation among its hardware cohorts as not being the sharpest knife in the drawer. In fact, the hub is considered downright dumb.

Don't worry. Just because the hub isn't the network equivalent of Einstein, doesn't mean it can't do its job. In fact, hubs are very reliable in that they are simple and the job they handle is simple. They act as a basic meeting place through which data is passed, and that is all that is asked of them. Another good thing about the simplicity of hubs is that because they are not very complex, they are usually very cheap. If there is one maxim that can be applied to both networking and computing equipment, its that the smarter the product you have, the more expensive it is likely to be.

And not only does our friend the hub have to suffer through the indignity of being called dumb in front of its friends, but it also can be seen as unnecessary in some circles (especially by network switches, which are seen by the hubs as snobs). This is for two reasons:

- You don't need a hub to build a home network with only two PCs or if you are building a wireless, phoneline, or powerline network. With a phoneline or powerline home network, you can connect two or more PCs, and the NICs in these PCs, directly to what is called a "bus" network. If you are building an Ethernet network with more than two PCs, you need a hub or some device to act as the main connection point.

- The hub can be replaced by a more intelligent device called a switch. A switch is a device that acts much like a hub in that it is a central station for your network, but it gives each connection more dedicated bandwidth (see the following sidebar, "The Switch: A Bandwidth Baron").

The Switch: A Bandwidth Baron

Network switches for office and home networks are becoming more popular. The switch is very similar to a hub in that it acts as the central station for a home network, but it is more efficient in that it provides each connection with more bandwidth. How is this different from a hub?

Well, because a network hub has only so much bandwidth to go around, it is like a man with a limited bank account. Let's call this guy Mike W. Because Mike W has only so much money to go around, every time someone comes and asks for money, he has to shrink the amount he gives to the other people in his "network." The "switch," on the other hand—whom we shall call Bill G—has plenty of bandwidth for each connection. If Bill has two people on his network, he can give each $100 (or, in the case of a network switch, 100Mbps). If six more people come and ask him for money, he can dig in his billfold and hand out six more $100 bills.

This is because Bill G, or the network switch, has a fixed amount of bandwidth for each port. The network hub has to share its total bandwidth, usually 10 or 100Mbps, with all the users on its network. This is usually fine on a small home network where users aren't constantly sending large files across the network, but in business networks and larger home networks, the dedicated bandwidth of a switch can be very welcome.

The good thing about this is that some day everyone will buy switches, and hubs will go the way of the electric typewriter. Switches have become very affordable over the past few years, and it is possible to buy a small four-port switch with speeds up to 100Mbps for under $80. And as is the way with all technology products, the prices can be expected only to drop further in the future.

We'll get more into the different networking setups in the next chapter, but for now it's important to remember that you can set up a home network with or without a hub. Figure 2.5 shows a basic home network using a network hub. As you can see, the hub is where the network comes together. This could also be a switch if the user decided to take advantage of the higher, dedicated bandwidth to each connection (see the preceding sidebar, "The Switch: A Bandwidth Baron").

FIGURE 2.5
A home network using a network hub.

Figure 2.6 shows a picture of an actual network hub. These devices are usually no larger than 6 to 12 inches wide and 2 to 3 inches thick. So don't worry, having network equipment in your house will not require you to build a network wiring closet similar to what you see in office environments.

NOTE

A *wiring closet* is a room dedicated to holding the equipment of a local area network and any large PCs that need to be accessed by multiple members within an office.

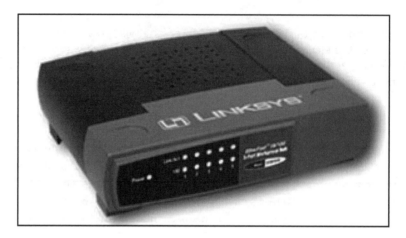

Figure 2.6
A network hub.

Network Cabling (or Lack Thereof)

So far we've discussed the different pieces of equipment that act as the way to connect to the network (the NIC) and as the network central station (the hub), but we haven't looked at the actual cables that connect these pieces of equipment together. Network cabling is very important to the network, and, as you'll see, different types of network cabling are used for different needs.

What About No-New-Wires Technologies?

The following discussion looks at cabling as one of the network building blocks. You might be wondering about some of the new technologies that enable you to connect without installing new cabling, referred to as "no-new-wires" technologies in the industry (no one ever said those "in the industry" were very creative). These new technologies include wireless, phoneline, and networking over power wiring.

We'll further discuss the different no-new-wires options for networking your home in Part II. Right now, however, we'll take a quick look at network cabling as a network building block. It is similar to the no-new-wires technologies in that it serves as the network "roads" or communications channels to send info from one network user to the next.

In a traditional network, there are different types of cabling for connecting your network equipment together. The different types of cabling vary primarily in their cost, speed, types of material, and actual connection type they allow you to make. This last characteristic has to do with the style of NIC that the cable connects to.

To Cable or Not to Cable

As you might already have discovered by reading this book, there are new types of home networks that use existing phone wiring, electrical wiring, or radio signals to communicate, not unlike your cell phone. These types of networks were built with the home network user in mind, because not everyone wants to install network cabling in their home. We will discuss in Chapter 4, "Your Home Network Planning Guide," the reasons you might want to choose one of these alternative methods of connecting your network, which include

Budget blower: Having network cables put in your walls and throughout your home might be a more expensive project than you want to undertake.

Renter beware: You rent your home and are not permitted to install cabling throughout your home.

Cabling mess: You aren't fond of the idea of having cables installed because this will require putting holes in your walls and snaking the cables from room to room.

Mobile Mabel: Many people think the freedom they have with a wireless connection is better than being tied to the wall with a cable. With a laptop or even a new device called a web pad you can freely roam the house and access different PCs or surf the Internet without being stuck in one place by a cord. Talk about cool!

There are basically three types of cabling you will use in a traditional local area network. These are *unshielded twisted-pair cable*, or *UTP*; a thin coax cabling called *thinnet*; or *fiber cabling*, a cable made of glass that transmits light instead of electric signals.

Each has its own benefits, as shown in Table 2.1. Each type of cabling is discussed in greater detail in Part II.

TABLE 2.1 Cabling Options for Home Networks

Cabling Type	Characteristics
Unshielded twisted	• Most common form of cabling pair (UTP)
	• Widely available in stores

TABLE 2.1 Continued

Cabling Type	Characteristics
	• Used with most Ethernet networks
	• Can operate at high speeds, up to 1000Mbps
	• Very affordable
Thinnet	• Smaller than old coax cables
	• Uses special twist-on connector
	• Not commonly used in today's networks
Fiber-optic cable	• Fastest cabling (fast as "speed of light")
	• Most expensive cabling
	• Used more in business networks and wide area networks

The type of network cabling you choose will depend on what type of network you want and what type of networking equipment (NICs and hubs) you use in your network. Each type of NIC, for example, uses a specific type of cabling. There are NICs for thinnet, for fiber-optic cabling, and for the different types of UTP cabling. Although you might feel a little intimidated by having to choose a type of network, it really isn't anything you will likely have to worry about. There are network kits today that include the appropriate cabling for your network. In most networks today, both home and business, UTP cabling is used for connecting different PCs.

Unshielded twisted-pair cabling comes in a few varieties, the most common of which is called "category 5" UTP. The category 5 is part of, you guessed it, the five types of UTP cabling you can use. The higher the number of cabling, the higher the quality in terms of protecting the cable traffic from interference. Category 5, or more commonly called Cat 5, is the most commonly used cabling for both home and business networks. In fact, in many business networks, Cat 5 UTP cabling is used for both voice and data traffic. Category 3 cabling is what has traditionally been used for phone networks in both home and business, but it is not recommended for use in home networks unless you are utilizing special phoneline-based networking equipment. This will be further discussed in Chapter 8, "Other Networking Technologies: Phoneline, Powerline, and Structured Wiring Ethernet."

Internet Sharing Devices

Most home network books have focused exclusively on the home local area network and have not mentioned the building block that enables the network to connect to and share an Internet connection. Feeling cheated? You should, and let me tell you why.

In addition to my job of writing this book, I work as a network industry analyst. This means I follow the industry of home networking and other networking markets and look for trends. Probably the most dominant trend that I and other home network industry analysts have noticed is that after people get a high-speed Internet connection, they want to share it. What does this mean? It means it's time to look at new devices that are emerging to more easily enable you to share this "fat pipe."

Although we won't get into too much detail about the new devices called residential gateways or home routers in this chapter, I will mention that these devices allow you to share a high-speed connection and also can provide such benefits as security against hackers, as well as enable new services such as streaming audio and video. Sound neat? They are, and we'll go into depth on home/residential gateways in Chapter 14, "Internet Sharing on a Home Network."

2

HOME NETWORK
BUILDING BLOCKS

NOTE

A *residential gateway* is an Internet sharing device that can also provide security and server functions, and can even become part of your home phone system to enable such things as call forwarding and ID. The interesting thing about residential gateways, or RGs, is that they come in many sizes and flavors. Some incorporate the high-speed modem; some connect directly to your modem and have a built-in Ethernet or wireless hub.

It's also important to mention that a residential gateway and home routers are not the only ways to share an Internet connection. We will discuss all the different methods in later chapters, but following is a list that shows you the different ways to share an Internet connection on a home network:

- With Internet-sharing software and a modem installed in your PC
- With a high-speed modem connected to a PC and this PC sharing the connection with the rest of the network
- With a high-speed modem connected to a residential gateway and then each PC on the network connecting to this residential gateway

Network Software

Although the most obvious building blocks for a network are those physical pieces you use to connect the different PCs on the network together, such as NICs, hubs, and cables, the network could not operate without another major building block: network software. The network software consists primarily of what is called a network operating system. As you read on, you'll also hear about another important piece of software (which is usually included in your operating system or the network hardware when you purchase it), called drivers.

Network Operating System

The network operating system is software that manages the resources of the network. This means that by using a networking OS you can control which PCs talk to which, and what resources will be available to other PCs such as files and printers. The great thing about looking for a networking OS for a home network is that more than likely, you already have one on your computer.

Chances are you have some version of consumer Windows on your PC. These include

- Windows 95
- Windows 98
- Windows Millennium Edition (ME)
- Windows XP for Consumers

With any of the standard Windows operating systems for consumers, you have everything you need built into the program itself to set up a home network. Windows has a central command center for your home network called Network Neighborhood in Windows 95 and 98, My Network Places in Windows ME, and X in Windows XP. All these central management centers look and operate the same way and can interoperate with each other.

In addition to the network command center, Windows also gives you a control panel to configure the network settings such as passwords, and permissions for which drives and PC resources to access, as well as non-network settings such as display and time settings.

In Figure 2.7 you see the My Network Places screen for Windows ME. As mentioned a moment ago, this screen or one like it is used in most versions of Windows. But what if you don't have one of the newer versions of Windows, or don't use Windows at all? Although most PCs in homes today use Windows 95 or one of the newer operating systems from Microsoft, it is possible that you have a version of Windows released before Windows 95 or a non-Windows operating system such as the following:

- Macintosh 7, 8, 9, and X
- OS/2
- Linux
- DOS

- Windows 3.11 (this *is* a Windows OS, but it does not have built-in networking)
- Windows NT and Windows 2000 (also Windows, but built for business PCs; the good news is that these were made with networking in mind)

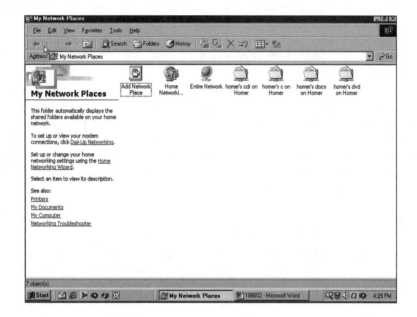

2

HOME NETWORK BUILDING BLOCKS

FIGURE 2.7
The Windows Millennium My Network Places screen.

The general rule is that the older the operating system, the harder it is to network. This book gives you in-depth instructions on how to set up a network in Consumer Windows (95, 98, ME, XP) in Part III, "Software Setup and Management." It also looks at how to set up a network in other operating systems such as those for Apple's Macintosh computers. This book does not, however, go in-depth on networking older Windows OS's such as Windows 3.11 and other less common OS's such as IBM's OS/2.

If you are using an older Windows OS such as Windows 3.1, I would strongly suggest that you consider upgrading your software to one of the newer Windows operating systems because your life will be much easier. Also, you will want to be sure that your PC is equipped to handle a home network. If you are not sure what makes a PC adequate, see the following sidebar, "My PC: Does It Have What It Takes?"

My PC: Does It Have What It Takes?

With all this talk about operating systems, you're probably asking yourself whether that old clunker sitting in your basement under the Christmas ornaments will work on your home network. In other words, does it have enough processor speed, memory, and general chutzpah to get on the network? That question can be answered by—what else—what kind of operating system you are using. If you are using an older version of Windows, such as Windows 3.11, you are also using an older PC, but one that can be networked.

But what if you are using one of those really old computers, the kind that is a candidate for the computer history museum? Will *these* work on a home network? Well, if you have a really old system such as the kind I remember using in my junior-high days, the kind that used to store programs on little cassette tapes, such as the TRS-80 or the old VIC systems advertised by William Shatner, your chances are not good. In fact, they're pretty much nonexistent. Old Bill Shatner didn't last long as a PC pitch man (nor as a prognosticator—he predicted the VIC-20 would become "the computer of the eighties"), and neither did these obsolete systems. If you are one of the hold-outs who actually still use one of these babies (when you're not watching *Star Trek* reruns), to you I say, "Get a life." That and get a new computer.

If you are using an older PC with an older processor (the central "brain" of your PC) such as a 386 or 486, running Windows 3.11 or DOS, you might want to consider upgrading your PC to a faster processor and at least Windows 95, if this is possible. In Part III we will discuss upgrading your OS and the minimum requirements it will take in terms of processor (that is, 386, 486, or Pentium) and memory (how many megabytes of RAM you will need).

Network Drivers

So what's a network driver? No, it isn't some guy who hauls around network equipment in a van, but instead an important piece of software that allows your network equipment, such as a network interface card, to talk to your PC.

Why do we need drivers? Well, since there are so many choices among networking equipment products and manufacturers, each product is just different enough from another that each needs its own set of instructions to talk to the PC operating system.

The good thing about network driver software is it is included in your operating system much of the time. Windows includes drivers to common networking equipment products. If the driver is not included on your PC hard drive where the OS sits or on your Windows CD included with your PC, it will likely be included on a floppy disk or a CD included with your network equipment.

One thing you should know is that a certain piece of network equipment will often need a different driver for each operating system. A NIC from vendor A might work with Windows 98, but if you decide to upgrade your OS to Windows XP, you might need to install a different driver.

Some day the need to install different drivers will likely go away. Microsoft and other large technology companies have developed what is called Plug-and-Play installation. In most cases, your installation of an NIC will be pretty seamless and trouble free because of this Plug-and-Play installation. Still, at times the user will be required to install a driver, or an older NIC will need to be configured manually.

> **NOTE**
>
> Although *Plug-and-Play* eased the installation of new peripherals to a PC, Microsoft and other large PC companies realized that users would soon require the capability to plug new peripherals or PCs in to the home network as simply as they could plug new devices in to their standalone PC. So they came up with *Universal Plug and Play*, aimed to do just that, allowing for "plug-and-play" installation of new PCs, devices, and even such things as your refrigerator to your home network.
>
> Of course, Universal Plug and Play (UpnP) will take time to develop, so don't expect a world where new devices are added to the network without any need for configuration by the end user. In fact, chances are you will not be able to fully benefit from UpnP for years to come, because it will require that the devices you attempt to plug into the network be UpnP compliant. Today there are very few devices on the market that can make this claim.

What About Other Home Network Building Blocks?

So far we've reviewed different building blocks you use to create a basic home network. Some building blocks, such as some form of network interface card and an operating system, are necessary for creating a home network. This discussion has served to introduce you to the basic building blocks you will need to understand to build a traditional home network.

As the home networking industry continues to evolve, there are new and emerging home network devices that are being created specifically to make the life of a home network owner simpler and more satisfying. These devices are built with the home network owner in mind—not only do these new technologies take advantage of the new connection technologies, such as wireless, phoneline, and powerline networking, but some are designed specifically to help the user do a specific task or activity that he or she finds desirable.

Table 2.2 has some examples of new products that are emerging to make the life of you, the home network user, more enjoyable. We will examine these in later chapters, specifically in Part V, "Unleash the Network," where we look at how to allow you to use some of these exciting new technologies. These might not be building blocks in the same sense as the previously discussed devices, but if you are building a home network to accomplish certain tasks specific to one of these devices, they certainly can be viewed as an important "building block" for your purposes.

TABLE 2.2 Emerging Home Network Building Blocks

New Products	What They Do
Digital MP3/music players/tuners	Allow you to play your MP3 or other digital music around the home, like a whole home stereo system.
Home gateway (aka residential gateway)	Connect to a high-speed modem, or are combined with a modem, and allow you to share your Internet connection around the home.
PC/network cameras	Allow you to watch another user and monitor home when away from home.
Network drives	Are large hard drives with a ton of space to act as a "media tank" or storage facility for large files and multimedia.
Wireless access points	Are essentially "wireless hubs" that are used in a wireless home LAN. They connect different users to the network with radio signals instead of cabling.
Firewalls	Protect you against hackers.

Wrap It Up

As you learned in this chapter, your home network, and all local area networks, have certain building blocks that are used to build a network. These building blocks include the following:

- Network interface cards, or NICs
- Network hubs or switches
- Cabling, such as category 5 unshielded twisted pair (UTP)
- An Internet access/sharing device
- Network software, such as your PC operating system and network drivers

There are other important "building blocks" designed specifically for a home network to give the user a desired type of functionality. These include Media/Music players, home gateways, network cameras, standalone network drives, wireless access points, and firewalls.

Network Relationships: Network Types and Topologies

IN THIS CHAPTER

After reading Chapter 2, "Home Network Building Blocks: What Makes Your Network Tick," you should understand the building blocks that you need in order to put together a simple but highly functional home network. These building blocks are used by nearly every type of local area network, both in the office environment and within the home.

Although we have explored the basic network building blocks, there are still a few network basics that would be helpful before we dive into talking about the different network technologies and choosing which will be best for you. Discussing these different basics will help you to better understand how networks are set up and then help you decide, based on your needs, which is best for you.

Network Basics: How the Building Blocks Come Together

In addition to the basic building blocks used in a typical home network, there are certain things you must consider when planning to put together a home network. "*Oh great,*" you're thinking, "*I knew there had to be a catch.*" *The building blocks were just too easy.* Well, if you're thinking this you're right in one sense: understanding the network building blocks *is* easy. And the other concepts described in this chapter about network basics are just as easy, and will help you decide how you want your network set up.

The discussion in this chapter centers around relationships between the PCs on your network. These relationships can be broken down into two categories: the control relationship and the physical relationship. If you think this is starting to sound like marital counseling, don't worry, I won't go into how to "reignite your hard drive."

The control relationship in your network is based on whether you want a *peer-to-peer* or *client/server* network. The physical relationship of your network is described as *network topology*. Both of these topics sound complicated, but they are not, as you'll see next.

Network Control: Peer-to-Peer Networks Versus Client/Server

In the world of local area networks, there are basically two choices of network control, or network types: peer-to-peer and client/server. The choice of these two networks basically determines the relationship each PC or device on the network has with the other in terms of control.

A peer-to-peer network is a true democracy. Each PC on the network is equal to the other in that the PCs can communicate with each other directly, and do not have a centralized PC monitoring and controlling the communication on the network.

A client/server network, on the other hand, has a central authority figure that controls the communication and access to resources on the network. This centralized controlling PC is called a server.

> **NOTE**
>
> *Servers* are PCs that control access to different resources on the network. In a home network, this can be such things as printers, a central storage drive, MP3 files, and anything you can think of that can take advantage of the server's capabilities. The server generally has a bigger processor and more storage than other PCs, or the clients, on the network.
>
> A network *client* is a PC on a client/server network that communicates to other PCs on the network community through the server. It takes advantage of the server's resources and is very similar to other "clients" on the network.

If the peer-to-peer network is like a democracy, the server in a client/server network is more a network "dictator." Don't worry; in reality, the server is not a bad guy, and there are actually sound reasons that many networks today are set up as client/server networks, which we will explore later.

But first, let's look at the relative characteristics of each type of network to help you better understand the differences. Table 3.1 outlines these differences.

TABLE 3.1 Peer-to-Peer Networks Versus Client/Server Networks

Peer-to-Peer Networks	Client/Server Networks
Each PC is an equal participant on the network	One PC acts as the network controller
PCs are not reliant on one PC for resources such as the printer	One PC controls access to network resources
Access to the network is not centrally controlled	Network access and security are centrally controlled
Can operate on a basic PC operating system	Need a special operating system
Are generally simpler and lower cost	Are generally more complex but give the user more control

3

NETWORK
RELATIONSHIPS

As shown in Table 3.1, there are definite differences between networks set up as peer-to-peer and those set up as client/server. It should be stated that most home networks today are set up as peer-to-peer, because this network type is simpler and works great for the needs of the home user. Because most home networks today are set up to perform basic but important tasks such as sharing an Internet connection or multiplayer gaming, there is no reason for a user to consider a client/server network. However, we will discuss each type more in-depth, and this information will help you decide how you want to set up your network.

Understanding Peer-to-Peer Networks

When all PCs on the network are set up to act as equals, this is called a peer-to-peer network. Every PC shares its files and resources with the other PCs on the network. Communication among PCs is a direct link with no central network controller, such as a server.

As shown in Figure 3.1, the two PCs on this simplified network engage in direct communication, or peer-to-peer. In reality, the network can look as simple as this figure, with the PCs talking directly to each other through one cable. We will look more at the actual physical configuration of the PCs and cables later in this chapter.

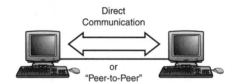

FIGURE 3.1

A basic peer-to-peer network.

A basic peer-to-peer network can also be set up in which a piece of network equipment can facilitate this direct relationship. Remember the discussion in Chapter 2, "Home Network Building Blocks: What Makes Your Network Tick," about the network hub? The hub can, as described before, act as the central station for the direct, peer-to-peer communication between the different PCs on the network, as shown in Figure 3.2.

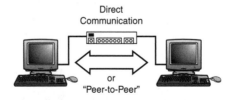

FIGURE 3.2

A basic peer-to-peer network using a hub.

At first it might not be apparent why you would want to use a hub in your network if you can connect them directly, NIC to NIC, with one piece of network cabling. We will discuss the benefits of each type of configuration in the second half of this chapter (in "Network Topologies"). For now you should know that it is easier to grow your network when you are using a hub, because you simply add a new connection from the PC to the hub.

Pluses of a Peer-to-Peer Network

The peer-to-peer network is the easiest type of network to set up. It does not require any software other than the operating system already on your PC, and it does not require the more complex configuration of a client/server network.

The following subsections cover all the advantages of a peer-to-peer network.

Simplicity

A peer-to-peer network is so basic that you don't need anything more than your PC's existing software, a couple of NICs, and some cable. In a wireless network, all the hardware you will need is two wireless NICs.

Peer-to-Peer Is Supported in Windows

Because most personal computers in homes today have some form of Windows, it is very easy to set up a home network. Of course, you need to have Windows 95 or a newer edition of Windows, but chances are that you do.

Low Cost

The cost to build a home network using peer-to-peer technology is lower than that for a client/server network because you do not need any special software or computer.

New Technologies for Home Networking Favor Peer-to-Peer

Technologies we will talk about in Part II, "Digital Plumbing: Network Wiring and Hardware Options," such as phoneline, powerline, and wireless networking, are built with the understanding that you will likely build a peer-to-peer network. This isn't to say that you can't build a client/server network with these technologies, but with these "no-new-wires" solutions, a peer-to-peer network is extremely simple.

What's Mine Is Yours

A peer-to-peer network allows each PC on the network to access resources on all the other PCs on the network. That Zip drive on Dad's PC, the laser printer downstairs on Mom's, the PC camera on Billy's PC—they're all part of the network community after you create a peer-to-peer network.

Potential Minuses of a Peer-to-Peer Network

Now that you have seen some of the advantages a peer-to-peer network can offer, you will explore some possible drawbacks peer-to-peer networks can hold. The following are the potential minuses of a peer-to-peer network.

Security

If a PC is on a peer-to-peer network, there is the chance that another PC on the home network will access files that the owner of the PC might not want accessed. Not that this will necessarily happen or that you have something to hide from other users (or do you?), but this is something to think about. However, Windows provides the capability to block access to certain drives, so this shouldn't be a worry for anyone who properly configures her network software.

PCs Down on the Network Can Cause the Network to Go Down

In some instances, a PC might not be working, either because of problems or because it has simply been shut off. In a basic peer-to-peer network that uses direct connections from PC to PC without a hub, this might cause a problem.

Network Speed

In a peer-to-peer network situation in which a hub or switch is not used (such as a phoneline network), it becomes a real possibility that the network can get bogged down when more than one user is using it at the same time.

Scalability

A peer-to-peer network is great for a home network with a handful of users such as three to five PCs. However, if one day you decide to go into business with Brad, your neighbor, and set up a network in your home, when you start to increase the number of users to 10 or beyond, you might want to consider moving to a client/server network.

Understanding Client/Server Networks

The other network type is a client/server network. As described earlier, client/server networks have more centralized control of the network through the network server.

As shown in Figure 3.3, the communication and services on the network are controlled through the server. The resources, such as Internet service and printer sharing, are controlled through the network server. If you were to set up passwords to get on the network, this would also be controlled through the server.

TIP

An important distinction to make here is that this does not mean that all communication needs to go through the server. In a situation in which a hub or network "central station" is used, Client A can communicate directly with Client B. However, the *permission* that enabled this direct connection was granted by the network "dictator," the server. Figure 3.3 is a conceptual diagram and doesn't show the use of a hub or switch that actually handles network "traffic."

NOTE

Network traffic is what we call the actual communication over the network. Network gurus like to use this term to describe how "congested" (see where we're going here?) or busy the network is.

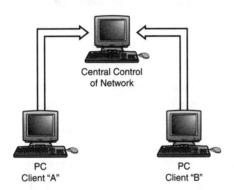

FIGURE 3.3
Central control through a client/server network.

Considering that a client/server network is generally more complicated and expensive than a peer-to-peer network, you're probably asking yourself why you would ever need one. Here are the circumstances in which you might want to consider using a client/server network:

- You expect that your network will grow over time and might exceed 10 users.

- You have a PC that has a noticeable advantage in processor speed and disk drive (storage) space.

- You need to control access to your network.
- You want to be able to have greater management and monitoring control over your network.
- You want to set up a Web server (a special server that creates Web pages on the Internet).

These are all reasons you should consider using a client/server network over a peer-to-peer network. A client/server network, because of a more robust operating system such as Windows NT or NetWare, allows the network administrator to have better control over who accesses what and allows monitoring of network traffic and usage patterns.

Choosing Between Peer-to-Peer and Client/Server: A Suggestion for Your Sanity

As you can see, you must weigh a few basic considerations when deciding between the two options. But to give you even more value from your investment in this book, I will make a suggestion that should ease your pain considerably:

Unless you feel very strongly that you should have a client/server network based on the answers you had to the previous questions, *by all means go with the much easier solution of a peer-to-peer network*.

So you might be shocked that I go so far as to suggest what you should use, but don't be. That's my job (and I'm an extremely nice person).

Not convinced? Let me go over a few reasons I believe you should consider a peer-to-peer network unless you are absolutely convinced a client/server is for you:

- As I've mentioned repeatedly, peer-to-peer networks are much simpler. They use your basic PC operating system and the newer operating systems, such as Windows ME and XP, have built-in wizards to help you create your home network.
- Network operating systems are more complex, and you will have to learn a whole new set of commands to get your client/server network operating to your liking.
- Client/server networks are more expensive.
- Most home networks have only five or fewer PCs, which is well within the capabilities of a peer-to-peer network.
- Most important, in a peer-to-peer network you can share files, share printers, create passwords, and do most of the things you do with a client/server network.

Don't be surprised by that last statement. A peer-to-peer network can take advantage of the resources of different PCs within the network. If one has a larger hard drive, make that one the PC where you store all your large music and video files. If you want to use dad's laser printer in the den, make sure you ask him nicely to allow sharing. For a home network, in almost all instances, you can do all the things you want to do with a peer-to-peer network.

Here's one more reason to consider a peer-to-peer network. As I've mentioned before, new products aimed specifically for home networks are coming to market, and many of these are beginning to fulfill functions that a server might have done in the past.

For example, home routers or residential gateways are available today to provide basic security against hackers and allow for Internet sharing, two functions that could have been administered by a server in the past. Media servers and network storage drives are available that allow you to store large multimedia files such as movies and music in a "media tank." Some of these products are even designed to plug right into your stereo system or TV so that they won't look like a PC sitting awkwardly in your living room.

Because I feel so strongly that a peer-to-peer network is a great fit for a home network, the rest of this book focuses mainly on explaining how to set up and use a peer-to-peer home network.

Network Topologies: How Your Home Network Comes Together

As you're learning, new home network technologies are making lives easier for people like you, me, and even dear old Grandma. Grandma, you ask? Certainly that nice little lady who knits me overly large sweaters and bakes the world's best apple pie (although her meatloaf might leave something to be desired) wouldn't want to set up a home network. Or would she?

Actually, don't be surprised if someday everyone has a home network. And chances are that when this happens, most people still won't know what the term *network topology*, or *neuro-photonic asynchronous reassemblator*, for that matter, means. This is because as home networking advances and becomes easier for everyone, traditional networking terms that were born out of the business-networking world will take on less meaning to the home user. The user won't have to put thought into such things as network topologies and other traditional networking considerations. Someday (within the next 10 years, but not quite yet), we'll just plug things in and they'll be networked. But because you are a curious sort, I'll briefly discuss network topologies with you, Mr. Pocket-Protector.

So, what is a network topology? In the simplest description in history of network topology descriptions (will someone alert the Guinness Book for me?), a network topology describes how network communication links or "roads" run from one PC to the other. In other words, it's the way the cables and networking equipment are arranged.

Why do we need to even think about this? Well, even in the case of a home network, it is important to think about how things are arranged or risk running into confusion and clutter down the "road." Network topology is important to consider when you look at how your network will evolve. To understand this, let's look at the different types of network topologies.

The Three Network Topologies

The three basic network topologies you need to consider for a home network are bus, ring, and star. Each of these looks and operates differently from the others.

Bus

Like its name, a bus topology is like a basic bus route going from point A to point B and point C. Our bus is very simple in that it is straight and simple as a direct connection between the PCs on the network. Of course, in real life, your bus network might not be as simple as shown in Figure 3.4. Not all PCs on a bus network sit next to each other in a straight line, but still the bus network has connections that are "direct and straight" from one PC to the next.

FIGURE 3.4

A "bus" topology.

The appeal of a bus connection is that it is simple to create. No network equipment other than a single cable and couple of NICs are needed. Some phoneline or powerline networks are not really called "bus" networks, but some can in essence be basic "bus" networks using the phone or power wiring in your home. The difference here is that you do not lay the cabling, but instead use your existing phone or powerline wiring.

The disadvantage of the bus network is that it relies on one cable, and if this cable were to become disconnected from one of the PCs or to break, the entire network would stop working. This would not be the case with a phoneline or powerline network.

Ring

A ring topology is much like it sounds: The different nodes or PCs on the network form a ring like that shown in Figure 3.5.

Ring topologies are probably the least likely to be used in a home environment. The type of technology used to make ring networks is called Token Ring, which is more expensive than other types of network technologies we will discuss in Part II.

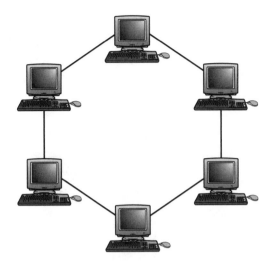

FIGURE 3.5

A ring topology.

> **NOTE**
>
> *Token Ring* is a technology for networking in which PCs communicate by sending an information "packet" around a ring until the packet finds the PC it was intended for. This technology is very polite in that a packet will not be sent by another PC until the packet circulating at a given time finds its destination. Token Ring, while being a very stable technology, is not as popular for new network installments and is not a good choice for a home network.

Star

The star topology, also called spanning tree, is the most common topology used in business networks, and is also very popular with home networks. This is because the star topology is used with the networking technology called Ethernet, which is also very popular.

> **NOTE**
>
> What is *Ethernet*? Ethernet, like Token Ring, is a kind of communication protocol, except that Ethernet operates over cable networks using a star topology as opposed to the ring topology explained previously. We'll go more in depth into Ethernet in Part II, but it's important to remember that Ethernet is an extremely popular and reliable way to network.

Star networks using Ethernet look like—what else—a star, with a center and several "spokes" reaching out from the center to the different PCs on the network. As shown in Figure 3.6, the network hub is the center of the star, with the different PCs connected through the hub.

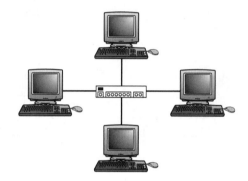

FIGURE 3.6
A star topology.

As to be expected, a network might in reality look a little different from the simplified picture in Figure 3.6, with the network hub sitting in one of the rooms of your house, and the cabling running throughout your walls to reach it.

Network Topologies with Wireless Home Networks

If you are one of those who are set on using a wireless network in your home (if you haven't decided, don't worry; we'll go over each way to network your home in Part II and help you reach a decision), you might be asking whether this discussion about how to set up the network cabling is even necessary.

Well, even if you are going to use a wireless network, this discussion about network topology is still useful in helping you to understand how a network communicates. With wireless LAN technology, there is usually a type of device that acts as a wireless "hub," taking and receiving the wireless signals from the different PCs equipped with wireless NICs and directing them to the other PC that the communication is directed to. This "wireless hub" is called an access point.

> **NOTE**
>
> *An access point* is a piece of equipment used in wireless LANs, both for home networks and for business LANs. The access point acts as a central transmitter and receiver (some technical types combine these to words to call the access point a "transceiver") for the radio signals that are going back and forth to the different PCs or those going out on the Internet.

You can think of a wireless LAN that uses an access point to communicate with the different end points on the network as acting like a star network. In fact, one of the wireless LAN technologies, called 802.11b, or Wi-Fi, refers to itself as "Wireless Ethernet." Remember, Ethernet is the most popular kind of star network.

But to make things more interesting (a polite word for confusing), not all wireless LANs use access points. Some are built to allow for the wireless NICs in each PC to communicate directly without going through a central access point or hub. These wireless LAN configurations are called "peer-to-peer." This term is familiar to you from our discussion at the beginning of this chapter regarding the different network types (peer-to-peer versus client/server). Although the term *peer-to-peer* is helpful in describing the direct nature of the communication within these types of wireless LANs, it should not be confused with the network type discussed earlier in the chapter.

You can learn all about wireless home networking in Chapter 7, "The Wonderful World of Wireless Networking."

Wrap It Up

You learned in this chapter about the types of relationships that can be used in networks. These relationships can be broken down into two categories, control and physical relationships.

The control relationship can be described in terms of peer-to-peer or client/server. Peer-to-peer networks describe network types in which every PC or device on the network is an equal. They share their resources and are not controlled centrally. Client/server networks are different in that control of the different clients' access to resources is administered by the server.

Network topology is a term used to described the physical relationship of your network connections. Home network topologies can be broken down into bus, ring, or star networks.

Your Home Network Planning Guide

IN THIS CHAPTER

Having a home network is like investing. If you spend time thinking about the subject, researching your needs and matching this information with what is available, you will find that with a little preparation, you will ultimately reach your goals. With investing, these goals might include financial security, some pocket money, and possibly even that little red sports car you always wanted. The key is that all these benefits didn't just drop into your lap (or your driveway) but were the result of good planning.

A good home network is similar. You want the benefits of a home network—increased productivity, access to your Internet connection or other resources throughout your house, whole-house entertainment or automation—and this is why you've decided to invest in building one. And, as with any investment, you need to plan.

The Four Pillars of Home Network Planning

A good home network plan addresses four main considerations, or pillars. Think of each pillar as a leg of a table. Without considering one of these pillars, you are in danger of seeing your plans tilt and fall and break one of your toes (ouch!).

What are the four pillars? Proceed!

Your Home (and Its Special Requirements)

Every home is different. Whether your house is new or old, big or small, you will need to cater your network to the special needs of your home.

Your Budget

A home network can range anywhere from a basic $50 Ethernet network to a $50,000 futuristic smart home. Chances are most home networks will fall somewhere in between (more likely on the lower end of this range).

Your Network Activities

It seems so basic that most people don't even ask this question, but perhaps the most important question in planning your network is what do you want to do with it?

Your Technical Know-How

Although a home network can be so easy that the most nontechnical person can install and operate one, there's no denying the fact that networks—both their installation and their operation—can be an intimidating endeavor. We'll consider how you can adjust various solutions to your particular comfort level.

Each of these pillars is important. We'll take a look at each in depth and then help you devise a home network plan accordingly.

Planning Pillar One: Your Home

As you know, every home is different. This will have an impact on how your network comes together. Homes are not like today's offices, because they were not built with networking in mind. This is especially true of the older houses, which often have old phone and electrical wiring. Newer homes, especially those in more forward-thinking community developments, might be "prewired" for whole home networking. We'll look at the differences in networking in new versus existing homes.

First, let's break down some of the basic things you need to consider when making sure your home network is right for your home.

Your Home's Size

Let's face it, some homes are bigger than others. Some are sprawling mansions with rooms upon rooms, whereas most are much more modest. Some are even downright cramped. The size of your home (or apartment or dorm) makes a difference in what type of network you put in. If you have ample room for your network gear, and even a server in the basement, that's great. However, if you are cramped in your current environment, and don't really want to use one of your PCs as furniture, you might consider a peer-to-peer network using a laptop, or even one of the newer (and smaller) information appliances.

Another size factor to consider is transmission from one network node (PC or whatever device you are using) to the other. If you are using wireless networking equipment, you might need to consider that some wireless LAN equipment has a limited distance for transmission, and might have trouble going through multiple walls. We'll talk about this subject in our discussions about wireless networks in Chapter 7, "The Wonderful World of Wireless Networking."

Your Home's Age

Your home's age will have a significant impact on what type of network you install in your home. If you are lucky enough to be planning your future home from scratch, you can consider putting in network wiring throughout so that you'll be "future-proofed" for all later network needs.

4

YOUR HOME
NETWORK
PLANNING GUIDE

NOTE

Future-proofing means preparing your home or network for the future. This term is popular among network types because they want to make sure that whatever network they build, it is not obsolete in a short time. If they plan ahead, they will buy network equipment or build their home so that they are "future-proofed."

Not all of us are lucky enough to be planning a new house. In fact, some might choose to live in older homes (you know, those one-of-a-kind "charmers" that require just a little work). And given the fact that most people who decide to install a network live in an existing home, they will have to give special consideration to their home's characteristics related to age. Such items can include the condition of network phone and electrical wiring and the condition of basements or attics (where wiring or network equipment can often sit).

The condition of your home's phone or electrical wiring is important if you are considering using phoneline- or powerline-based networks. As I mentioned previously (and we'll go into depth in Part II, "Digital Plumbing: Network Wiring and Hardware Options"), there are special types of networking equipment that allow you to network over your existing in-home wiring. However, if your home is older than 25 years or so, you might have trouble with some of these solutions. This is because both phoneline and powerline quality can be expected to degrade over long periods. Also, certain homes have phone wiring that might not be suitable for whole-home phoneline networking. We will go into some of the problems that phoneline networks might have in older homes, but if you do have an older home, you might want to consider a wireless or new-cabling solution.

Planning Pillar Two: Your Budget

The cost of networking your home can run the gamut. Today, the cost of Ethernet or phoneline-based networking cards can be less than $25 per NIC, and many of the new PCs you buy already have networking products built in. If your budget is unlimited, you can have a whole-home networking cable system installed as well as home automation and control technology that could set you back tens of thousands of dollars.

Table 4.1 shows examples of the types of networking equipment and the costs of these products. The good news is that there is networking equipment to fit any budget, from the smallest to the most extravagant.

TABLE 4.1   Cost Comparison for Different Home Networks

Network Type	Price Range (Total Cost for All Equipment)
Standard Ethernet network for three PCs with a hub and three NICs	$50–$200
No-new-wires network using phoneline or powerline powerline technology for three PCs	$75–$150
Wireless LAN for three PCs	$200–$400
Whole-home wiring system	$1000–$15,000
Smart home automation system for entire home	$100–$20,000

As you can see, the cost of home networking equipment has quite a range. From the fattest wallets to the tightest budget, there really is a solution for everyone. There are also different types of equipment you might want to purchase to add to your home network. In Table 4.2, you'll see prices of network-related technologies you might want to consider to gain additional value from your network. Some of these products or technologies might be included already with your PC or as part of your existing "bag of goodies"; if that's the case, you don't have to worry about the price of these products because you already own them! Or, if you're looking to expand your network to a new PC or information appliance, you might have to factor the cost of these products into your home network plans.

TABLE 4.2 Cost of Other Stuff You Might Want for Your Home Network

Other Stuff	Price Range
New desktop PC	$700–$2,000
New laptop PC	$1,000–$3,000
New high-speed modem (DSL or cable)	$0–$200 (might come with your subscription)
Residential gateway (might include high speed modem in an "all-in-one" solution)	$100–$300
Zip drive or network storage drive (large hard drive that connects directly to the network as opposed to your PC)	Zip: $100–$200 Network Drive: $300–$700
MP3 audio receiver	$100–$300
Networked PC camera	$100–$200

As you can see, a home network allows you to do many things, and there are specific products that allow you to get extra value out of a home network. But don't be intimidated by the cost of some of these products or the network equipment itself, because as you will see with the two contrasting examples given next, you can spend very little or very lavishly, depending on your tastes and budget. I'll show you how two people take two different approaches to networking their homes.

First we'll look at Paul Pinto, a 29-year-old single man living in Seattle, Washington. Paul is currently working as an office temp, trying to getting his fledging band, "The Naked Greenspans," a record contract. Paul wanted a home network to share his DSL connection with his roommate, Mo. Paul decided to share because he realized he could split the cost of the DSL connection with his roommate and still have the effective throughput of a DSL connection at half the cost.

Obviously, Paul most likely does not have a lot to spend on a network. Yet you are probably getting the sense that he did not need a lot to accomplish his home-networking goals. In Table 4.3, you'll see the additional cost of everything Paul needed in order to set up his home network. To show you what he also used but didn't pay for, we'll look at what network building blocks were used even if they did not cost Paul any additional money.

TABLE 4.3 Paul Pinto's Home Network Budget

Item	Cost to Paul	Note
PCs on network	$0	Paul is using his old Pentium II system he bought two years ago. Mo is using his Dad's laptop he "borrowed" about six months ago.
Network interface cards	$80	Paul bought two NICs, one for himself and one for his roommate (he owes Mo for last month's power bill.)
DSL modem	$0	The modem came with Paul's DSL service. He and Mo need only one because Mo accesses the DSL modem through the network.
Five-port hub	$40	Paul thought the extra ports might come in handy because he is thinking of asking his girlfriend, the one he met over the Internet, to move in soon.
Network software: Windows 98	$0	This came with the PC.
Network cabling	$10	
Total Network Cost	**$130**	Paul might need to spend an extra $50 for a NIC and some cable if his girlfriend, Venus, decides to move in.

As you can see, Paul was able to put together a network for well under $200. This network allows him to share a high-speed Internet connection, play the occasional game of SPLAT head-to-head with Venus, and share his latest lyrics with Mo.

If Paul had decided to install a wireless network, the cost could have been anywhere from $75 to $200 more, depending on which type of equipment he decided to use—a little more expensive, but still affordable enough for a struggling musician.

Next we'll look at Barry Beemer, the 40-year-old founder of a company that specializes in true-to-life replicas of Elvis Presley. His company, TheKingLives.com, is doing a thriving business, and this has allowed him to live quite comfortably, including a recent purchase of a large mansion in Memphis, Tennessee. Barry decided to make his new home truly wired, including a whole-home wiring system and some of the latest home automation technologies.

In Table 4.4, you'll see the breakdown of Barry's budget for his smart home. Barry decided to fully equip his smart home with high-speed networking technology, a centralized smart home management console, all built around a structured wiring solution. This budget includes the cost of new PCs and stereo equipment, most of which many folks would already have paid.

TABLE 4.4 Barry Beemer's Home Network Budget

Item	Cost to Barry	Note
Five new PCs	$7,500	Barry decided to move his personal "entourage" (what he calls his business team) into his mansion.
Structured wiring solution	$5,000	This included a central wiring closet, integrated cabling (Cat 5, coax, and fiber).
Centralized home automation/control system	$5,000	Barry bought a system that controls his lighting, heating/air conditioning, and 12-foot Electric Elvis statue through a centralized keypad.
Installation of wiring and homeautomation	$2,000	Many times this is included in the cost of the packages themselves.
New networked cameras for surveillance	$1,000	Barry feels he is being stalked by a former girlfriend who calls herself "Priscilla."
Ethernet switch and NICs	$350	Enough NICs for three desktop PCs.
Wireless LAN access point and two wireless NICs	$450	Barry opted for an office-grade solution, although he could have bought a cheaper system for wireless networking.
Cable modem	$0	This came with his service.
Total Network (and then some) Cost	**$21,300**	Barry figures he'll have to sell five "Flaming Elvises" to pay for his new Smart Home.

Clearly Barry decided to go all out. It is important to note, however, that *the data networking equipment—other than the wiring—cost Barry only $800*, and this was enough to network up to 10 PCs with traditional Ethernet (he bought a 10-port switch) and two wirelessly. The cost of the PCs was included only to illustrate what the cost would be if someone such as Barry decided to buy all he needed. The structured wiring system, though it cost Barry an additional $5,000, was one of the nicer systems available and was not necessary if Barry decided to string the cable through the home himself.

The structured wiring solution, clearly a nice addition to a whole-home network, cost $5,000. This included a centralized wiring panel and phone, network, and cable TV jacks in every room of the house. The home automation system included a centralized management touch pad and controlled all lighting and most electric home systems such as heating, air-conditioning, and the home security system. This set Barry back another $5,000.

A Network to Fit Any Budget

It is clear from looking at two different network installations that you can spend very little or much more to set up a network in your home. One thing you should understand from these examples is that it doesn't take very much to install a basic network in a home, even for a large or more expensive home.

Planning Pillar Three: Your Network Activities

One of the most important things you'll need to understand and plan for is what exactly you plan to do with your home network. The needs of different individuals vary widely, even within the same household.

Consider the Needlemeyer Family. Ned Needlemeyer and his wife, Nelly, live in a nice four-bedroom house with their two children, Nina (15 years old) and Nick (9 years old). One day Ned was reading a magazine article about how affordable and easy it is to put in a home network, and he decided to ask the family whether they'd like to have one in their home. When he did bring it up over dinner that night, Ned was surprised at how enthusiastic his family was about a home network. Here are some examples of the different responses Ned heard:

- Nelly: "I could use the network to share your DSL line, as well as set up an intercom to tell Nick when it's time to quit playing Doom and come eat. I could also hook up a Web pad and check on recipes over the Web in the kitchen."

- Ned: "I think I'll use it for sharing my Internet connection and allow everyone to use my laser printer."

- Nick: "I'll use it to play SHREDDER against Daryl and Adam over the Internet, and stream my Greenday MP3s downstairs."

- Nina: "Dirk [Nina's boyfriend] and I can use the network to connect our PCs when he comes over to do homework with me."

Ned proceeded to finish his meal and realized that a home network would indeed be a good investment for his family. Besides being a scarily "traditional" family, the Needlemeyers are pretty representative of other families who find that each member of a household might have a very different reason for accessing the network. Some of the things impacting network activities include the following:

- Each family or household member might have very different interests.
- Different ages mean that each member will likely participate in different activities on the network.

    (Children's activities are likely to be very different from that of their parents.)
- A network set up for a home office will likely have very different activities on it than one set up primarily for entertainment.

It pays to sit down with all the members of the household and find out what they want to use the home network for. Some things may be beyond the wishes of certain family members, but doing such an interview will help you better understand how your network will be used and thus help you plan it most efficiently.

Planning Pillar Four: Your Technical Know-How

As you will find out in Part II and Part III of this book, you do not need to be a technical guru to set up a home network. Windows PCs (as well as Macs) have built-in basic commands that I will walk you through to help set up your home network. Many companies sell products designed specifically for people who do not have a technical background so that they can quickly and easily set up a home network.

So although setting up a home network requires practically no knowledge, there are more advanced networks that might require some level of network knowledge. One such situation we have already discussed is setting up a home server using a network operating system. Although NOS's such as Windows NT or Windows 2000 for Servers are similar to Windows solutions for desktops in look and feel, they are nonetheless still more complex to use than if you were to set up a peer-to-peer network using the built-in capabilities of Windows for desktops.

And even though I will show you the basic steps of how to set up a network, there are those who absolutely refuse to touch the wiring or even think about plugging things such as NICs into PCs. My mom is one of those people. For her, or for you if this is the case, I would suggest either appointing a person you know (if they're really nice) to do this or hiring a network installation specialist.

Network installation might not be the only reason you want to bring in someone to help you with your network. Here are some other reasons you might consider using the services of a specialist in setting up your network:

- You are installing network cabling that requires tearing up walls and other changes to your home infrastructure.
- You are installing a complicated network including a network server that acts as a Web server.
- You want to install a non-self-installable home control/automation system.
- You want to tie your home network to electrical-system control, in which case you might want to consider an electrical contractor.
- You are building a new home, in which case you can use your builder/contractor or someone this person has contracted with who specializes in new home wiring systems.
- You want to use the special skills of a home system integrator who is knowledgeable about home data as well as audio/visual networks to ensure that your design, layout, and functional needs are met.

The technical know-how required for installation of a small network is minimal, but when you need to expand beyond the basic peer-to-peer network (which, by the way, meets the needs of most households), you might consider the services of a specialist.

> **NOTE**
>
> It's also important to remember that as technologies advance, less and less knowledge will be required of the end user. If you think networking is simple today, all I can say is you ain't seen nothin' yet. Companies involved in the networking space know that things need to be simple for consumers of their products, and they are working hard to make things easier. Advances in ease of installation and maintenance of this equipment will only get easier in the future.

Time to Plan the Pillars

Okay, now that we've reviewed the basic fundamental "pillars" that need to be considered when you're planning a home network, it's time to start planning. Don't worry, this won't get too involved, and it might actually take only a few minutes for some of you who already know the answers to many of these questions.

Table 4.5 shows a set of questions based on the different planning pillars. Some will require a simple yes or no; some might involve a little more research such as talking to different members of the household or looking up the age of your house. Either way, I would suggest answering each question as best you can so that at least you have a basic understanding of your specific situation, which should allow you to make a plan to address all the different "planning pillars."

TABLE 4.5   Questions to Ask Yourself When Planning Your Home Network

Questions	Implication
How many members of the household will use the home network?	This will impact size and amount of home network, and whether you need to address certain needs of others.
How old is my home? Also, do I think I can use my in-home phone or electrical wiring? Will my home network be installed in multiple areas of the house?	If your home is older, you might have problems using existing wiring. If you are planning on having network cabling installed, you will need to decide how to run it through the house. You will want to draw a network map to help you plan where you need to run cabling and place different equipment such as network hubs and residential gateway.
How much do I plan to spend on my home network?	This is a crucial question; as you've seen, there is a wide range of prices for different home network configurations.
What do I need for a home network, and what do I already have in terms of equipment and software?	As you've seen, you might already have much of what you need, or someone in your home might have the necessary network building blocks to get started.
What will each member of the household use the network for?	This is very important because it will help you determine the network needs of each before you purchase and install the network.
Will children be using the network?	Children might have special needs in terms of using the PC or network security.
Are there any special features of your network or smart home that will require the skills of a specialist?	If you just need help with network setup, you can ask a friend or family member; if it's a specialized skill such as installing a high-end home automation system, you should consider hiring a system installation specialist.

4

YOUR HOME
NETWORK
PLANNING GUIDE

This list does not include every question you could ask, but these are the key issues that will help you to plan your home network.

A Few Other Things

If you've gone through all the steps we've talked about to this point, you'll have a good idea of how to plan your home network. However, there are a few other things I thought I'd mention to make sure that your move to getting wired is a smooth one.

Remember to Allow for Head Room

One thing to keep in mind is that your network needs today might not be your needs six months or a year from now. If you foresee adding new members to your household, you should make sure that you can expand easily when they come on board. Okay, so maybe that new baby won't be getting "connected" right away, but Spike the live-in boyfriend might want to check the latest scores on his favorite teams, and you'll want to have a hub or switch with enough ports for him. Or, that home business you've started is going to grow faster than you expected, and you'll need to add a server or more PCs within the next 6 to 12 months. Whatever your future needs are, it helps to do a little planning.

Organization Plan

One thing that you'll find makes your life as a home network user and manager infinitely easier is creating an organization plan. It might not seem like much, but after you make your purchases of home network equipment and begin to assign network IDs and passwords, you could soon find yourself awash in a case of information overload. The best way to make sure you are prepared for the potential network equipment problems (they can happen!) and user questions is to keep all your information organized in one place. This will include receipts, customer support numbers, user profiles, and any other relevant network information.

Are You Ready?

Well, now we're about to have some fun. We've talked about the different important network concepts you'll need in order to get started, and helped you make a plan for creating a network that meets the special needs of your home and its inhabitants. Now, believe it or not, we're ready to start building that little hummer. But before we start on Part II, let's review what we've learned in this chapter.

Wrap It Up

When creating a home network plan, you need to consider four basic "planning pillars":

- The special characteristics of your home
- The budget for your home network—remember, home networks can range anywhere from under a $100 to over $20,000 depending on complexity and how advanced your equipment is

- The activities you and those you live with plan for the home network

- The technical know-how needed for installation of any advanced network or smart home equipment

You'll also want to plan for any changes or growth you might have on the network. You will also save yourself future headaches (and wallet-aches) if you create an organization plan for your network.

Digital Plumbing: Network Wiring and Hardware Options

PART II

IN THIS PART

Home Network Equipment: Choices, Choices, Choices

IN THIS CHAPTER

There is a network for everyone. No matter what a person's unique situation is, regardless of where he lives and what his budget is, he will find a wide range of choices of network equipment that will fit the bill.

As you know from reading Chapter 4, "Your Home Network Planning Guide," you are no different. Your home, budget, housemates, and technical abilities all will impact what kind of network you decide to invest in. If you haven't read Chapter 4 (shame on you!), you should at least review the first section, which outlines each of the planning criteria, or planning pillars, that will determine what your unique situation is and what type of network you will want to have.

Let's Get Started!

Now that you have a foundation in the basic networking concepts or building blocks, as well as an understanding of what your particular needs are, you are ready to go shopping for network equipment. This chapter will give you an overview of the different technology options, and their price ranges and capabilities, and will look at how you actually go about buying these products. Where many books fall short is in helping you actually go out and get your network, but not this one! You'll learn about the different options for acquiring and even installing your home network. You'll also find appendixes at the end that list the different product manufacturers and some areas where you can buy these products.

What Are My Choices?

Networking equipment comes in various options. These are just a few of the types of networking equipment you can buy today:

- Ethernet equipment using new cabling
- Wireless networking equipment
- Phoneline networking equipment
- Powerline networking equipment
- Whole-home wiring systems called structured wiring packages
- Internet sharing devices called home routers/residential gateways

With this much variety, everyone can find a particular type of network equipment to fit his or her situation. In Table 5.1, you will see the different options and the costs, benefits, and potential drawbacks of each.

NOTE

This particular chapter focuses mainly on setting up data, entertainment, and communications networks. Chapter 21, "Smart Home: Home Automation Networks," has a special section focusing on home automation/smart home networks. However, I will mention, when relevant, how the technologies discussed in this part of the book overlap and are integrated with smart home technologies.

TABLE 5.1 Home Network Comparison

Network Equipment Type	Cost Range	Benefits	Drawbacks
Traditional Ethernet equipment and cabling	$80–$200 to network three PCs	Cheap technology that is reliable and widely available; highest speed alternative	Need to install new cabling
Wireless LAN	$200–$400 to network three PCs	No need for cabling, can move throughout house and seamlessly remain on network	Higher cost relative to Ethernet or phoneline networking equipment
Phoneline networking equipment	$80–$150 to network three PCs	Very cheap and no need for network hub or new cabling	Might not work well in older homes; some rooms might not have phone jacks; slower than Ethernet
Powerline networking	$150–$250 to network three PCs	No need for new cabling; there are more power outlets per room than phone jacks	Might not work well in older homes; possible interference with other electrical equipment; slower than Ethernet

TABLE 5.1   Continued

Network Equipment Type	Cost Range	Benefits	Drawbacks
Whole-home wiring systems (aka Structure Wiring)	$500–$10,000	Great solution for new homes; ensure each room is wired for network, entertainment, and communications	Highest cost solution; still need to buy Ethernet networking equipment; will likely need installation specialist
Internet sharing hardware	$100–$300	Provides Internet sharing with other benefits such as firewall, Ethernet hub	Can do sharing with software-only solutions

Each solution has its own unique cost, benefits, and solutions. The good thing is that you can choose whichever one fits your unique situation. We will briefly discuss each option and why you might find a given option right (or wrong) for your situation. For a more in-depth look at each technology, check out the chapters that follow in Part II, "Digital Plumbing: Network Wiring and Hardware Options."

Good Old Ethernet

If you go into an office today where there's a local area network, chances are that it is running on Ethernet. This is because since Ethernet's early days it has proved reliable and widely available, as well as very affordable. Why not take this same popular technology and use it for your home network?

Well, many people are doing just that. In fact, in the days before home networks became such a hot topic (only a few years ago), most people who did set up a home network used Ethernet technology. And even with the arrival of new networking technologies specifically geared toward the home environment, more people than ever are choosing to use Ethernet because of its low cost and reliability.

Ethernet equipment and UTP cabling are available at your local electronics or PC store. To make things even easier for new network users, there are such things as "network kits" that include a couple of Ethernet NICs and a hub or switch, often for under $100. Also, because most high-speed modems such as DSL or cable have an Ethernet port, you can connect directly with an Ethernet connection to your PC or into an Ethernet switch or Ethernet supporting residential gateway.

To determine whether Ethernet is what you want, you might consider the following questions:

- Are you looking for reliable and time-tested technology? If so, Ethernet is for you.

- Do you want the highest speed technology available? If so, Ethernet technology allows you to go up to 100Mbps with equipment from your local store, and up to 1000Mbps (gigabit speeds, or 1000 megabits per second) with equipment available to office network users.

- How do you feel about running cabling in a room or through your home? If this is no problem, Ethernet is a great solution. If you are not excited about possibly putting holes in your walls, you should consider a no-new-wires option.

- Do you have a tight budget? If so, Ethernet is very affordable and should be highly considered.

One thing for sure: Ethernet is not going away, and it is likely to continue to rise in popularity over the coming years as more people explore home networks. To learn more about Ethernet networks, including how to set up and install the appropriate drivers, see Chapter 6, "Understanding and Installing an Ethernet Network."

Wireless Networking

Wireless is wonderful—you have the capability to walk around your home with a laptop or wireless Web tablet and surf the Web, play games, listen to your digital audio. Of all the technologies available to the home user, wireless networking will likely see the greatest increase in popularity in coming years.

It used to be that wireless networking technology was hard to find and was much more expensive than traditional Ethernet networking. Well, this has changed and you can now find wireless networking equipment at any local electronics or PC store, or even through your PC company when you buy a new computer. As for cost, wireless LAN equipment is still a little more expensive than Ethernet or phoneline networking equipment, but it is coming down rapidly in price. Today it is possible to find wireless NICs for under $100.

> **CAUTION**
>
> One thing you should know about wireless is that there are various technologies and standards for allowing networking equipment and other devices to communicate. We will take a look at these (and whether you should even care) in Chapter 7, "The Wonderful World of Wireless Networking."

When considering whether to go "wireless," you should ask yourself the following:

- Do I really want to be able to access the network and the Internet anywhere in my home (including out on the back deck)? If you answered yes, you should strongly consider wireless networking.
- Do I have an older home (30 years or older) in which telephone- and powerline-based networking might not work as well? If so, wireless is a great option.
- Do I cringe at the thought of someone stringing cable around my home, through my walls, and under my carpet? If so, wireless will help you avoid this mess.
- Am I networking a laptop PC or a couple of laptops? If so, wireless networking makes a lot of sense for mobile PCs.

Although a little slower than most types of Ethernet equipment in use today, wireless networking technology is quickly catching up and is on its way to becoming one of the most popular home networking technologies. For more information on wireless networking, including the different technologies and standards, be sure to read Chapter 7.

Phoneline Networking

It used to be that the phone wiring in your home was just for sending your voice signal to others. Boy, have things changed! With new technology from an industry standards group called the Home Phone Networking Alliance (HPNA), networking equipment is available that allows for networking PCs or other HPNA-based equipment over the copper phone wiring in your home.

Phoneline NICs connect into the same phone jack that your phone does, so there is no need for anything other than two NICs, and a little phone cable to connect your PC to the phone jack, and you're networked! And believe it or not, you can operate your phoneline network simultaneously with voice calls. This is because phoneline networking technology and voice calls operate at different frequencies.

> **NOTE**
>
> *Frequency*—R.E.M asked, "What's the frequency, Kenneth?" Well, I'll tell you. A frequency is like a channel in communication. Different frequencies are available over wired networks such as phonelines, as well as wireless networks. Networks operating at different frequencies do not interrupt one another, so when a phoneline network is operating on frequency A, and your voice call is on frequency B, they can coexist peacefully and simultaneously.

Is a phoneline network right for you? Ask yourself the following questions to find out:

- Do you want an easy-to-install network that avoids installing new wiring? Phoneline is a good option for this type of network.
- Do you have phone jacks in every location where you would like to have a network-connected PC or device? If so, you should look at phoneline networking.
- Are you budget conscious? Phoneline networking is extremely affordable.

Phoneline networking equipment is available through retail stores, online stores, or large PC manufacturers. We'll take a deeper look at phoneline networking in Chapter 8, "Other Networking Technologies: Phoneline, Powerline, and Structured Wiring Ethernet."

Powerline Networking

As with phoneline networking, companies in the technology industry realized that it would be very convenient for home users to be able to network over their existing in-home wiring. Except that instead of phone wiring, this group, called HomePlug, decided to develop a standard for networking over your in-home AC power wiring.

The HomePlug standard is new. Products for networking using the HomePlug standard will be available in late 2001. Unlike phoneline networking technology, which started out at 1Mbps and has now moved up to 10Mbps, HomePlug decided to jump right to the higher speed 10Mbps.

If you are considering powerline networking technology, you should answer the following questions:

- Do you want a network that does not require new cabling? If so, powerline is a good option because most homes have multiple power outlets (often even in the same room).
- Are you interested in using the latest in new home networking technology? If so, HomePlug-based networking technology will certainly fit the mold.

- Do you work in an environment where a lot of high-power electrical devices are plugged into your power outlets? If you are in an industrial environment or your home uses a lot of construction equipment or tools, this might disrupt your network.

Powerline networking is an exciting new technology that will make it easier for many people to get wired. You can read more about powerline networking in Chapter 7.

Whole-Home Wiring Systems (Structured Wiring)

So what if you really want to do this connected home thing right? You want to install a home wiring system in which you can place your home network switch or hub in a central network wiring closet, and have the network cable as well as phone and even cable TV wiring run throughout the house to outlets with different connector ports for each type of connection? If this is what sounds good to you, you should look at a structured wiring package.

Structured wiring systems, though more expensive than a basic Ethernet or other types of networks, are still within reach of many. A very basic structured wiring system can be found for under $1,000, but the cost goes up quickly from there. Still, if you want to have your home future-proofed for new technologies such as faster Ethernet (a Gigabit Ethernet) and also be able to have whole-home audio and video, you should definitely look at structured wiring as an option.

> **NOTE**
>
> Structured wiring systems are most often installed in new homes. Because a new home is often an "open canvas" when you are constructing from the ground up, it is much easier to have the advanced wiring installed before all the drywall and other finishing touches are installed. This does not mean that you cannot have a structured wiring system installed in an existing home, but you should be aware that a professional installer will need to put holes in some of your walls (which, I would hope, they patch up when they're done!) to install a structured wiring system.

What About the Internet? Internet Sharing Hardware

The previous pages of this chapter talked about the variety of in-home networking technologies available. Although having a wide variety of technologies to fit the different needs of home networkers is important, just as crucial to many is the actual connection to the Internet and how this connection is shared. As you know from reading Part I, "Getting Going: Networking Overview and Planning," a big reason people are getting home networks is to share their Internet connection—dial-up connections and, more and more, high-speed connections using DSL, cable, and even satellite Internet services.

There are a few ways to share your Internet connection, which we will review in Chapter 14, "Internet Sharing on a Home Network." One of the options is to use a special piece of equipment called a home router, also known as a residential gateway. Residential gateways can come in different sizes and capabilities, but you should know the following about them:

- Residential gateways include home networking "ports" such as Ethernet, wireless, phoneline, and powerline connections.

- The residential gateway is referred to by various names, such as a routers, home gateways, or home network "hubs" (not to be confused with a traditional Ethernet hub).

- Residential gateways can include the modem as well as the home network connections in one box, but many of the early ones simply connect to the modem through an Ethernet connection.

- Residential gateways are used by many because they incorporate the capability to share one IP address. (An IP address is the "Internet address" you are using as part of your agreement with your Internet service provider to surf the Internet. You can learn more about IP addresses in Chapter 10, "Getting Around the Home Network.")

You can buy basic home routers, which are basic residential gateways, at a retail store, and soon you will be able to get more advanced residential gateways through your Internet company when you order your service.

Residential gateways and home routers will increasingly become popular ways to provide Internet sharing capabilities and Internet security. Many RGs incorporate firewalls for strong security against hackers.

NOTE

A *firewall* is a piece of equipment or software (or both) that protects your LAN against mischievous no-good types who can sneak their way in though the Internet connection onto the network. Those networks that are connected to an "always on" connection such as a DSL or cable modem connection are especially at risk because they are always connected. We will discuss Internet and network security in length later in the book.

Where to Get Home Network Equipment

Now that you have an idea of some of the options in networking equipment, you are probably asking yourself where you can get some of this stuff. Once again, I'm way ahead of you. Table 5.2 shows the ways you can buy home network gear. In my day job as an analyst, I call these locations or methods to purchase gear "channels." But because I sound like a nerd saying "channels," I'll just call them storefronts.

TABLE 5.2   Different Home Network Storefronts

Storefront	What's Unique?	Examples
National computer and electronics superstore	Large selection of networking equipment for home and small office	Best Buy, CompUSA, Circuit City, Fry's, Radio Shack
Office superstores	Smaller selection, but definitely will carry brand names	Office Depot, Office Max
Warehouse stores	Minimal selection if at all, cheap	Costco, Sam's Club
E-tailers (online stores)	Usually large selection, easy comparisons with other e-tailers, must add shipping cost	Amazon.com, Buy.com, MicroWarehouse, Egghead.com
Computer and networking catalogs	Large selection, good info, must pay shipping, most catalogs have Web sites to order from as well	CDW, Insight, Creative Computers, Black Box
PC company	Can order networking equipment with a new PC as well as other PCs you might have, company can install NIC or equipment for you	HP, Gateway, Dell, Compaq, IBM

By no means is this list exhaustive. You can certainly buy networking equipment in many ways, including through your local neighborhood store as easily as you could from a national store. With that local touch, you might even get better service. Also consider network specialists who might be willing to sell you equipment and do the installation for a reasonable price. Other possible "storefronts" include your contractor if you are building a new home, and your broadband service provider. This last one might surprise you, but many DSL and cable modem ISPs realize that there is a rising demand for home networking and are beginning to sell home network equipment (in addition to the modem) to their subscribers. This might include an Internet sharing device such as a residential gateway.

I would suggest that you buy from a location with a good return policy and, if possible, knowledgeable salespeople. I can honestly say, after spending ample time in different storefronts, that the salespeople's knowledge of networking equipment is spotty at best. However, this situation is getting better as more people demand networking equipment. I predict a day when the salespeople at the local electronics store will be as knowledgeable about NICs as they are about PC processors and cell phones. The good news is that many of the equipment vendors themselves have 1-800 numbers for call-in support as well as Web sites where you can get help.

Also remember that networking connections will begin to be integrated into all sorts of devices we use every day. Gaming consoles from the likes of Sony and Microsoft will someday have Ethernet connections, and home appliances will someday have the capability to be remotely monitored and connected to some form of network. These changes will allow networking to be easier and more pervasive in our lives. However, these changes are coming slowly; so you'll still have to look for a good place to buy networking equipment and (thank goodness) you'll still have to read the rest of this book.

Wrap It Up

You've learned in this chapter that there are various solutions for your networking equipment needs, each with its own benefits. I've broken down the different networking technologies into the following:

- Ethernet
- Wireless
- Phoneline
- Powerline
- Whole-home wiring systems (structured wiring)

You can buy your networking equipment through various storefronts, including the following:

- Large computer and electronics stores
- Office equipment stores
- Warehouse stores
- E-tailers or online stores
- Catalogs
- PC companies
- Other places such as your home builder/contractor, network installation specialists, or even your Internet service provider

This chapter briefly introduced the choices available to you for your home network. The following chapters in Part II will go in depth on the available solutions, as well as tell you how to install the different networking equipment choices.

Understanding and Installing an Ethernet Network

IN THIS CHAPTER

Ethernet is the big kahuna of modern local area networks. Sure, there are different networking languages. Some work with Ethernet; some operate in place of Ethernet entirely. But in today's business and home networks, a large majority of networks in use today are using some form of Ethernet.

After reading Chapter 5, "Home Network Equipment: Choices, Choices, Choices," you should know whether you think an Ethernet-based network is right for you. This chapter will tell you everything you want or need to know about Ethernet, including the following:

- An overview of how an Ethernet network works
- How to select which Ethernet "flavor" is appropriate for your home network
- How to install an Ethernet NIC
- Ethernet hub placement and cabling tips

An Ethernet Primer

Because you've heard quite a bit about this thing called Ethernet, you're probably wondering how it actually works. For those of you who are less curious about the inner workings of the technology and want to get going on installing your Ethernet network, you can skim this section of the chapter and move right on to the section "Choosing from Among the Different Flavors of Ethernet." For you curious sorts, the next few sections will give you a good understanding of how Ethernet works.

Ethernet as a Communication Protocol

So you know a little bit about the history of Ethernet and how it works, but do you know what exactly Ethernet is? Ethernet is both a communication protocol and a cabling scheme. What is a protocol? A protocol is basically a set of rules and conventions for communicating between devices. In this way, a protocol is really like a language, because languages have their own conventions and rules, as well as words, for communicating.

Who Oversees the Ethernet Kingdom?

Ethernet's growth as a network technology has been in part due to the fact that it's a widely accepted standard. Most networking standards are monitored by a group called the Institute of Electrical and Electronics Engineers, or IEEE (pronounced "I-triple-E"). Besides being, as you might expect, a bunch of wild and crazy guys and gals, the members of IEEE oversee technical standards such as those for Ethernet. Being big on math, these guys also assign each standard a number, Ethernet's being the 802.3.

Ethernet has its own set of rules for communicating between devices. These rules define how long each communication chunk of data, also known as a packet, is. These rules also determine how fast each packet will travel and how each packet is formatted. The Ethernet protocol even has rules for how the communication between devices is to be conducted. These rules of conduct are based on what is called CSMA/CD—short for Carrier Sense Multiple Access with Collision Detection.

How does CSMA/CD work? An Ethernet network using CSMA/CD operates like a person trained on the rules of polite conversation. Much like this person would listen first to see whether anyone else was talking, an NIC that is ready to send some information from a PC will listen first to hear whether there is any "noise" from another computer on the wire. If there is no other communication, the NIC will send its communication packets. However, as with any conversation, it is possible that two NICs might start talking at the same time. If this is the case, there will be what is called a collision, meaning that the packets run into each other and do not arrive at their destination. Because Ethernet is a pretty resilient protocol, it has built-in capabilities to recover in the case of a collision and have signals resent after a brief period of silence. All this happens so fast that most likely you would not ever notice any slowdowns related to packet collisions.

Ethernet as a Cabling Scheme

Ethernet not only dictates how the communication is formatted and executed (what the protocol part of Ethernet does), but also has rules for what kind of cabling to use and how the cabling is set up. In Chapter 3, "Network Relationships: Network Types and Topologies," we examined the different network topologies for cabling, including star and bus. Both of these topologies can be used in an Ethernet network, depending on which type of network cabling you use.

In the section "Choosing from Among the Different Flavors of Ethernet," we will discuss all the options available to you in terms of cabling and the relevant topology. We will also make your life simpler by suggesting which option to choose for your particular situation.

What About the Different Speeds?

Ethernet is not just Ethernet, but it's Fast and Gigabit Ethernet too! These prefixes tell you how fast an Ethernet network communicates. The original Ethernet technology operated at 10Mbps, which means 10 million bits per second. Back in the 1970s and early 1980s this was blazing fast, but before you knew it, those at the IEEE realized they'd need to move data at faster rates as more traffic came on to the network. They soon developed a standard for Fast Ethernet, which operated at 10 times the speed of Ethernet, or 100Mbps.

Fast Ethernet networks are plenty fast for a home network. But in case you're an extreme user, or building a high-speed office network, there is the next step up in speed, called Gigabit Ethernet. Gigabit Ethernet moves at a scorching 1000Mbps, 10 times the speed of Fast Ethernet and 100 times that of the original Ethernet.

If you think Gigabit Ethernet seems fast, there is a new standard in development for 10 Gigabit Ethernet. This standard, which will not be finished until sometime in 2002, will be for very high-speed networks in large data centers and for aggregating multiple Fast and Gigabit Ethernet connections in a large business network.

Ethernet is plenty fast for many home networks, but because the cost difference between Ethernet and Fast Ethernet is minimal, if you have a choice you'll want to go with the higher speed Fast Ethernet. Making your choice even easier is the fact that today most Ethernet NICs, hubs, and switches are dual-speed, meaning they operate at either 10 or 100Mbps depending on how fast the other parts of the network they are connected to operate. So if you have a 10/100 (dual-speed) NIC, it will sense whether the hub it is talking to can communicate at Fast Ethernet speeds, and if it can it will move to the higher speed. If not, it will automatically adjust to communicating at the lower 10Mbps speed.

Choosing from Among the Different Flavors of Ethernet

Because you have more knowledge about the inner workings of Ethernet than you could ever possibly put to good use, we'll now spend some time discussing something you'll definitely need to know about before installing your Ethernet network: the types—or flavors—of Ethernet. This is because each requires its own type of cabling, its own topology, and its own type of special connector, as well as having its own benefits (some more than others!).

> **NOTE**
>
> A *connector* is the type of physical interface that is on the end of the network cable that connects to the NIC or hub. You can see what a connector looks like by referring to Figure 6.2, later in this chapter.

As you'll recall, in Chapter 2, "Home Network Building Blocks: What Makes Your Network Tick," we briefly discussed the types of network cabling:

- Unshielded twisted pair
- Coax
- Fiber

Because there are different types of cabling for Ethernet, there are essentially different flavors of Ethernet that operate over a particular type of cabling, each requiring a specific type of topology as well as connector. Table 6.1 shows the types of Ethernet, with the corresponding cabling, connector type, and topology.

TABLE 6.1   The Different Ethernet Flavors

Ethernet Flavor	Cabling Type	Connector	Topology
10/100BASE-T	UTP (unshielded twisted pair)	RJ-45	Star
10BASE-2	Thinnet (also called coax)	BNC, T-connector, terminator	Star or bus
100BASE-FX	Fiber	SC connector	Star

Now we'll discuss each flavor of Ethernet, looking at the types of cabling needed, the connectors for each, and what your network topology should look like. The first Ethernet flavor we'll discuss is 10/100BASE-T, which is the most commonly used type for home networks.

TIP

If you are looking at installing an Ethernet network for your home, you should strongly consider a 10/100BASE-T network. 10/100BASE-T Ethernet is the most commonly used type of Ethernet for both business and home networks. 10/100BASE-T Ethernet NICs and hubs are the most widely available of Ethernet equipment (and are extremely affordable), and the most common type of network cabling is unshielded twisted pair (UTP), the kind used with 10/100BASE-T Ethernet networks.

10/100BASE-T (UTP) Ethernet Networks

As you know by now, 10/100BASE-T Ethernet networks are the most common type of office and home Ethernet networks in use today. In fact, for the prospective home networker, if you go to the store and buy a home network "kit" that comes with a couple of NICs, a hub or switch, and some cabling, more than likely this kit is a 10/100BASE-T network.

The 10/100BASE-T Ethernet networks use a star topology. This means that when you set up a 10/100BASE-T network, you will need a hub or switch to connect all the different endpoints. Figure 6.1 demonstrates a basic two-PC 10/100BASE-T network. The network uses Cat 5 cabling and connects to the hub and the different endpoints using RJ-45 connectors. You can connect two PCs directly without a hub (but not more than two PCs) in a 10/100 BASE-T network via a crossover cable. However, I strongly recommend using a hub or switch to allow for growth of your network—and hubs are extremely affordable.

> **TIP**
>
> Network kits are a great way to get started networking. These kits are available at any large electronics retailer or online, and they come with everything you need to start a two-PC Ethernet network. For under $100 (sometimes under $50), you get all the necessary building blocks for a small Ethernet home network. If you want to simply network a couple of PCs in a room or in an adjacent room, all you might need is one of these network kits. Wireless and phoneline networking kits are also available.

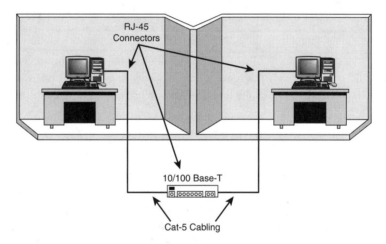

FIGURE 6.1

A two-PC 10/100BASE-T network.

As you've learned, each cabling type has its own connector. Cat 5 cabling uses RJ-45 connectors. If you are wondering what the heck one looks like, Figure 6.2 is a picture of an RJ-45 connector used in a 10/100BASE-T network.

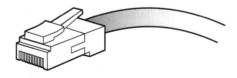

FIGURE 6.2

An RJ-45 connector.

RJ-45 connectors come as part of the cable, and they connect into the hub port or NIC slot. These connectors don't look all that different from phone connectors, which go by the name of RJ-11 connectors (or jacks). If you look closely at an RJ-45 connector, it is wider than an RJ-11 connector and has more little metal "pins" (which look like little copper strips) than an RJ-11. An RJ-45 has eight pins, compared with six for an RJ-11.

Recall from Table 6.1 that the 10/100BASE-T Ethernet network uses unshielded twisted pair cable. UTP is broken into different categories, and the category of UTP used in today's home 10/100BASE-T networks is Category 5 (Cat 5) UTP. You can purchase Cat 5 UTP cabling as a separate purchase or as part of a network kit. If you purchase a network kit with two NICs and a hub, you will likely receive two lengths of cable ranging anywhere from 10 to 20 feet. Those cables with RJ-45 connectors on both ends are called *patch cables*. If you need a longer cable than is provided in a kit, you can purchase cabling separately in different lengths at any store that carries networking equipment. You can also connect two shorter patch cables using what is called a *coupler*.

What About Cat 3 and 4 Cabling?

If there is a Cat 5, or Category 5, of unshielded twisted pair cabling, there has to be other categories, correct? In my best Ed McMahon voice: You are correct, sir!! In fact, there are seven categories, but all you really need to know about is Cat 5, and to a lesser extent, categories 3 and 4.

As you've probably figured out, the lower you go in the category ranking, the lower the quality of the UTP cabling. The type of cabling used for plain old phone wiring to carry voice calls in office buildings and homes is Cat 3. Cat 4 is a little higher quality, but it isn't very common today. You could conceivably use Cat 3 cabling for your home network, but it isn't a good idea because you are likely to experience slower speeds and loss of information. There is a recent trend toward using Cat 5 UTP cabling for voice calls as well, and some progressive companies are putting their voice and data traffic on the same Cat 5 cabling. This type of *integrated network* takes special equipment.

If you're a cabling snob, you could use Cat 6 and Cat 7 UTP cabling, but this is not necessary. Only really high-speed networks in offices necessitate Cat 6 or 7 cabling, and chances are you'd have to go to a special networking store or reseller to find this type of cabling.

Ethernet 10BASE-2 (Thin Coax/Thinnet) Networks

Although most home networks using Ethernet will be 10/100BASE-T, the second most common will likely be 10BASE-2 networks. 10BASE-2 networks are also called Thinnet or thin coax networks. With 10BASE-2 networks you use a star or bus topology. With a bus topology, you can hook the different PCs on the network together using a common cable.

The connector on the end of coax cabling is called a BNC connector. Like any type of plug-in connector, a BNC connector has a male piece (the plug-in piece) and a female side (the port side on a 10BASE-2 hub or NIC). For a bus network like the one shown in Figure 6.3, you will also need to have what is called a T-connector. T-connectors are three sided connectors that

- allow you to connect a thinnet cable coming from computer A into a connector that
- connects into the NIC in computer B and
- then connects the NIC in computer B to the strand going to computer C.

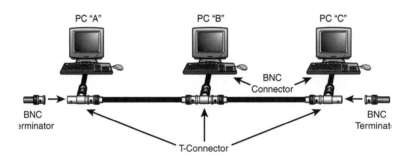

FIGURE 6.3

A 10BASE-2 bus network using BNC connectors, T-connectors, and BNC terminators.

For each PC that is on the "end" of the network, meaning that the cabling terminates at this PC, you will also need to use a BNC terminator, which plugs into a the third side of a T-connector that is not being used to connect to another PC. Figure 6.3 illustrates the use of all three connectors in a 10BASE-2 bus network.

As you can see in Figure 6.3, a 10BASE-2 network requires much more variation in the type of connector needed. In a simple three-PC network, this is what you need:

- The BNC connectors included on the thinnet cabling
- The T-connector to connect the different pieces of cabling and connect to the NIC itself
- A BNC terminator for capping off the T-connectors on the end of the network

CAUTION

One word of caution for a 10BASE-2 network: The thinnet/coax cabling you use must be rated at what is called 50 ohms. An ohm is a measure of electrical resistance. When you buy thinnet, the packaging should tell you whether it is 50 ohms. When terminating the open connection in a T-connector with a BNC terminator, you must use one that is 50 ohms as well.

Ethernet 100BASE-FX (Fiber) Networks

So you really want to go fiber, do you? Fiber-based Ethernet networks are the fastest type of local area network, with technologies to go up to a gigabit per second and beyond. However, in a home network, chances are you will never need to go to these types of speeds.

Before you decide to go with a fiber-based network, ask yourself the following questions:

- Do I want to pay extra for fiber as my network cabling, when I can use a 10/100BASE-T (using UTP cabling) to achieve the same speeds?

- Do I want to pay extra for the Ethernet hardware, because the NICs and switches for fiber-based Ethernet are more expensive and are not generally available at the usual computer or electronics retailers?

- Am I prepared to deal with the extra expense of using a professional installer, because fiber cabling is much more difficult to install?

The last thing I want to do is discourage someone from achieving home network nirvana (ah, isn't that what we're all after?), and fiber-based Ethernet networks certainly are the créme de la créme of home networks. So if you do want to pay the extra expense for fiber-based cabling and Ethernet equipment, by all means do so. If you are building a new home and want to install the best network money can buy, 100 or 1000BASE-FX is a good choice. Fiber cabling can also be included as part of a structured cabling package when you build a new home.

How Does Fiber Cabling Work?

Fiber cabling is very different from other network cabling. The major difference is that fiber cabling has a core of glass, or optics, which carries light.

> **NOTE**
>
> *Optical networking* is that which uses light instead of electrical pulses. Because nothing travels faster than light, optical networking is seen as the fastest way to network, usually for long distances such as the network connections at the core of the Internet.

The signals that are sent across the network are changed from electric signals to optical signals. The change to optical signals is the reason for the high speeds made possible through optical fiber.

Fiber-based Ethernet networks use star topologies similar to those in a 10/100BASE-T Ethernet network. A hub or switch is required to connect the different endpoints.

Have You Decided Yet?

If you are planning to install an Ethernet home network and you haven't decided on the flavor of Ethernet, Table 6.2 should help you make up your mind. Here we take a look at the expense of each type of network, as well as the level of installation difficulty and available speeds.

TABLE 6.2   Ethernet Network Flavor Rankings

Ethernet Flavor	Cost	Difficulty	Speed
10/100BASE-T (Cat 5 UTP)	Cheapest	Easiest	Up to 100Mbps (can go to 1000Mbps with Gigabit Ethernet equipment)
10BASE-2 (Coax/Thinnet)	More Expensive	More Difficult	Up to 10Mbps
100BASE-FX (Fiber)	Most Expensive	Most Difficult	Up to 100Mbps (can go to 1000Mbps with Gigabit Ethernet equipment)

Clearly the solution with the most benefits for the least amount of trouble and expense is 10/100BASE-T. Of course, there might be reasons you choose to go with another variation of Ethernet, such as you want to use existing cabling that might already be installed in your home. I've probably made it clear which Ethernet flavor I think you should use, but if not, let me say it again: If you have no particular leanings one way or the other, for Sweet Sassy Molassey's sake, go with a 10/100BASE-T network!

There, I feel much better.

Now that you've made your decision, on to the tough stuff: installation of your Ethernet network.

Installing the Network Interface Card

Now, it's time to roll up your sleeves and install your NIC. Up until now it's been a matter of choosing what type of network you want. Now you have to actually do your first installation, that of the NIC. Whether it's an Ethernet, wireless, phoneline-based, or powerline-based network, there's a good chance you will need to install some form of NIC. The nice thing is that you have some choices that will make things easier for you, and these all start with the type of PC slot you want to connect to. Before I show you how to physically install the NIC, we'll take a quick look at how NICs differ depending on the type of PC slot they fit into.

PC Bus Types

A PC slot is also called a bus (not to be confused with the bus topology).

> **NOTE**
>
> *Bus* is a generic term for the different types of slots for connection of communications and peripherals to your PC. There are many kinds of bus types, most of which we will subsequently discuss.

The bus type of the NIC must match up with the PC bus you are using to connect to your NIC. Because many PCs have multiple slot/bus types, you can often choose the type of NIC depending on which bus you think you'd like to connect to. Table 6.3 shows the different PC bus types available and gives a description of each.

TABLE 6.3   PC Bus (or Slot) Types for NIC Cards

Bus Type	External or Internal to PC	Desktop or Laptop	Description
PCI	Internal	Desktop	Most common PC bus type, requires internal installation
USB	External	Both	Easiest installation, requires no opening of PC, can use USB NICs for desktop or laptop
ISA	Internal	Desktop	Older PC bus type, requires most complicated NIC installation
Laptop bus (PCMCIA or CardBus)	External	Buses specific to laptop PCs	Bus used for adding NIC or modems to laptops

TIP

The type of NIC bus you choose will be a separate decision from the type of network you choose (Ethernet, wireless, phoneline, powerline, or can-and-string). Each type of network technology has most of the different types of NIC bus types to choose from.

As you can see, the bus type you choose to connect your NIC to will depend on these factors:

- Whether you are hooking up a laptop or desktop PC.
- Whether your PC has available USB slots, which are often available on the front of the PC as well as the back. Some new PCs come with as many as four USB slots (fewer for laptops).
- The ease of installation and whether you would like to "get under the hood" and install a PCI or ISA NIC.

If you are installing a NIC on a desktop, you will need to choose from among a PCI, ISA, and USB NIC. PCI NICs are the most common for new Ethernet installations, as well as for wireless, phoneline, and powerline. Because the ISA bus is gradually being phased out and many new PCs are not sold with ISA bus slots, I suggest going with a PCI or USB NIC if you have these choices.

A USB NIC is a good choice if you do not want to open your PC, and all the different technologies have USB NICs available. The only drawback of USB is that the speed for the bus—

meaning the speed at which information comes in and out of the computer—maxes out at 10Mbps. This means that Ethernet and the alternative technologies have the speed "capped" at 10Mbps when USB NICs are used.

For laptops, you will want to go with a PCMCIA or CardBus bus type for your NIC, or with a USB NIC. The PCMCIA or CardBus slots are on the side of your laptop, the same slots where you would install a modem. You can get a combo NIC/modem if you want to conserve slot space on your laptop. Most laptops now have USB slots on them, but usually only one or two. This can be a disadvantage because many other peripherals for your computer now come with USB connections, and to use these, you might need to disconnect your NIC or get a USB hub.

NOTE

USB hubs are special devices that allow you to expand the number of USB connections you have on a desktop or laptop PC.

TIP

If your choice is between a PCI NIC and an ISA NIC, you will want to go with a PCI NIC if possible. This is because there are extra steps that make installation of an ISA NIC more complicated. Also, many new PCs do not have ISA slots, but all have PCI (and USB) slots.

Scalpel Please—Preparing for NIC Installation

You'll want to do a few things to prepare before you do the actual installation. Your preparation checklist should include the following:

- A small screwdriver, usually a Philips (the kind with the four wings).
- A clean workspace such as a desk or workbench with room for your PC, tools, and network equipment.
- A small container to hold screws and other small items.
- Clean hands—make sure that your hands are clean and that you have no extra jewelry on your hands. Also, before you install your NIC, be sure to touch the metal chassis of your PC to eliminate any static electricity that might be harmful to the internal components of your computer.

The Installation

Now that you've looked at the PC bus connection and have chosen the appropriate NIC, it's time to plug the NIC into the PC. This section describes the physical installation of your NIC into your PC. Although this information applies to Ethernet NIC installation, it can also apply to other technologies we will discuss in later chapters, such as wireless, phoneline, and power-line.

The installation of the NIC requires the actual physical placement of the NIC into the appropriate PC bus slot. You will also need to install NIC drivers (the software that allows your NIC hardware to work with your PC) as part of the installation process. After we review the physical installation of the NIC, we will look at installing network drivers. The two almost always go hand in hand.

CAUTION

Before you do install the NIC, you will want to review the manual or installation guide for your NIC and see whether it comes with any special instructions. You will also want to make sure that you turn the power off for you PC, and unplug your power cord to make sure you don't accidentally turn it on. Newer PCs often aren't completely turned "off" even after you have gone through the power-down process by logging off your PC. The safest way to make sure that your PC is truly off is by disconnecting the power cord.

Installing a PCI NIC

The installation of a PCI NIC is a simple process. The PCI bus is very common, and PC manufacturers have made this installation process very much a plug-and-play experience.

Figure 6.4 shows a typical PC motherboard. The PC motherboard not only has your PC's processor, memory, and other smaller components that make it run, but also has bus slots for PCI and ISA to add additional functions like sound cards, video cards, and (what else?) networking cards. As you can see in the graphic, PCI slots are generally white and smaller than ISA slots.

Before you install your PCI NIC, be sure to review Figure 6.4 so you understand what a PC motherboard, as well a PCI slot, looks like.

The steps you'll want to take for the physical installation of a PCI NIC are as listed here:

1. Make sure once again that the PC is shut down.
2. Move your PC to a desktop or workbench where you will have plenty of room to put your tools and network equipment.

3. Take off the cover of your PC. If you are not sure how to do so, refer to the manual that came with your PC. If you still are not sure, you might want to get help or consider a USB NIC, which wouldn't require opening your PC.

4. Locate an empty PCI slot. Your PC will likely have up to five PCI slots, some of which might be taken by such things as modems or sound cards. Use one that is not in use.

5. Take out the metal bracket behind the PCI slot. This will allow the NIC to have its RJ-45 jack exposed for cable installation. Remove the screw that holds the metal strip in. Save the screw, which will be used for securing the NIC after it is installed.

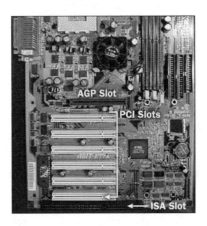

FIGURE 6.4
A PC motherboard.

CAUTION

Before you pick up the NIC and install it, be sure to touch the metal cover of your PC to eliminate any static electricity that might be in your body. The small electrical charge from your finger could harm the sensitive electronics on your PC's motherboard if not eliminated.

---

6. Line up the bottom of the NIC with a PCI slot. Press down gently and make sure that the NIC is being inserted properly. After the NIC is lined up correctly, press down firmly until the NIC is fully inserted. You can tell whether the NIC is fully inserted by whether the NIC's metal bracket fits where the small piece of metal was that you unscrewed in step 5. See Figure 6.5 for an illustration of this step.

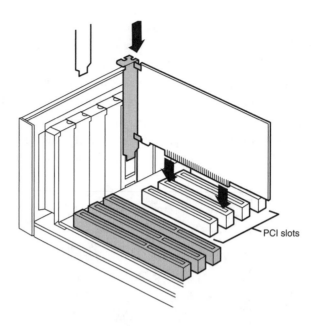

PCI slots

FIGURE 6.5
Installation of a PCI NIC.

7. Insert the small screw into the NIC's metal bracket and secure tightly. Be careful not to drop the screw onto the motherboard. If the screw does drop, you should use a pair of needlenose pliers to retrieve it.

8. Put the cover of your PC back on. Reinsert any screws and make sure the NIC is in place after the PC is reassembled. Make sure the RJ-45 jack is accessible from the back of the PC.

9. Plug the power cord back into the PC.

Installing Network Drivers

Now that you've completed the physical installation of the NIC, you will need to install the network drivers. As you might remember, drivers are the software components that enable your NIC to talk to your PC. They are a very important part of the installation process, without which your network would not work.

The task of installing a device driver is simple. Today most operating systems operate using what is called Plug and Play. Plug and Play is the automated detection and installation of the drivers necessary to allow a device to properly work.

If you have Windows 95/98/ME or XP, it is likely that your PC supports Plug and Play. However, it is not always guaranteed that the device you are installing, in this case a NIC, has the necessary drivers in Windows to be properly installed. If this is the case, the installation wizard will notify you and let you know if you need to install a disk or CD-ROM that is provided with the NIC.

To install a NIC using plug-and-play installation, follow these steps:

1. After you have physically installed the NIC in the appropriate slot, turn on the PC and wait for a screen that says New Hardware Found. The Add New Hardware Wizard will look like that shown in Figure 6.6.

FIGURE 6.6
The New Hardware Installation Wizard in Windows.

The wizard will guide you through the installation process of a plug-and-play NIC. When it appears on your screen, it will likely have identified the manufacturer and model of the device you are installing.

NOTE

If your PC does not detect your NIC, you need to use the Add/Remove New Hardware option in Windows, which will search for the NIC.

To reach this option in Windows 95/98/ME, click Start, Settings, and then Control Panel. In Control Panel, click on Add New Hardware to launch the window.

In XP, click Start and then Control Panel, and under Pick a Category, click the option for Printers and Other Hardware. Then click the option on the left for Add Hardware.

2. The wizard asks whether you want to install the hardware driver automatically or install from a list. Choose Automatic Installation and click Next.

3. Your PC searches for the appropriate driver and installs it automatically. If it comes back with a message indicating that it cannot find the appropriate driver, click Back and choose the install driver from the list provided.

4. You will likely have received a floppy disk or CD-ROM from the manufacturer of the NIC with the appropriate drivers on it. After you have chosen the Install from List option and have installed the disk or CD-ROM, click Next. The wizard might prompt you to indicate what drive you are searching on.

5. Your PC will likely have found the driver by now, and you can follow the prompts to finish the installation of the driver. If Windows still cannot find the driver, another option might be to look on the NIC manufacturer's Web site for the latest drivers. Some manufacturers do not always have the latest drivers in Windows or on a disk or CD-ROM, but often will post them on their Web site.

6. When you are done, Windows will ask whether you want to restart your PC. Make sure that all your other programs are closed, and click Yes.

Installing NIC Drivers Manually

Sometimes Windows will not identify the NIC automatically and you will have to install the drivers manually. This is not difficult because you can utilize the Add New Hardware Wizard to manually select the installation of a network adapter (Window's term for a NIC).

In Windows 95/98/ME, follow these steps:

1. Go to the New Hardware Wizard by clicking Start, Settings, Control Panel, and then clicking on Add New Hardware.

2. Click Next twice to allow the wizard to search for a device. You then get the option to have Windows search for new hardware that is not plug-and-play compatible, or you can select the device. Click the option No, I Want to Select the Hardware from a List, and click Next.

3. Choose Network Adapters and click Next. You then can choose from a list of manufacturers. Click the appropriate manufacturer.

4. You then are given a list of different models. Check the box that came with your product to find the appropriate model number.

5. If you cannot find the appropriate model, click on the Have Disk button below the models screen. Choose the appropriate disk and then click OK. Windows then searches the disk for the appropriate driver.

To do the same in Windows XP, follow these steps:

1. Click Start, Control Panel, and then Printers and Other Hardware. Click Add New Hardware on the left.

2. In the Add New Hardware screen under the Installed Hardware box, click Add a New Hardware Device.

3. Select the option to install the hardware manually, and click Next.

4. Choose Network Adapters to get a pop-up window similar to that of Windows ME. From here, select your manufacturer and the model, and follow the instructions on the screen.

Troubleshooting Driver Installation

If you are still having trouble installing your NIC, you might have a faulty product or one with a noncompatible driver. You might consider calling the customer support number provided with the product, or e-mailing a support representative if a general support e-mail address is given. You can also check the manual provided to see whether there are any suggestions for troubleshooting the installation process. If all else fails, you can take the NIC back to the store of purchase and exchange it for a new NIC. The risk here is that you will have the same problem. You might consider exchanging the model you purchased for a new model.

Installing a USB NIC

It is not always necessary to install a NIC inside a PC. If you would rather use a USB NIC, all you need to know is the location of your USB port. From there you simply plug in the device, and that's it. Of course, you still need to install the NIC drivers, which should for all intents and purposes be the same as those illustrated in the earlier section about installing NIC drivers for a PCI NIC.

In Figure 6.7 you will see what a USB port looks like. You will find USB ports on the back of most computers built after 1996. Many newer PCs have USB ports on the front of the PC as well. Laptop PCs often have USB ports on the side.

FIGURE 6.7

A USB port with USB connector.

If your PC does not have a USB port, you can add one through an add-in host adapter. Most USB add-in host adapters are PCI-based, so this means adding a USB port by taking up one of your PCI slots. This might seem like double the effort, but you may ultimately like having the flexibility of having a USB port on your PC, because USB ports allow you to add different peripherals, besides NICs, in a hot-swappable fashion.

> **NOTE**
>
> *Hot-swappable* means you can plug and unplug devices from your USB port while the PC is running. This is different from the PCI slot, which requires that you shut down the PC and then take off the PC's cover when unplugging a card. USB connections are built from the ground up to be plug-and-play, or hot swappable. *Hot-swappable* is a term that is not necessarily specific to USB, but refers to any type of equipment that can be exchanged or disconnected while running.

Installing a PC Card NIC for Laptops (PCMCIA or CardBus)

The installation of a PC Card—the name for a NIC that uses a PCMCIA or CardBus slot in a laptop—is almost as simple as that of a USB NIC. The only additional complication to the physical installation of a PC Card into a laptop is the need for what is called a dongle.

> **NOTE**
>
> A *dongle* is a small piece of cable with an RJ-45 jack on one end (for the Cat 5 UTP cabling) and the connector to the PC Card on the other. Because PC Cards for laptops are too thin to have an RJ-45 jack on the actual card, you need this special adapter called a dongle to connect the LAN cabling to the PC Card.

Figure 6.8 shows how the dongle fits in between the PC Card—which has been inserted into the PCMCIA or CardBus slot in the side of the laptop—and the LAN connection.

Certain types of PC cards are made for networking laptops that do not require a dongle. These special cards are double-height and take up two slots on your laptop, but they are more convenient because it is easy to lose the dongle for the other types of PC Card NICs.

Installation of an ISA NIC

The installation of an ISA NIC has a few more considerations than that of a PCI NIC. The ISA bus on a PC looks a little different from a PCI slot, as shown previously in Figure 6.4. The major difference with the installation of ISA NICs is that they are not Plug and Play, meaning that there are special settings that must be configured for the installation. These can be adjusted through software or on the NIC itself. These special settings are called the IRQ—which means interrupt request—and I/O address. You will want to look at the installation manual of the ISA NIC to understand how this is done.

Understanding and Installing an Ethernet Network

CHAPTER 6

101

6

UNDERSTANDING
AND INSTALLING AN
ETHERNET NETWORK

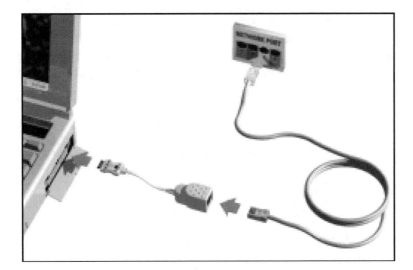

FIGURE 6.8
A PC card installation in a laptop using a dongle.

CAUTION

It is strongly recommended here that you carefully read the manual about how to set IRQ settings. If you do not correctly set up IRQ settings when installing your ISA NIC, the equipment will not operate correctly or, worse, can cause problems with your PC. My recommendation is to use a PCI NIC and avoid this step altogether.

Putting It All Together: Hub and Cable Placement

The biggest disadvantage to installing an Ethernet network is the fact that, at some point, you will have to run cabling. The difficulty of this task is largely dependent on how far the different PCs in your network are situated from each other; a simple in-room network can be as easy as running the cable from one PC to the other and tucking the cable under the baseboard. A network with PCs in non-adjacent rooms or on different floors of your home will require more work, because you will have to drill holes in your walls and run the cable from room to room.

If you haven't done so already, it might help you to visualize your network by drawing a map of your home. In Figure 6.9, a simple line diagram is used to plan for a network. You can use drawing software such as Visio to draw your network map, or simply sketch it using a pencil on a sheet of printer paper. The map does not need to be a "work of art," but just a basic visual guide for you on where you want the different PCs in your network to be situated. Figure 6.9 shows a view of a single-story home from the top. If you have a two-story home or a home with a basement, you might want to draw the home from the side, especially if you are considering having the network run to the different floors of the house.

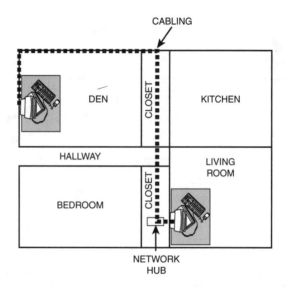

FIGURE 6.9

A home network map for Ethernet network.

You might want to start by drawing a simple diagram of your home and where your PCs will be situated on the network. After weighing the different options described next, you can fill in where you want to locate the hub and how the cabling is run.

Placing the Hub

One of the main considerations in building your Ethernet network is where you will place the hub or switch. These are the main things to consider in placing the hub:

- You will need an electrical outlet nearby.
- Consider whether you have a basement to put the hub in; a basement can be a good centralized place for connecting the different cable runs.
- Consider whether you have room next to one of your PCs to place your hub. Most hubs are pretty small and can be placed next to one of your PCs fairly inconspicuously.

If you are using a structured wiring system as the cabling solution for your Ethernet network, the system will have a central wiring station where you can place your hub.

Running the Cables

Running the cables from your PC to the network hub and vice versa is the most work intensive part of installing your Ethernet home network. If you have a multiroom network and the idea of drilling holes in your walls and running cable through your attic or crawl spaces does not strike you as a fun way to spend your Saturday afternoon (or any afternoon, for that matter), you should stop right here and consider hiring an electrician or a network installation specialist. If, on the other hand, this is the kind of work you relish (and like to brag about to your golf buddies), you can read on to learn what things you will need to consider in such an installation.

Take a Network Walk-About

By now you should know which rooms you will run your cabling to. Drawing your network map gave you a good idea of where each PC will sit and what "path" your network cable will take to connect the different PCs. However, you will want to take a closer look at the network path to determine what lies ahead in terms of the actual cable installation. In other words, you will want to go on a network "walk-about."

A network walk-about means taking your map and a pencil, and walking around your house to examine the network path more closely. You will want to take notes and see what things might help or hinder your installation. Some things to watch out for:

- You will want to note any sharp corners. You will need to be careful when you install the cabling not to bend your cabling at a sharp angle because this could damage the cabling, especially fiber-optic cable.

- Look for easy points of entry for putting the cable through the walls. Closets are a good location to run cable from room to room, or from one floor to the other.

- Make sure the cable is not under a rug in a heavy traffic area, because repeated foot traffic on top of cabling can damage the cable.

- Look at where your cabling will cross electrical wiring. You will want to make sure the cabling runs at a 90-degree angle to the electrical wiring so as to minimize interference.

Cabling Room to Room

The installation of cable from room to room will require drilling holes into the walls, or at the very least running cabling parallel to heating ducts or pipes. Before you drill the holes you will want to get a stud finder from your local hardware store to make sure you do not drill into wood studs, electrical wiring, or plumbing.

When pulling the cabling through the wall, you should consider having someone on the other side of the wall to assist you. Be sure to figure out where the hole will be on both sides by having someone listen while you knock on the other side of the wall. This will eliminate any potential "misfires" in the drilling process. When you are stringing the cable through the drilled hole, you might want to use a coat hanger to help pull the cable through.

If you are connecting computers in adjacent rooms, you can possibly position the PCs close to the same area in the wall and drill one hole for the cabling. If you are connecting a PC to a different floor, you should consider running the cabling up through a closet. You can drill the hole into the closet ceiling and have someone upstairs to pull the cabling through.

One way to avoid drilling holes in your walls is to run your cabling alongside heating or air ducts. You can sometimes go from one floor to another by finding room beside a duct.

Another way you can run cabling from room to room is through your attic or crawl spaces. When you are running a cable in non-adjacent rooms, this is an option you will want to give serious consideration. Being able to run cabling from one end of the house to the other by only drilling two holes (one into your ceiling or floor, and one out) is handy. Many cable TV installers use this option today when running cable TV coax cabling around the home. You will want to be careful, especially if you are walking up in the attic, not to misstep on an unreinforced area, or you risk coming down through the ceiling along with your network cabling.

Got Cabling?

Before you have all your holes drilled, you will want to make sure you have a good idea of how much cabling you will need. This will make things easier after you have everything drilled so that when you begin to string the cable, you don't risk installing a cable that is too short. Cabling that is too long is not a problem, because it is easy to have the extra cable length wrapped up behind the PC or hidden out of sight in a closet or attic.

Cable is sold in premanufactured lengths, anywhere from 10 feet to over 500 feet. You should know what each cable segment of your network is in terms of rough linear feet, and then buy a cable length at your local computer store to match each segment. If you are buying Cat 5 cabling, the premeasured segments will come with RJ-45 jacks on each end. If you have a segment that is not long enough, you can connect two lengths of cabling with an RJ-45 coupler to make one longer segment.

When installing your cabling, you should consider running the cabling to each wall where you can install a wall jack. From there you can connect from the hub or PC to the wall jack using patch cables. Patch cables are usually 10 feet or shorter in length and often come with your NIC or hub purchase. This method allows you to avoid having cables hanging out of walls when you disconnect or move a PC on the network. You can purchase wall jacks for network connections at a local electronics store.

Coax cabling can be bought in premeasured lengths from a cabling and wiring specialist (see your local Yellow Pages), or you can create your own custom lengths. You can do this by buying some bulk coaxial cabling, cutting it to your measurements, and then attaching special twist-on connectors. You will want to consult a networking cable specialist to learn how to attach the twist-on connectors to the cable segments.

Wrap It Up

Ethernet has firmly established itself as the king of local area network technologies. The assembly of a basic Ethernet network is not difficult after you are familiar with the basic concepts of Ethernet networks, such as the following:

- Ethernet has a few "flavors" that determine which type of cabling, topology, and connectors to use.

- Of the different Ethernet flavors, 10/100BASE-T for operation over Cat 5 UTP is the easiest to install and the most widely available.

- Networking kits offer a great way to get all the necessary networking building blocks for a basic network installation.

- NICs differ slightly depending on what type of PC bus they plug into; the different PC buses include PCI, USB, PC Card (PCMCIA or CardBus), and ISA. Which bus types are available on a given PC is largely dependent on the age of the PC and whether it is a desktop or laptop.

- The physical installation of an Ethernet NIC is very easy, especially among plug-and-play PCI, USB, and PC Card bus slots.

- You should draw a network map to help you figure out where you want to place the different PCs, the hub, and the network cabling.

- You might want to consider using the services of a network cabling specialist if you are not comfortable with stringing cabling through walls, attics, or crawl spaces.

- You should strongly consider purchasing the different cabling segments in premanufactured lengths at your local computer or electronics store, to avoid the more complicated process of attaching cable connectors onto the cabling.

The Wonderful World of Wireless Networking

IN THIS CHAPTER

The world of communications is rapidly becoming a wireless one. From the satellite beaming news around the world to the mobile phone you (or that annoying guy next to you in the movies) carry with you everywhere, wireless communication has already become an indispensable part of our life.

Wireless networking is no different. The same basic radio communication technology that makes up the foundation of other wireless communications is also at work in a wireless local area network. Signals are transmitted and received over invisible radio waves. The following technologies use radio technology:

- Cellular phones
- CB radios
- Satellites
- FM and AM radio
- Television broadcast
- Cordless phones
- Wireless LANs

Although wireless LANs use the same radio technology as many other forms of radio communications, they do have their own special characteristics. And not only do they have unique characteristics when compared to other forms of radio, but they also operate quite differently than other forms of wired networking. This chapter explains how a basic wireless LAN works, the different wireless LAN technologies (yes, there is more than one), and how to set up and install your wireless home network.

Introduction to Wireless LANs

As you now know, wireless LANs are different from wired LANs in that they use the air, rather than some form of wiring, as their transportation medium. The advantage of this wireless form of communication is self-evident: you don't need to go through the hassle of stringing cable from one end of the house to the other.

For you skeptical types, this probably sounds too good to be true. Well, aside from a few unique characteristics that you must recognize, most people who do install a wireless LAN find the benefits of untethered networking well worth it.

After reading Chapter 5, "Home Network Equipment: Choices, Choices, Choices," you should know whether a wireless network is right for you. Just in case you are still wondering about the differences between a wireless network and a wired one, Table 7.1 compares a wireless LAN (WLAN) to a wired Ethernet network.

TABLE 7.1 Wired and Wireless Network Comparison

Characteristic	Wireless LAN	Wired Ethernet LAN
Speed	1–10Mbps, depending on technology	10–1000Mbps
Hardware Cost	$150–$400 for a two-PC network	$50–$150 for a two-PC network
Distance	150-300–foot radius	150 meters between nodes
Amount of Up-Front Installation Work	Low	Low with exception of cable installation in multi-room network
Ease of Use	Very easy	Very easy

As you can see, the speed of a wired network will always beat that of a wireless network, and usually for a lower cost. At least this will be the case for the foreseeable future. But with the amount of freedom and lack of up-front work for installation of a wireless LAN, many home users find it well worth it to pay a little extra to go wireless. And the speed difference is usually not an issue, because the 10Mbps available through wireless LANs today is plenty of bandwidth for most home users.

Communicating Wirelessly in a LAN

A wireless LAN communicates by transmitting information from one transceiver to another. A *transceiver* is nothing more than radio jargon for any communication device in a radio network that can both transmit and receive a signal. Don't worry, you won't have to go the store and ask for a couple of transceivers, because these devices are integrated in the wireless LAN equipment you'll be buying.

Within a wired Ethernet network, the standard distance that communication can travel is up to 150 meters. The distance that wireless communication can travel in a wireless LAN is usually anywhere from 150 to 300 feet in any direction from the transceiver. This area of operation for a wireless LAN is generally called a cell. Figure 7.1 shows a typical cell in a wireless LAN.

As you can see, the WLAN cell is a circular area of operation that spreads out from the center. At the center of the WLAN, also known as an infrastructure wireless LAN, is an access point cell, as shown in Figure 7.1. An access point essentially acts as a wireless LAN hub. Remember how the network hub acts as a central station for the communication on a LAN network? The access point performs the same function in a wireless LAN.

One important thing to note is that not all wireless LANs require an access point. Those that do not require an access point operate in what is called ad hoc (or peer-to-peer) mode. You may recall the term *peer-to-peer* from our earlier discussion of different network types, in which the peer-to-peer network was compared to a client/server network. Understanding the different types of network configurations is helpful in understanding ad hoc wireless LANs and WLANs using an access point.

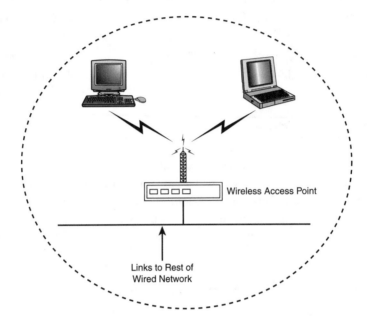

FIGURE 7.1
A wireless LAN cell.

Ad Hoc Versus Infrastructure Wireless LANs

As in a peer-to-peer network, an ad hoc wireless LAN is a network in which all PCs equipped with a wireless LAN NIC communicate directly with one another. There is no need to go through some form of centralized device—in this case called an access point—to communicate.

With an infrastructure WLAN, it is necessary to go through an access point. In addition to acting as a hub, the access point acts in many ways like a server in a client/server network, essentially controlling all communications between the different PCs on a wireless LAN network.

Access points also generally have a wired Ethernet connection so that all PCs on a wireless LAN can connect to the wired network. In an ad hoc wireless network, the PCs get onto a wired network by communicating through one of the peers that is equipped with both a wireless LAN NIC and a wired Ethernet NIC.

In Figure 7.1 you saw how two PCs communicate using an access point. In Figure 7.2 you'll see how PC "A" gets on the Internet by communicating with PC "B" in what is an ad hoc wireless LAN. PC "B" is equipped with both a wireless LAN NIC and an Ethernet NIC, which allows it to communicate to a cable modem. PC "A" is going peer-to-peer with PC "B" to get onto the Internet.

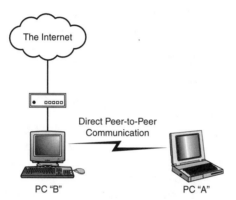

FIGURE 7.2

A wireless LAN ad hoc network.

The good thing is that—depending on which standard you choose for your wireless LAN—you can choose whether you want to use an ad hoc or infrastructure wireless LAN. The major downside to infrastructure wireless LANs is that they generally cost more, because access points can run anywhere from $200 to $400. Some vendors are now combining the access point with four or more Ethernet switch ports, allowing the user to easily combine a wireless LAN network with a wired Ethernet network.

Tell Me About Spread Spectrum

Spread spectrum is the method in which most wireless LANs communicate today. Spread spectrum systems use methods for quickly manipulating the frequency of the signal, so as the different data packets travel from the transmitting antenna to the receiving antenna, they will travel over different frequencies.

There are two kinds of spread spectrum systems: frequency hopping and direct sequence. Signals in frequency hopping spread spectrum (FHSS) systems hop around on a range of different frequency bands. If you think of the signal as moving on a pogo stick around the frequencies—and there are about 80 different slots in Home RF and other frequency hopping standards—you would see the signal move randomly among the bands.

Direct sequence spread spectrum (DSSS) system signals do not hop around, but instead are sent in a specific sequence that is randomly generated and altered by the sending system. The receiving system then decodes, or demodulates, the sequence of the different bits.

So You Think Actresses Can Just Act?

One of the most interesting stories about frequency hopping spread spectrum systems is how they started. Most people are surprised to find out that it wasn't some pocket protector–wearing scientist who invented frequency hopping, but was instead a famous actress of the day named Hedy Lamarr, whom you can see in Figure 7.3. Lamarr, who appeared in such 1930 and 1940s era movies as *Samson and Delilah* and *Lady in the Tropics* (and also turned down the lead for *Casablanca*), was the co-inventor of the frequency hopping technology with another famous person, film-score composer George Antheil.

The story goes that the two were chatting one night at a 1940 Hollywood dinner party, and they got to talking about World War II. Lamarr, who had previously been married to an Austrian arms dealer, had fled Austria to get away from her husband. She did not like the fact that he had been selling arms to Nazi Germany and Mussolini in Italy. Lamarr outlined her idea that night and the next night for a sophisticated radio jamming technology for use in radio-controlled torpedoes. The foundation of this knowledge came from Lamarr's memories of hearing her former husband, Fritz Mandl, discuss weapons with his customers.

What began that evening as a conversation between an actress and a composer resulted two years later in a patent being awarded to the two, as well as the beginning of the foundations for much of modern wireless communication technology. Frequency hopping technology not only was used by the military in WWII for avoiding detection of transmissions by the other side, but helped create the techniques used for many wireless LANs, as well as cordless phones.

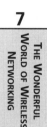

FIGURE 7.3
Hedy Lamarr, actress and co-inventor of frequency hopping.

Important Differences Between Wireless and Wired LANs

As you know, wireless networks are very different from wired networks. Although the most obvious difference is that no cables or wires are used to connect the nodes on the network, there are other important differences you should know about. The major differences involve security and the distance and barriers between transceivers.

Wireless LAN Security

First of all, let me soothe your fears. Wireless LAN networks are plenty secure. The chances of having some weirdo listen in on your wireless LAN signals are pretty remote.

Okay, now that I've said that, you should be aware that there are security concerns specific to users of wireless LANs. The reason for these concerns is that wireless LANs use wireless signals. Think about it: with radio signals that are sent by any wireless communication device such as a wireless LAN NIC (or a cellular phone), the information you are passing is transmitted over airwaves and can, theoretically, be listened to by anyone within the signal radius.

This means that if a really technical (and not very nice) person had the knowledge and equipment, he could conceivably sit outside your home listen in on the signals passed around on your wireless LAN. He may even be able to communicate with a PC on your wireless LAN and get information from that PC, such as your financial records.

What can you do about it? Well, thankfully the folks who make wireless LANs are smart (heck, you'd have to be smart to make this stuff) and have built technology into their products that enables you to protect yourself against wireless LAN snoops. The safeguards used for wireless LAN security are called authentication and encryption.

Authentication is the process in a network of validating whether users are who they say they are. Authentication methods vary from the most basic, a password that you type, to advanced methods such as authentication tokens or biometrics.

> **NOTE**
>
> *Biometrics* is a way to verify someone's identity using his or her own body. Typical biometric identification methods include fingerprint and retinal (eye) scans. Because each person's fingerprint or eye is as unique as the variations in snowflakes, biometrics is recognized as the most secure method of identification.

> **NOTE**
>
> *Authentication tokens* are electronic cards that only the user has and that the user needs in order to log onto the network. Sometimes these tokens are called smart cards, and in some areas of the world they are used for other things such as credit-card and ATM transactions.

Although authentication will allow you to keep unauthorized users from logging on to your network, you still need to protect against unwanted interception of the data contained within your wireless LAN signals. This is where encryption comes in. Encryption is the process of converting information into a secret code for transmission. Encryption is used not only in wireless networks, but also for when information is passed over public networks such as the Internet.

For the different WLAN standards, you should know that each has its own type of security built into it. We will look at how to ensure that the security for your WLAN is activated. Also, we will discuss some additional steps you can take for overall network security in Part VI, "Running and Securing Your Network."

Wi-Fi Security: Safe Enough for Home Networks?

A lot has been said in the news about what is perceived as a security "hole" in Wi-Fi wireless LANs. In fact, a bunch of smart guys at the University of California at Berkeley wrote a paper outlining the weaknesses of the security built into Wi-Fi wireless LANs and how those with the technical aptitude and determination could sneak onto a Wi-Fi wireless LAN.

Although you should be aware of the potential for a security violation with a Wi-Fi or any wireless LAN technology, the likelihood of someone "snooping" around your wireless LAN in your home is remote. If you turn on the wireless LAN encryption that is built into your wireless LAN, you should be safe from potential hackers or snoopers. However, if you are interested in using a Wi-Fi wireless LAN and want to be extra safe, you should see whether a vendor's equipment supports security that goes beyond basic WEP, or Wireless Equivalent Privacy, the standard security for 802.11b/Wi-Fi security.

The good news is that even though the basic security for Wi-Fi wireless LANs is plenty strong for most home networks, most manufacturers have taken extra measures and added their own security features to their wireless LAN products. Also, the IEEE working group is hard at work creating more robust security for all Wi-Fi wireless LANs.

Wireless LAN Transmission Barriers and Distance Limitations

One of the basic facts of life with wireless LANs is that they will never be able to transmit across distances comparable to those with wired Ethernet networks. As you saw in Table 7.1, the range with wireless LAN networks is anywhere between 150 and 300 feet. This compares with up to 150 meters for wired Ethernet links, which is up to three times the distance. And, unlike wireless LAN links, wired Ethernet links do not have to face transmission barrier issues.

Transmission barriers for wireless LAN links are any solid barriers that block or slow down the transmission of the radio signals. These can include walls, large objects such as refrigerators, and even people. Most wireless LANs experience some level of degradation when they try to transmit through walls, which are the most common transmission barrier.

NOTE

Degradation of wireless LAN transmissions is the slowing down of signals as they encounter barriers. Most signals in a wireless LAN do not altogether stop when hitting barriers such as walls, but instead they slow down, or degrade.

One of the considerations you will want to think about when deciding whether a wireless LAN is right for you is how long the transmission will have to travel within your home. Homes that are large or have many floors may experience some level of signal degradation. Some wireless LANs may even experience what are called "dead spots" in coverage, which are areas where a transmission cannot reach a wireless transceiver. These dead spots may be areas that are physically far away or are behind multiple transmission barriers.

Walls may be the primary transmission barriers for wireless LANs, but they are not the only ones. The following list covers the types of transmission barriers, including certain types of materials that might be part of a wall:

- Metal that is part of a wall or something large such as a refrigerator may impair wireless LAN signals.
- Radio signals from other devices such as a microwave oven may impair wireless LAN signals.
- Thick masonry such as that used in older homes can act as a barrier. Some walls in older homes have thick mason blocks that are harder to transmit through than basic drywall and insulation.
- The existence of a large number of walls, such as those in a house with many rooms, can impede or altogether stop wireless LAN signals.

The best thing for you to do when using a wireless LAN in a home is to have one of the transceivers on the network—such as the access point—centrally located. If the access point is in the middle of your home, it will be within reach of different network nodes within a certain radius. If you were to put the access point in the wireless LAN on the far end of the house, you could have some serious degradation problems when trying to transmit to the other nodes on the network.

The Different Wireless LAN Standards

It's important that *before* you go out and buy your home network, you learn about the different standards for wireless LANs and which should you use.

> **NOTE**
>
> A *standard* in networking is an agreed-upon method for creating technology products that interoperates across different manufacturers' versions of the technology. Standards are good things in that they allow you to have a product from one company that communicates with a product from another company.

If you've done any research on your own or simply happened across an article on wireless home networks, you've probably heard different terms such as Wi-Fi, Home RF, and Bluetooth. These are different standards for wireless networking, and each has its advantages and disadvantages.

> **CAUTION**
>
> It might not be immediately clear when shopping for a wireless LAN which standard each manufacturer's equipment adheres to. However, if you look closely at the packaging, you will be able to find a label that identifies which standard the product is based on.

Wi-Fi Wireless LANs

Wi-Fi is the name of wireless LANs based on the standard called IEEE 802.11b. You might remember the numbers 802.1 from our discussion about Ethernet. Like Ethernet, 802.11b is a standard that has been created by the IEEE (remember, it's pronounced I-triple-E), which is the primary body responsible for networking standards. Because folks at the IEEE are good at creating technology standards and are not good at marketing, some creative types fortunately came up with the term Wi-Fi to signify that a piece of wireless LAN equipment is based on the 802.11b standard.

Although Wi-Fi wireless LANs were originally targeted at business networks, the folks who make equipment based on Wi-Fi soon realized that Wi-Fi would make good home wireless networks as well. The speed of the current generation of Wi-Fi networks tops out at 10Mbps, although someday in the future you will be able to buy higher speeds. Most Wi-Fi wireless LANs are set up to act in infrastructure mode, in that they employ an access point. However, all Wi-Fi wireless LANs allow for configuration as an ad hoc network.

Home RF Wireless LANs

Home RF is the name for a standard developed by the Home RF working group. Home RF is a wireless LAN standard developed with home networking in mind. The focus from the get-go was on creating low-cost wireless technology that would also support such things as sending voice calls as well as computer traffic, all in a home environment.

Like Wi-Fi networks, Home RF uses what is called spread spectrum technology for sending data over the air. If you would like to know more about this means as well as the different types of spread spectrum technology, see the section "Tell Me About Spread Spectrum," earlier in the chapter. One thing you should know about current spread spectrum technologies is that because most operate today in what is called the 2.4GHz frequency spectrum—along with some other electronic devices such as (believe it or not) your microwave oven—and because of the operation of other devices, there is a chance for some amount of interference.

Home RF wireless LANs were designed from the beginning to act as ad hoc networks. Home RF network equipment usually consists of just two or more NICs and does not require the extra expense of an access point. Wi-Fi networks do not require access points either, but they are primarily designed to operate using an access point.

Radio Frequency and Spectrum

The terms *frequency* and *spectrum* are part of the unique language used by wireless communication aficionados to describe the universe of radio communications. Radio waves are sent from transceivers such as those in your wireless LAN over various frequencies. Different frequencies are assigned to each type of network, and the difference between frequencies is how fast the radio signal oscillates, which is a fancy word for fluctuates. Radio-wave oscillations that make up the different frequencies are measured in what is called hertz (no, not the car-rental company). You might have heard of the different hertz measurements, such as megahertz (MHz) and gigahertz (GHz). These are measures of how fast the radio signal fluctuates.

The measures of radio frequency are assigned different bands, which are called spectrums. Different frequency bands—or spectrums—are used in different kinds of radio networks. Some common spectrums for types of radio networks include the following:

- *Cell phones*—824MHz to 849MHz
- *Cordless phones*—40MHz to 50MHz, or 900MHz
- *CB radio*—26.96MHz to 27.41MHz
- *FM radio*—88MHz to 108MHz (hence the range of 88 to 108 on your FM dial)

Home RF speeds range from 1.6Mbps to 10Mbps. The first generation of Home RF products released in 1999 operated at 1.6Mbps. New products released in late 2001 are based on a higher-speed standard by the Home RF working group, to allow for Home RF systems to operate at 10Mbps. These higher speeds are roughly the equivalent of the current Wi-Fi products. Don't worry about buying 10Mbps Home RF if you own Home RF equipment based on the lower speed, because the old Home RF and the new Home RF equipment have been designed to interoperate.

What About Bluetooth?

Bluetooth—besides being a name for a Viking sailor—is a name for a new wireless communication technology. It seems that since its inception in 1998, countless articles have appeared in newspapers and magazines about how every little device, from cell phones to Palm Pilots, would someday communicate with each other using Bluetooth technology.

Although this will possibly be the case at some point in the future, you should know that Bluetooth was designed to act as a cable replacement for short-range communication (much like infrared in remote controls is used to talk to your TV), not as a whole-home wireless LAN technology. Most devices using Bluetooth will be small, and you will not find wireless LAN products at your local computer store based on Bluetooth. Someday Bluetooth technology may enable your PC to talk to small devices such as your cell phone or a PDA, but Bluetooth is not designed for wireless LANs.

Which Standard?

Chances are you shouldn't have to think too much about which standard you should choose for wireless home networking. Each standard uses reliable technology. Still, there are some differences you should know about. Table 7.2 shows how Wi-Fi and Home RF stack up. The characteristics that are discussed include speed, security, distance, cost, and number of manufacturers.

TABLE 7.2   Wi-Fi and Home RF Wireless LANs

Characteristic	Wi-Fi Wireless LANs	Home RF Wireless LANs
Speed	11Mbps	1.6–10Mbps
Security	Okay; should be fine for home LANs	Good for home LANs
Distance	300-foot radius	150-foot radius
Cost	$200–$450 for a two-PC network	$150–$250 for a two-PC network
Number of Manufacturers	Plenty	Shrinking; some vendors are moving to Wi-Fi

The speed and cost aspects of the different standards should be self-explanatory. We discussed how the distance between wireless LAN transceivers can impact the signal quality, as well as how different barriers can impede signals. With 802.11b you can use a centrally placed access point to help communicate among the different nodes on the network. A Home RF–based network could have a centrally placed PC to help communicate between itself and the other nodes on the network, but you might have problems when communicating with any device farther than 150 feet, or less if there are a lot of walls or other barriers.

If you have a larger home, you might want to consider using Wi-Fi wireless LAN because the distances the signals travel are farther and a centrally placed access point is your best bet for reaching all the nodes on the network. If your home is so large that there is serious signal degradation even with a centrally placed access point, you might consider using two access points if you want access to your wireless LAN around the home.

As you learned in the previous section about security, it is important to at least recognize that wireless LANs have some special security concerns. Each standard has its own safeguards using encryption and authentication. The main difference between the two standards is that Home RF is based on the more secure frequency hopping method of sending signals, whereas Wi-Fi relies on direct sequence. See the section "Tell Me About Spread Spectrum," earlier in the chapter, for details on each standard.

The security measures for each technology should be sufficient for the home user. If you are especially concerned about security using wireless LANs, you should consider using a wireless LAN product that is developed for office networks, which usually have stronger encryption and authentication techniques. You can usually tell office wireless LANs by their higher prices.

Another important consideration when choosing between the two wireless LAN standards is the number of manufacturers that make equipment based on each standard. Part of my day job is to monitor how the different standards are doing commercially. One of the trends noticeable in 2001 is that some of the large companies that have made Home RF–based products are beginning to shift toward supporting Wi-Fi as the primary wireless networking technology for the home.

Part of the reason for this shift is the belief by these companies that it would be easier if there were only one technology standard for the office, as well as the home. Chances are that if you have a wireless LAN in your work, it is based on Wi-Fi, and if you are using a Wi-Fi wireless LAN you can pretty easily take your laptop home and put it on your Wi-Fi home network.

TIP

If you want to ensure that you buy wireless LAN technology that has the widest support possible, you should choose a Wi-Fi based product. With the current momentum in the industry towards Wi-Fi, you can be sure that a wider range of products from a greater number of manufacturers will be available when compared to Home RF wireless LAN products.

Tomorrow's Wireless LAN

Don't think that wireless LAN companies are content with only 11Mbps. The next generation of wireless LAN technology is around the corner, because companies are making wireless LAN systems that operate at 22Mbps all the way up to 54Mbps. Much of the buzz regarding the next-generation wireless LAN technology is around the higher-speed standard called IEEE 802.11a. Why 802.11a is the higher-speed standard for WLAN systems after 802.11b (or Wi-Fi), only a radio engineer could know (or want to know), but the great thing is that eventually wireless LAN systems will go much faster than they do today, someday even close to the speed of Fast Ethernet.

In addition to 802.11a, another technology being developed is called 802.11g. This is a higher-speed wireless LAN standard that will allow 22Mbps networking. The advantage of 802.11g is that equipment will be compatible with older equipment based on the 802.11b standard, something that is not the case with 802.11a.

The bad news is that you likely won't see higher-speed wireless LANs based on 802.11a in your home network for at least two to three years. The technological kinks are still being worked out, and the initial systems built on this technology will likely be too expensive for home use, instead being placed in office environments.

This doesn't mean that many companies aren't interested in seeing these higher speeds in the home. Some of the companies most interested in pushing the higher-speed wireless LAN technology into the home are consumer electronics companies such as Sony and Panasonic, who envision the day when they will be able to beam video signals around your home from their video recorders and set-top boxes.

Installing a Wireless LAN

The installation of a wireless LAN is extremely simple. There are no wires to string from room to room, and the installation of the network interface cards is just as plug-and-play as that of Ethernet and phoneline NICs.

Before you install the NICs and access points, you should think about where you want each node on your network to sit. If you are connecting two or more desktop PCs, it is likely that these will be stationary. If one or more laptop PCs are on your network, you should think about the primary places you will be using the laptop and what its positioning is relative to the other PCs. Remember that wireless LANs are different from wired LANs in that the communication quality will vary depending on characteristics such as transmission barriers and short variations in distance.

You might want to draw a map of your wireless LAN, much like we suggested with an Ethernet network. This will allow you to see how many walls separate the different nodes and give you a rough idea of the distance between nodes. If you are using an access point, you need to give some thought to determining where a central place is for this device.

Configuring Your Wireless LAN

The basic installation of a wireless LAN NIC requires physically plugging in the NIC, installing the network drivers, and configuring the wireless network using special configuration software provided by your equipment vendor. To understand how to physically plug in your NIC and install the network drivers, review Chapter 6, "Understanding and Installing an Ethernet Network."

After you have installed your wireless LAN and have installed the necessary drivers, you must configure your wireless LAN. Because a wireless LAN is, as you know, different from other technologies in that it uses radio signals and operates in either infrastructure or ad hoc mode, there are special configuration characteristics you must consider. Most wireless LANs come with a configuration utility, which is an interface that allows you to tweak the settings on your wireless LAN to your preferences. Figure 7.4 shows one such configuration utility.

FIGURE 7.4

A Wi-Fi wireless LAN configuration utility.

> **CAUTION**
>
> This example refers specifically to the installation of a Wi-Fi wireless LAN. The configuration utility may differ between different Wi-Fi equipment as well as with Home RF–based products. Be sure to refer to the instruction manual with your equipment to ensure that you are using the configuration utility with your equipment correctly.

In many instances, the configuration utility for your wireless NIC and access point can be started from the system-tray icon in Windows, whether it is 95/98/ME or XP. The configuration utility icon for your wireless LAN will often look like that shown in Figure 7.5. The icon looks like a small access point with an antenna. In addition to being the way to access your wireless LAN configuration utility, the icon also helps you monitor the performance of your wireless LAN after it is operational. The icon in Figure 7.5 shows a fully operational wireless LAN card because it is green and shows a signal from the antenna.

FIGURE 7.5

The system tray with a wireless LAN configuration utility icon.

If you have the small access-point icon on the lower-right corner of your Windows screen, you can access the configuration utility by double-clicking on the icon.

If you cannot see your configuration utility from the system tray icon, it can be for one of the following reasons:

- You are using a Home RF–based wireless LAN.
- Your configuration utility needs to be accessed through the Start menu on Windows.
- You have not yet loaded the software for your wireless LAN that includes the configuration utility.

To get your wireless LAN configuration utility through the Start menu on Windows, you need to do the following:

1. Click on the Start menu at the lower-left corner of Windows.
2. Under Programs, look for the folder that lists the name of your NIC or access point. It should be something like Start/Programs/*Wireless LAN NIC Name*/Configuration Utility.

In the wireless LAN configuration utility with a Wi-Fi wireless LAN, there will usually be four tabs. Each tab has a specific purpose. The tabs, as shown previously in Figure 7.4, are listed here:

- *Status*—This tab shows the signal strength on your wireless LAN connection, showing whether the NIC in your PC is connected to the wireless LAN and at what speed.
- *Configuration*—This is the primary tab you use to configure the wireless LAN NIC.
- *Encryption*—This tab is for setting up your wireless LAN NIC for security using encryption.

- *About*—This tab holds important info from the manufacturer such as the driver version and hardware version, which you might need if you ever talk to a customer support representative for troubleshooting.

The Configuration Tab for a Wi-Fi Wireless LAN

The most important tab when you're setting up your wireless LAN NIC or access point for receiving a signal on the network is the Configuration tab. The Configuration tab allows you to adjust the following for your wireless LAN:

- *The Station Set ID or Service Area*—This configuration setting, which goes by different names, is the information that identifies all the different nodes on a wireless LAN on the same group. This ID must be the same for each node on the network. Some manufacturers will allow you to pick Any as an option for the service area or ID.

- *Network Mode*—This setting allows you to choose between ad hoc and infrastructure mode (see Figure 7.6). Remember that ad hoc mode allows the different wireless LAN NICs to talk directly to each other in a peer-to-peer fashion, whereas infrastructure mode is used when you have an access point on the network.

- *Tx Rate*—This is the speed of your wireless LAN. You will have a range of choices from 2Mbps to 11Mbps, as well as possibly an automatic option. You should go with the highest speed or automatic if this is an option.

- *Channel*—Many wireless LANs have the option of choosing a channel for communication. You need to make sure that all the nodes on your wireless LAN are on the same channel, or that you choose the automatic option.

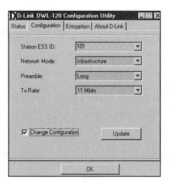

FIGURE 7.6

The Configuration tab on the wireless LAN configuration utility.

The Encryption Tab for a Wi-Fi Wireless LAN

As you learned earlier in the chapter, because wireless LANs use radio signals, they are susceptible to a hacker listening in on the signals being passed between your network, if they are within the transmission radius of one of the wireless LAN nodes. To protect against this type of unwanted access to your wireless network, Wi-Fi–based equipment has the capability to use encryption. The configuration utility for Wi-Fi LANs will usually have an Encryption tab that allows you to enable security for your wireless LAN. Figure 7.7 shows what the Encryption tab looks like.

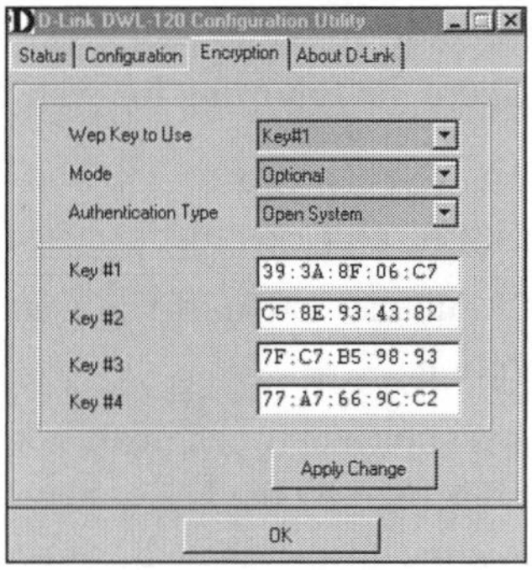

FIGURE 7.7

The Encryption tab on the wireless LAN configuration utility.

Wi-Fi–based systems use what is called Wired Equivalency Protection, or WEP. WEP is the encryption scheme that takes the data traffic on your wireless LAN and encodes it to prevent hackers from sniffing around your network.

WEP uses what are called keys. Keys are a necessary part of encryption, because they are essentially the secret decoder ring for your network.

NOTE

Encryption keys are what are used to encode and decode the transmissions on a wireless network. Keys are usually long strings of hexadecimal characters (which means letters and/or numbers) that each side of the transmission must know. It makes sense, because you must have the "key" to unlock the meaning of each message.

Keys in a WEP encryption scheme range from 40-bit to 128-bit. The more bits the key has, the more secure the network, because there are more numbers to decipher.

> **CAUTION**
>
> One downside to encryption is that it slows down your network because each transceiver must take the time to encode or decode the key when sending and receiving information packets. Although the computational chips on the NICs are fast, they still slow down somewhat with encryption.

The Encryption tab for each manufacturer differs slightly, so you will want to read the manual with your equipment carefully to see how to set up encryption on your wireless network. You will likely have the option to configure the following for your network encryption:

- Whether you want encryption. You can choose not to use encryption at all if you feel secure that your network won't be accessed by unwanted visitors.

- Whether you want 40- or 128-bit encryption. If you want a more secure network, you should choose 128-bit encryption.

- A mode option, usually with a choice between mandatory and optional. Mandatory requires that WEP encryption is used by the NIC you are configuring and any node it is communicating with. Optional means that the NIC or access point can communicate with any other node whether WEP is activated or not.

- Your security keys. You may have the option to enter your own security keys. Often this means just typing a random string of numbers. You must make sure that the keys are the same for each node on the network. You may also have the option of having the configuration utility generate the numbers for you.

What If My Wireless LAN Won't Communicate?

The previous sections talked about configuring your wireless LAN. Installing a wireless LAN NIC or access point and configuring it to communicate is simple. But if you are having problems, you might want to check the following:

- Are the nodes on your network too far apart? Remember that most wireless LANs have a radius of 300 feet or so.

- Are there many walls between nodes?

- Do the walls that your wireless LAN is transmitting through have transmission-resistant materials, such as metal, in them?

- Are there other devices that might interfere with radio transmission, such as a microwave oven or cordless phone, within close proximity?

- Are your wireless LAN nodes using the same standards-based technology—that is, are they all Wi-Fi or Home RF and not both trying to communicate on the same network?

Wrap It Up

Wireless LANs are wonderful for the mobility and ease they afford their users. No other network technology allows the user to roam freely throughout their home without the mess of cords and plug-in jacks.

Wireless LANs have some unique characteristics when compared to wired LANs:

- They are usually more expensive, so you pay a premium for the mobility that you get with a wireless network.

- They have distance limitations that the user must be mindful of, because they are susceptible to transmission degradation when transmission barriers such as walls, metal objects, and other radio devices are in close proximity.

- Security is a concern that a wireless LAN owner must give consideration to, because any wireless communication is less secure than wired communication.

- You can set up your wireless LAN in ad hoc or infrastructure mode, depending on which better suits your needs (as well as whether the standard your wireless LAN is based on allows for both).

- There are two main standards you should be aware of when looking at wireless LANs: Wi-Fi (also called 802.11b) and Home RF. Bluetooth is a wireless communication technology but is not designed for whole-home networking.

- Configuring a wireless LAN is easy; your manufacturer will provide you with configuration tools or utilities to aid in the process.

Other Networking Technologies: Phoneline, Powerline, and Structured Wiring Ethernet

IN THIS CHAPTER

Man (or Woman) Can't Live off Ethernet and Wireless Alone

The world of home networking is more than just Ethernet and wireless. In fact, over the past few years, new technologies that utilize in-home phone or electrical wiring have emerged, focused specifically on the needs of the home networker. And as you are aware from our previous discussions, structured wiring is a whole-home cabling solution that allows you to send high-speed Ethernet (as well as video and voice communications) around the home over high-quality integrated cabling. This chapter reviews each of these technologies, shows you how they work, and then looks at how to install the different choices.

Phoneline Networking: How to Use Those Phone Wires for More Than Just Talking

Good ol' phone wiring. We talk on the phone for hours upon hours every day and don't give any thought to how these pairs of copper wiring just sit there and do their job, transferring our voice signals from the handset onto the wire and out onto the phone company's voice network. It's pretty amazing to think about the process, but because making an ordinary phone call has become such an integral part of our everyday lives, most of us don't give it a moment's notice.

Many of us have already begun to use phone wiring as a way to send data signals onto and around the network. Our dial-up modems are in actuality pieces of networking equipment, allowing us to communicate on the Internet through our Internet service provider. Much of the same technology that allows us to communicate on a modem is used for phoneline networking.

So How Does Phoneline Networking Work?

Phoneline networking can be thought of as Ethernet networking that communicates over in-home phone wiring. It sends and receives packets the same way Ethernet does, using the "listen first, then send" method of packet delivery. In fact, phoneline networking uses the same CSMA/CD technology that Ethernet uses to make sure that all the nodes on the network can communicate.

One of the most interesting things about phoneline networks is that they work simultaneously with phone conversations. Some people have shied away from phoneline networking because they fear that they would interrupt their phone conversations. No wonder, anyone who has picked up a phone while dialing into the Internet over a dial-up modem has probably heard that screeching sound. But unlike dial-up modems, phoneline networks work at a different frequency range than that of phone conversations.

Phoneline networks work in some ways like air travel. In this age of air travel, the sky is filled with different traffic as jets, planes, helicopters, and the occasional rocket zoom by and almost never meet (ouch!). Because plane collisions aren't a good thing, the different air traffic is given certain space in which to travel, so as to avoid any close calls. Phoneline networking, voice traffic, and even high-speed digital Internet connections over phonelines such as DSL (as opposed to analog connections such as a dial-up modem) are given different "lanes of traffic," or frequencies, in which to travel as well. Technical types call this technique frequency division multiplexing.

TIP

Frequency division multiplexing, or *FDM*, is a technique in which different types of communication operate over different frequency spectrums. Special filters are used to select the frequency each type of traffic passes over. FDM allows for "peaceful coexistence" of voice, fax, and data networking traffic.

Phoneline networking was developed by a cross-industry organization called the Home Phone Networking Alliance, or HPNA. The HPNA consisted of networking, PC, software, and chip manufacturers who knew that not everyone wanted to install wiring or even use wireless technology, and who figured out that phone wiring isn't all that different from Ethernet Cat 5 cabling.

The Home Phone Networking Alliance: Getting It Done

The computer and technology industry had known for years that it was possible to connect PCs and other devices over phone wiring, but there had never been a standard to do so. The Home Phone Networking Alliance, or HPNA, was formed with the idea of creating such a standard, and in June 1998 the group was announced.

The initial group included 11 companies, including many large computer, chip, and networking companies. One of the initial companies was Tut Systems, which is a maker of DSL equipment (see Chapter 13, "Getting Online the High-Speed Way," for an explanation of DSL). Tut had the initial technology on which the HPNA based its first specification. Tut used much of what it had learned for sending information over phone wiring using DSL for creating "Ethernet over Phone Wiring," or HPNA 1.0. HPNA 1.0 allows for speeds up to 1Mbps.

The first specification was approved and published at the end of 1998, and by the middle of 1999, products that allowed people to network in their home over phone wiring at 1Mbps were on store shelves.

> The HPNA was not satisfied with 1Mbps. The companies involved had decided early on that they needed to move to higher speeds, and by the end of 1999, a new specification (HPNA 2.0) and products operating at 10Mbps were on store shelves. HPNA 2.0 was based on technology from a company called Epigram, which was soon to become part of communications-chip specialist Broadcom.
>
> HPNA was seen by many in the industry as a rousing success. The usual wait is at least two to three years for a new technology to make its way through a lengthy standards process, but from the time HPNA was formed to the time products were on store shelves was less than a year. Other organizations, such as the one for powerline networking, have since followed a similar path exemplified by the Home Phone Networking Alliance.

In Figure 8.1, you'll see what an HPNA phoneline network looks like. This network truly takes advantage of the in-home phone wiring, putting not only PCs on the network but other devices such as a network camera and a cable set-top box as well.

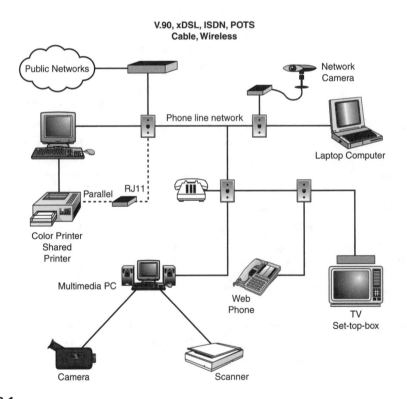

FIGURE 8.1

An HPNA phoneline network.

How Do I Know It's a Phoneline Network?

One of the most confusing things for those shopping for networking equipment is the fact that many types of equipment look alike. You really have to read the packaging to determine whether it is a phoneline network, Ethernet, wireless, or powerline. Luckily, those at the HPNA knew they had to identify their products by stamping each package with an insignia. In Figure 8.2 you'll see the HPNA stamp of approval, which tells you not only that the product is a phoneline networking product, but also that the product has been approved by the HPNA and is interoperable with other HPNA networking equipment.

FIGURE 8.2

The Home Phone Networking Alliance seal of approval.

Before you buy any product for networking over phonelines, you should verify that it was approved by the HPNA. You should be able to find the little blue home with a phone plug and the HomePNA insignia on the box.

Setting Up a Phoneline Network

As you've learned from reading previous chapters, phoneline networks are similar to other networks in that you will likely need to install a network interface card (see Chapter 2, "Home Network Building Blocks: What Makes Your Network Tick," for a description of a NIC) and software to make the network run. This chapter shows you how a basic phoneline network is physically set up, as well as how some equipment manufacturers have created special software to make for easy installation of a phoneline network. However, for installation of the drivers and software for phoneline NICs (as well as any other NIC type), see Chapter 9, "Setting Up Home Network Software."

It Works Like Ethernet, Without Hubs and Long Cables

Setting up a phoneline network is simple. The beauty of phoneline networking is that all you need for the physical installation are the NICs and phone cabling—the same kind you use to connect your phone into the phone jack in the wall—and you're ready to set up your network.

In case you haven't purchased your phoneline network, you can either buy standalone phoneline NICs or buy a phoneline networking kit. Phoneline networking kits usually come with two NICs and two phone cords to allow you to connect your NICs into the wall. Most

8

OTHER
NETWORKING
TECHNOLOGIES

standalone phoneline NICs also come with phone cords. I suggest that you buy a kit if you are connecting two PCs. The kits not only will come with all the equipment necessary, but also will save you money compared with buying two NICs separately. This advice goes for any type of networking technology.

Phoneline NICs come in most of the same bus types as Ethernet NICs (see the section "PC Bus Types" in Chapter 6, "Understanding and Installing an Ethernet Network," for an understanding of the different PC connections and NIC bus types). The two main bus types for phoneline NICs are PCI and USB based. Like Ethernet, with a PCI NIC you will need to install the card inside the PC. USB NICs allow you to avoid opening the PC by plugging into one of the PC's USB ports.

Figure 8.3 shows you how a two-PC phoneline network is set up. The concept couldn't be simpler: You plug in the phoneline NIC to each PC and then run the phone cabling to the phone jacks. Phoneline networks use RJ-11 jacks, as opposed to the RJ-45 jacks used by Ethernet networks. It's easy to tell the two apart: RJ-45 jacks are wider, containing eight different colored wires, whereas RJ-11 jacks are smaller, containing only four wires. The best test is to try plugging the jack into the wall jack you use for your telephone. If the jack slides into the socket, snaps in place, and fits snugly into the wall plug, it's an RJ-11 jack. If you can't get the jack into the wall plug, it's an RJ-45. It's vice versa if you're testing the jack in the NIC card: If the jack doesn't snap in place, creating a snug fit, it's not an RJ-45. If you slide the jack into the NIC slot and it falls out or is very loose, there's a good chance it's an RJ-11 jack.

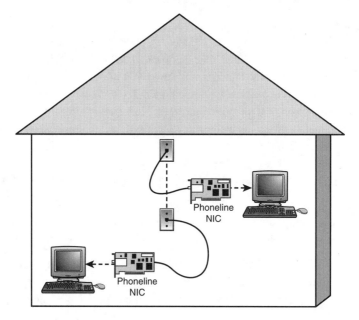

FIGURE 8.3

A two-PC phoneline network.

Figure 8.3 shows you how two PCI-based NICs would be used in a phoneline network. The PCI NICs are installed inside the PC, and you would plug the phone cord into the visible RJ-11 jack on the back of the PC.

You could easily use a USB-based NIC instead, and in this case the NIC would sit outside of the PC, connected to the PC via its USB port. The same phone cord would then connect the USB NIC into the phone jack in the wall. For laptop PCs, you will need to use a USB NIC because PCI NICs can be used only with desktop PCs.

CAUTION

Before you install your phoneline network, read over the product manual as well as Chapter 10, "Getting Around the Home Network." The physical installation of your NICs will need to be followed by driver installation, and some manufacturers even require you to install the drivers/software that accompanies the NIC before installation. The products manual will tell you in which order to install the NIC and software, and Chapter 10 will tell you how to install drivers for the different Windows operating systems.

If you are planning on using or continuing to use the phone jack where you plug in your PC, you can buy a two-jack converter from any local electronics store such as Radio Shack. Some of the USB phoneline NICs come with a two-port option, allowing you to plug in the phone cord from your phone as well as the cord coming from the phone jack in the wall.

NOTE

You might be asking, "What about mixing phoneline and other networks such as Ethernet?" Well, phoneline NICs won't communicate directly on an Ethernet network, but you can buy phoneline-to-Ethernet bridges that allow a phoneline product to communicate on an Ethernet network. Also, Windows XP will allow users of phoneline, as well as other types of networking equipment such as wireless or powerline, to communicate with all the various networking technologies. For example, if you have a PC equipped with a phoneline NIC and a powerline NIC, the bridging function in Windows XP will allow these different technologies to communicate on the same home network.

Power to the People: Networking over In-Home Electrical Wiring

A potential problem with phoneline networking is the simple fact that not every room in a home will have a phone jack. If your home is like many other homes, you might have a phone jack in your kitchen and your den, and maybe one in one of the bedrooms, but chances are that unless your home was recently built or you've had the phone company come out to install extra phone jacks, you won't have a phone connection everywhere you want a network connection.

Not so with power outlets. If you take a casual look around the room you are in now, you'll likely see more than one power outlet. In fact, most rooms have two to three outlets. This multitude of outlets allows you to have much more freedom in installing your networked PC where you like it, because you don't have to worry about having a couple of phone jacks in out-of-the-way places in your home.

An Industry Is Born

"So what," you say, "I have a bunch of power outlets, but don't tell me I can actually network things over the same wiring that powers my electronic gadgets such as the microwave and stereo." Believe it or not, the capability to connect things over in-home power wiring has been around for three decades, starting in the 1970s with a technology called X-10.

X-10 is a low-speed home control and automation technology that thousands of hobbyists have used over the years to do such things as automatically turn their lights and other home systems on and off. Although X-10 is not exactly high-speed networking technology, it's still a communication protocol that allows communication over electrical wiring.

NOTE

X-10 was the first home automation technology widely available. Its origins were in the 1970s when a company called Pico/X-10 (what else!) started selling products based on its patented technology to retailers such as Radio Shack and Macy's. Soon techno-geeks all over the United States were gobbling up these little control modules that allowed you to turn your lights and appliances off and on from a centralized location, as well as set up routines that turned these things on or off at certain times of the day. X-10 also helped to better the lives of people with disabilities, allowing for control of home systems that would otherwise have been impossible for certain people with handicaps. For more on X-10 and home automation technologies, see Chapter 21, "Smart Home: Home Automation Networks."

Other technologies exist for home control and automation, but only recently have companies looked at doing high-speed, Ethernet-like communication over powerlines. The first company that released powerline networking products goes by the name Inari. Inari, formerly called Intelogis, had a product called PassPort that allowed anyone to network PCs over in-home power wiring at 350 kilobits per second (1Mbps is 1000Kbps). The company has since decided to develop chips for powerline networking to sell to other companies and has announced that products will be available using its technology in 2001. Inari's PassPort NIC is shown plugged into a power outlet in Figure 8.4.

FIGURE 8.4
The Inari PassPort powerline NIC.

While Inari continued to push its own technology, another group of companies formed an industry group by the name of HomePlug Powerline Alliance, or HomePlug. The goal of the HomePlug alliance to is to develop a high-speed specification for networking over powerlines.

NOTE

HomePlug: Creating High-Speed Powerline Networking

HomePlug first formed in April 2000. Like the HPNA before it, HomePlug is a group of different technology companies that came together to develop a standard where there was none before. Like HPNA, the group has moved quickly to develop a standard and will have products available on store shelves less than two years after the group's formation, by Christmastime, 2001. You can learn more about HomePlug at www.homeplug.org.

How Does This Stuff Work?

HomePlug and Inari products work similar to phoneline-based networking products, except that you plug the NIC into the power outlet instead of the phoneline. The big difference between phonelines and powerlines is that whereas phonelines were developed from the beginning as a communication medium, powerlines were not. This does not mean that networking cannot be done over powerlines; in fact, efforts are underway to allow people to get their Internet access over their powerlines. Imagine your local electric utility also acting as your Internet service provider!

Talk About Power Surfing

Power companies have long known about the capability to send voice messages over powerlines. And in the past few years, the idea of sending Internet signals over the power grid into people's homes has gotten quite a bit of attention.

Think about it: Roughly 66% of U.S. households have cable service, and less than half meet the requirements for DSL, another form of high-speed Internet access. But everyone who lives in a house or apartment has power (unless they forgot to pay their bill!).

Utility companies in Europe have been experimenting with powerline Internet. In Germany a utility called RWE is working to bring Internet over powerlines to 16,000 homes, and another utility named Oneline AG is planning to connect another 10,000.

The capability to provide Internet access to homes over powerlines is not easy to achieve, especially in the U.S. Much of the reason behind the early efforts in Europe involved the differences in the power grid across the Atlantic and in the U.S. In Europe, a power transformer is responsible for providing power to approximately 300 to 400 homes. The transformers in the U.S. power only 5 to 6 homes. The capability to provide Internet access over powerlines is directly linked to configuring the transformer, and with the U.S. transformers being responsible for only 6 or fewer homes, this would create a much bigger (and costlier!) job.

Needless to say, powerline Internet, like powerline in-home networking, is still in its early stages. But don't be surprised if someday you get a call from your local electric company, offering to provide Internet access for an additional $19.95!

The powerline network in your home will be set up much like the phoneline network, in that you will have a NIC for each PC, which will communicate directly with the other PCs. Figure 8.5 illustrates a basic powerline network.

A couple of key differences exist between setting up a powerline network and setting up other networks. Specifically, you might find the following with a powerline network:

- *The NIC may be plugged directly into the power outlet*   You may have to plug the NIC into the actual power outlet, rather than having the NIC installed in the PC with a PCI slot or into a USB port.

- *The NIC and the power connection might be the same thing*   One of the benefits of powerline networking is that you can, theoretically, get power for your device as well as connect it to the network through the same connection. No PCs exist today that have this capability, but some PC companies plan to eventually allow for your PC to be networked simply by being plugged in.

- *There are special security concerns with powerline networking*   Because each home shares a transformer with other homes within its neighborhood, your neighbor could conceivably get on your network without your even knowing it. It's difficult to stop the network transmissions in your home without special filters. When you do buy a home network for powerline networking, be sure to see whether the equipment has security precautions. The PassPort network allows you to create a secure network, and HomePlug networks incorporate security measures as well. For more on security for your network, see Chapter 18, "Home Network Security Overview."

- *You need to be extra careful with powerline networks; after all, you are working with powerjacks*   Although this point may seem self-evident, there are some people who may need to be warned. Anytime you are working with anything electrical, you should be careful.

- *Powerlines are noisy and prone to interference*   One of the great challenges for creating a powerline network is the high level of variation of electrical surges on the network. In any given home, simply turning on a hair dryer can create quite a bit of electrical "noise" and possibly interfere with the network. In fact, with a HomePlug network, a noisy source such as a microwave or hair dryer can drop the bandwidth down from the usual 10Mbps to 1Mbps, a factor of 10! The manufacturers of powerline networking equipment have taken great pains to overcome the problem of electrical noise.

8

OTHER
NETWORKING
TECHNOLOGIES

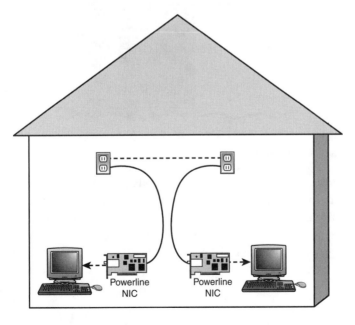

FIGURE 8.5

A basic powerline network.

Setting Up Your Powerline Network

Setting up a powerline network is much like setting up other no-new-wires networks. You mainly need to be concerned with installation of the NIC. You should read the manual for each product; as you read previously, powerline NICs might be a little different in that, depending on the model, they might be able to plug directly into the power outlet.

The Inari PassPort is one such product. A kit from Inari (or Intelogis, the company's previous name) comes with a couple of powerline NICs (they call them adapters) and a special power-line adapter for hooking up a printer. The kit also comes with a power strip to hook your PC into to avoid electrical interference.

The installation of NICs is simple. In the case of Inari/Intelogis, you take one of the adapters and plug it directly into the power outlet. You then hook the adapter to your PC through a parallel port, which auto-senses the adapter; your Windows PC will then start an installation wizard.

Like many manufacturers of phoneline equipment such as Intel, Inari/Intelogis has created its own installation and management administrator. In Figure 8.6 you'll see the administrator window, which works within Windows to help you set up and manage a powerline network.

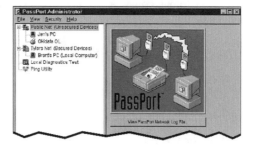

FIGURE 8.6

A powerline network administrator window.

For an in-depth look at the physical installation of a NIC, see "Installing the Network Interface Card" in Chapter 6. After your NIC is installed in the machine (or plugged into the outlet and then hooked up to your PC), you need to install drivers and configure your operating system. See Chapter 10 for in-depth instructions on how to do this. Again, your specific product *might* have its own software for installation and management of your network, but I would strongly recommend that you refer to Chapter 10 before attempting to install and configure your network.

> **Is a Powerline Network for Me?**
>
> Brand-new technology can sometimes scare people away. Powerline networking is no different, and many people *might* ask, "Do I even want to use this technology when I can use Ethernet or wireless networking?" Well, only time will tell, but one thing that should alleviate your fears is the support of many large manufacturers of this technology. Soon you will see not only NICs that operate over powerlines, but broadband modems and home routers as well.
>
> Also, many people believe that powerline networking holds great promise as a network backbone technology. Because powerlines reach around your home, what technology is better for distributing data and content to the different endpoints of your network? In fact, powerline has an advantage over wireless in that it will be able to send information around the network without the same level of degradation of the signal that you would get with wireless LANs.
>
> If you are still doubtful, that is fine. As new products come to market and a wider audience begins to use these technologies, you *might* become more comfortable and decide that powerline networking is for you.

Structured Wiring Solutions

Structured wiring solutions are different from the other solutions in that they do not consist of the networking hardware per se. Instead, they are whole-home wiring systems that can be installed to allow you to hook up Ethernet networks—as well as video, audio, and communications systems—throughout your home on one wiring system.

What Are They and Why Would I Want One?

The problem with most wiring in homes that are more than a few years old is that the wiring is not sufficient for all the things people want to do today: Internet access, networking, in-home communications, new forms of entertainment such as whole-home digital television and audio. Even as many of these new technologies gain ground among consumers today, the fact is that most homes are still being built as though most of us just made a few phone calls, read the newspaper for all our information needs, and watched TV using a rabbit-ear antenna.

Enter structured wiring. Structured wiring packages are advanced wiring systems that allow homes to take advantage of all the new communication technologies. Although most homes have just a couple of copper wires, homes with structured wiring have higher-grade Category 5 copper wiring, integrated in one cabling package with coax (for television and audio distribution) and possibly even fiber.

But structured wiring systems don't just stop with the cabling. They also include both a central distribution box for interconnecting the different cables and network devices and special service outlets in each room for easy access and setup of the network.

The Distribution Box

The distribution box is really the centralized maintenance box for the network, as well as for home communication and entertainment. Instead of your having to deal with all the cables of a structured wiring system just hanging hodge-podge in some closet, the distribution box gives you an organized and sturdy box for interconnection of the different cabling.

Most distribution boxes allow for a place to take all feeds, such as your high-speed Internet, telephone, and cable TV, and then interconnect to the different nodes around the home. You can also store your Ethernet hub in a distribution box for networking to the different PCs around the home over the Cat 5 cabling within the structured wiring assembly. See Figure 8.7 for a diagram of a distribution box within a structured wiring system.

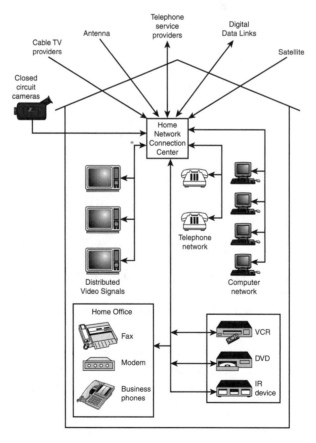

FIGURE 8.7

A conceptual diagram of a distribution box within a structured wiring system.

As you can see, a structured wiring system using a distribution box can be much more than a centralized place to hook network wires. In Figure 8.7, you see how televisions, telephones, fax machines, and the PC network all are connected into the distribution box. Figure 8.7 is a conceptual drawing of the structured wiring system utilizing a distribution box. Figure 8.8 shows you what an actual distribution box looks like.

FIGURE 8.8
A distribution box in a structured wiring package.

The Service Outlet

In addition to the integrated cabling and the distribution box, a structured wiring system includes the actual outlets that go in each room and allow you to plug into the network. These outlets allow for different types of plug-in jacks and are often configurable depending on the needs of the particular room, as well as the desires of the homeowner. The outlets can support RJ-45 jacks for network connections, RJ-11 jacks for communications, and coaxial connections for video, as well as stereo output binding posts for connecting to speakers via speaking cabling.

A service outlet featuring RJ-11, RJ-45, and coax connections is shown in Figure 8.9.

The availability in service outlets in each room makes for extremely convenient connections to any form of network.

Before You Go and Buy a Structured Wiring System

Structured wiring systems represent what is possible in getting a truly "wired" home. With integrated cabling that allows you to connect to any kind of network through a centralized distribution box and highly flexible service outlets throughout the house, if anyone had their choice, why wouldn't they pick a structured wiring solution?

As with anything that provides benefits, there are costs associated with a structured wiring solution:

- The cost of the system itself, which can range anywhere from $1,000 up to $10,000 for a highly advanced system with all the bells and whistles
- The cost of installation for a structured wiring system

FIGURE 8.9

A structured wiring service outlet.

Although it is possible, if you are a fairly competent technical person, to install a structured wiring system by yourself, I highly recommend that you use a trained and certified installation representative. This is because the installation of a structured wiring solution requires tearing holes in walls, working with the network interface unit on your home, and performing other jobs that are best left to those with proper training.

Those who have their home built for them or are looking to buy a new home with a structured wiring solution can talk to the builders and see whether they currently have a relationship with a structured wiring installer, or whether they do the work themselves. If they do not have structured wiring installation as an option, you might ask them to contact a home systems installation specialist.

Many structured wiring companies have directories to specialists certified to install their products. If you want to have a structured wiring solution installed in your own home, you can look up a specialist on the companies' Web sites. In Table 8.1 you'll see some of the more well-known structured wiring companies and their Web addresses.

TABLE 8.1 Structured Wiring Manufacturers

Structured Wiring Manufacturers	Web Site
Home Director	www.homedirector.com
OnQ Technologies	www.onqtech.com
Greyfox Systems	www.greyfox.com
Residential Cabling	www.residentialcabling.com
Monster Cable	www.monstercableManufacturers.com

Wrap It Up

The choices for home network technologies are many, from the traditional wired Ethernet to wireless to technologies that take advantage of your in-home phone and power wiring. Those who want to have the most advanced network systems in their home can have structured wiring systems that enable whole-home distribution of not only network communications but entertainment, voice, fax, and music as well.

Phoneline networking is a new technology that essentially allows you to do Ethernet-type networking over your in-home telephone wiring. Phoneline networks are easy to set up in that they require a few NICs and telephone wires.

Powerline networking, which is newer than phoneline technology, allows you to plug into your power outlet and send networking signals over in-home electrical wiring. Powerline networking products are not widely available today, but they should be by the middle of 2002. Someday you will be able to just plug in a device such as a PC or a digital music player, and it will both get its power and be networked through the same connection.

Structured wiring is the ultimate in home networking. Most systems are composed of three components:

- The integrated wiring, which usually consists of two Cat 5 cables, two RG-6 coax cables, and sometimes fiber.
- The distribution center, which serves as the centralized connection point for both the in-home wiring and those connections coming from outside the house such as cable TV, high-speed Internet, satellite TV, and your phone communication.
- The service outlets, which are the configurable plug-ins that reside in each room. These allow you to connect to the distribution center.

8

OTHER
NETWORKING
TECHNOLOGIES

Software Setup and Management

IN THIS PART

Setting Up Home Network Software

IN THIS CHAPTER

No More "Hard" Parts

If you're reading this, it's likely that you are done with the hard part of network installation—at least the hard-*ware* part. You've also gotten your feet wet with home network software through the installation of your network drivers, which is part of the installation process for NICs. We will examine how to configure the other software components that are part of your PC operating system to allow your home network to work like a charm.

You might be relieved to know that when you're setting up and configuring your software to run a home network, much of the work is automated. Microsoft, as well as PC and networking companies, has invested a lot of money and effort in making things run as smoothly as possible during setup of a home network. Believe it or not, many of the problems that pop up in running a home network are due to problems with or misunderstanding of the software. This chapter shows you how to avoid these problems and get your network software working in harmony with your network hardware.

This chapter will walk you through the following:

- We will review the basic configuration tasks involved in setting up a home network. Because there are slight variations between the different Windows operating systems, we will first look at how the operating systems differ for home networking purposes. We will also briefly review non-Windows operating systems such as those for the Macintosh computers. For a more in-depth look at setting up a Macintosh network, you should look at Chapter 12, "Networking with Macs."

- We will also discuss whether you should use a home network wizard to set up your home network. Many Windows PCs come with an easy-to-use wizard that makes network setup easier by masking some of the complexities of networking; this chapter discusses the benefits of using a wizard and how to access the wizard in Windows.

- The heart of this chapter examines the required software components in setting up a Windows-based home network. We will look at what each component does, and then we will see how to determine whether this component has been installed and, if not, cover the basic steps necessary to do so.

Don't worry, it's easier than it sounds. Before long, you'll be running your home network!

A Word About Windows Operating Systems and Home Networking

Even if you're a casual computer user, you likely are aware that there are many different operating systems.

> **NOTE**
>
> An *operating system* (OS) is the software that enables your PC to do basic tasks. It also manages how system resources such as memory and processor power are allocated. Microsoft Windows is an operating system.

Even Windows, which is by far the most common OS in use today at home and at work, has many different versions. What makes my job a little harder (and this book such a great investment!) is that each OS differs slightly in regard to network setup. I'll go over the differences when explaining how to set up a network.

These are the main Windows operating systems in use today on home PCs:

- *Windows 95*—This OS is usually on older PCs bought before 1998.

- *Windows 98*—Windows 98 is installed on PCs that are newer than four or five years old. There are two versions of Windows 98. Windows 98 Second Edition (or SE) has more built-in networking functions, including the Home Networking Wizard and Internet Connection Sharing. As you learned previously, the Internet Connection Sharing function is what allows you to share a dial-up or broadband connection with the built-in capabilities of your Windows operating system.

- *Windows Millennium Edition (or Windows ME)*—Windows ME became available in 2000 and is similar to Windows 98 SE in terms of networking functions.

- *Windows XP for Consumers*—This is the newest Windows operating system. XP is the easiest OS to use for a home network because a big focus was put on home networking. The capability to set up networks is automated in many ways, and we will review how to take advantage of XP's functionality.

There are other Windows operating systems that were designed primarily for use in business environments, including Windows NT and Windows 2000. Although these operating systems can be networked, they were developed primarily for business environments with more advanced needs than those of the home networker.

9

SETTING UP HOME NETWORK SOFTWARE

Windows XP: Networking for the Masses?

The folks at Microsoft knew that to get folks to buy their new operating system, they had to build in some obvious benefits that were not in previous versions. They also knew that the demand for home networks, as well as broadband, is skyrocketing. So what did they do? Made XP very network-centric.

What does this mean? Well, it means that many of the basic functions built into XP are geared toward networking and Internet sharing. They built in such things as an easier user interface for networking, and more help functions to answer questions about networking. Also added was a basic firewall for broadband Internet connections, which helps protect PCs on the network from security threats.

One of the other benefits of Windows XP is that it was built using the same technology used in Windows 2000, which is the business operating system from Microsoft. Because Windows 2000 is built for business networks, it is much more stable. As a result, Windows XP is also much more stable, a good thing when you are doing such things as building a home network.

What About Other Operating Systems?

As you probably know, the world is not made of Windows. Truth be told, there are other very viable operating-system alternatives. Networks using the Apple Macintosh and those running the Linux operating system are used by millions worldwide, and they are just as easy to set up and use as those based on Windows. The next few chapters focus on Windows-based PCs, because Windows is the most common operating system in use by consumers. However, it is important to note that the same equipment used for Windows home networks can be used just as well on alternative operating systems. To learn how to set up and run a home network using an operating system for Macintosh computers, refer to Chapter 12.

Using an Installation Wizard to Configure a Home Network

One of the things that has been implemented to make your life easier is the use of installation wizards for network setup. Windows Millennium Edition and Windows XP operating systems employ home network "wizards." Wizards guide you through the setup process, which helps shield the user from some of the more complex and arcane terms and configuration screens that are inevitably part of network setup.

Should you use the home network wizard that is part of your operating system? The fact is that many people do not care to learn about network configuration, and there is nothing wrong with that. They simply want to use their networks and no more! If this is the case, follow the instructions given next to get access to your home network wizard in either Windows ME or XP. This wizard will install all the necessary network software components to get you up and running with your home network, such as the network client, network protocol, and network services component.

However, if you are intent on learning a little about navigating your PC and setting up a network at the same time, I would suggest not using the wizards and setting up your home network yourself, installing the necessary network software components through the basic steps discussed in this chapter.

Accessing the Home Network Wizard in Windows ME

Accessing the home network wizard in Windows ME is simple. All it takes are a few steps and you will be well on your way to networking. In Figure 9.1 you'll see what the home network wizard in ME looks like.

FIGURE 9.1

The Windows Home Networking Wizard.

To access the home network wizard in Windows ME, do the following:

1. Double-click the My Network Places icon on your desktop. The icon will have two PCs and a small globe behind it, and it is usually below the My Computer icon.

2. When the My Network Places window displays, as shown in Figure 9.2, double-click on the icon for the Home Networking Wizard. You'll then need to follow the instructions for setting up a home network.

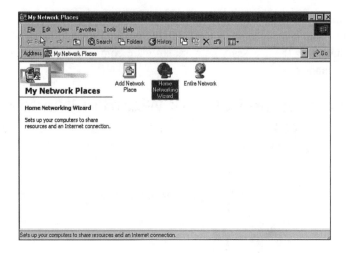

FIGURE 9.2
The My Network Places window in Windows ME.

Accessing the Home Network Wizard in Windows XP

1. Click the Start button on the lower-left side of the screen.

2. From the Start menu, click on Control Panel.

3. From the Control Panel, under the Pick a Category menu, click on Network and Internet Connections. This selection gives you the menu shown in Figure 9.3.

4. From Network and Internet Connections, click on the icon that reads Set Up or Change Your Home or Small Office Network, which launches the network setup wizard.

> **NOTE**
>
> In Windows XP, the home network wizard is called the Network Setup Wizard. Despite the different name, the wizard accomplishes the same function as the Home Networking Wizard in Windows ME.

> **NOTE**
>
> One of the nice benefits about Windows XP when compared to previous versions of Windows is that many of the pop-up menus, such as the one shown in Figure 9.3, are browser-based. This means that the different icons act as links in a home page, and a navigation bar at the top of the screen allows you to do such things as go back to previous screens.

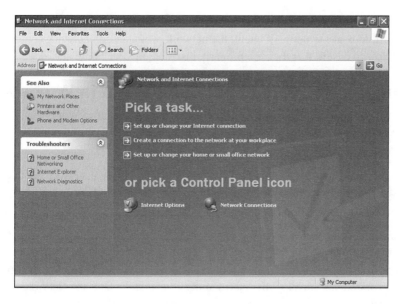

FIGURE 9.3
The Network and Internet Connections menu in Windows XP.

Network Software Components

The network software consists of several pieces. Each of these pieces is called a "network component." Network components are similar to the concept of network building blocks we discussed in Chapter 2, "Home Network Building Blocks: What Makes Your Network Tick" In fact, one of the building blocks of the network software we discussed in Chapter 2 was the network driver. A network driver is the software component specifically geared toward enabling the networking hardware installed in your PC (the NIC) to talk with the PC's operating system.

You learned in Chapter 6, "Understanding and Installing an Ethernet Network," how to install network drivers when we discussed the installation of a network interface card. Although drivers are an important part of the software components necessary to create a home network, there are other very important software components you will need to know about or at least be aware of. These include the following:

- *The Network Client*—This is the software component that allows a PC on the network to access the different services and resources on a network.

- *The Network Protocol*—Network protocols are what enable the communication between different devices over the network. In fact, the most popular network protocol, TCP/IP, is the native language of the Internet.

- *Network Services*—Network services are resources on the network that you can share with other PCs. The most common of these is file and printer sharing.

9

SETTING UP
HOME NETWORK
SOFTWARE

Because we reviewed driver installation in Chapter 6, we will not go into detail in this chapter. Instead, we will look at the network client, the network protocol, and network services as components and how to ensure that they are properly installed on your home network.

Installing the Network Client Component in Windows

As you learned earlier, the network client is the software component in Windows that allows you to access services across the network. It is your network "key," opening the door for you to the network.

In Windows XP, the Client for Microsoft Networks is loaded onto your PC by default when Windows is installed. However, it could possibly have been turned off, so we will review how to make sure that it is enabled.

For Windows 95/98/ME, you might need to add the Client for Microsoft Networks, which is simple to do, as you will see in the next section. There is also a minor difference between these older versions of Windows and Windows XP: in Windows 95/98/ME you have the option to add other network clients such as Microsoft Family Logon and Client for NetWare Clients. I recommend that you use Client for Microsoft Networks because this is the primary client used for most home networks and is the client that is supported in all versions of Microsoft Windows.

Installing the Client for Microsoft Networks in Windows 95/98/ME

Installing the network client in older versions of Windows is a quick and painless task.

> **Tip**
>
> Before you begin the installation of the network client or other networking software components, you should make sure that you have your Windows installation CD, which came with your PC when you purchased it. Your PC might ask for the CD as you walk through the following steps.

Here's what to do:

1. Click the Start button, choose Settings, and then double-click the Network icon.
2. In the Network window, on the Configuration tab, look in the section labeled The Following Network Components Are Installed. The Client for Microsoft Networks should be at the top of the list of components, as shown in Figure 9.4. If you do not see this icon, you will need to install it.

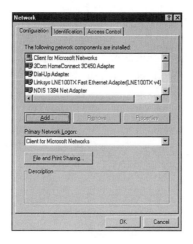

FIGURE 9.4
The Network window in Windows 95/98/ME.

3. In the Network window, click the Add button. You will see a dialog box with the words Select Network Component Type at the top. In the dialog box you will see the choices of Client, Protocol, and Service, as shown in Figure 9.5.

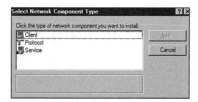

FIGURE 9.5
The Select Network Component Type dialog box.

4. Click on Client and then click the Add button.

5. You might get more than one option under the Manufacturers; choose Microsoft. Under the Network Client choices, choose Client for Microsoft Networks and then click OK. You now should have installed the Client for Microsoft Networks.

6. Click OK again, and say Yes when your PC asks whether to reboot.

Installing the Client for Microsoft Networks in Windows XP

As stated previously, the network client in Windows XP is installed and turned on by default. However, it is still helpful to know how to check whether the client is turned on. To do so, follow these steps:

1. Click the Start button, select Control Panel, and then click the Network and Internet Connections category.

2. In the Network and Internet Connections window, click on Network Connections, which is under the Control Panel icon section at the bottom of your screen.

3. In the Network Connections window, under the heading LAN or High-Speed Internet, click once on the Local Area Connection icon. When it is highlighted, click the right button on your mouse to get a pop-up menu. Choose Properties to launch the Local Area Connection Properties window, as shown in Figure 9.6. This is the equivalent of the Network window in Windows 95/98/ME.

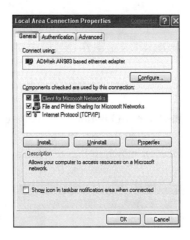

FIGURE 9.6

The Local Area Connection Properties window in Windows XP.

4. Look in the section Components Checked Are Used by This Connection to see whether the Client for Microsoft Networks is checked and active. If not, click the check box and click OK.

Installing the Network Protocols Component in Windows

Without the use of network protocols, home networks, or any other network for that matter, would not exist. Luckily, this important software component is easy to add and use in Windows. Like the Network Client, it has been installed in Windows XP by default and should be turned on by default. With Windows 95/98/ME, you will need to install the network protocol.

Of course, you should know that TCP/IP is only one of the choices for network protocols, but it is certainly the most popular and the most powerful. We will look briefly at another network protocol called NetBEUI later in the chapter, but our discussion about protocols will center on TCP/IP.

TCP/IP: The Mother of All Network Protocols

TCP/IP, often referred to simply as Internet Protocol, or IP, is truly the mother of all network protocols. IP is used as the main protocol to connect the millions of PCs on the Internet. It is also the primary network protocol used for communication in business and home networks.

How did TCP/IP become so popular? Well, it is widely used on the Internet because it was developed by the U.S. Government's Department of Defense in the late 1970s and has since been designated as the primary protocol of the Internet for long-distance communication. The popularity of the Internet combined with a need for a widely available communication protocol across different business networks catapulted IP into wide use at most of the big operating-system manufacturers.

You might also want to know that TCP/IP is the name of a full suite of Internet protocols, and TCP and IP themselves are only two of these protocols. However, the industry has come to recognize the term TCP/IP as the name for this family of protocols that help to enable today's LAN networks and the Internet.

Installing Network Protocols in Windows 95/98/ME

To install the network protocol in Windows 95/98/ME, follow these steps:

1. Click Start, select Settings, select Control Panel, and then double-click the Network icon.

2. Click the Add button.

3. In the Select Network Component Type dialog box, click on Protocol and then click the Add button.

4. You will see the Select Network Protocol dialog box, as shown in Figure 9.7. Under the Manufacturers you might see more than one; click on Microsoft.

5. After you click on Microsoft, you will see a choice of different protocols. Select TCP/IP and click OK.

6. When you click OK on the Select Network Protocol window, you will be asked whether to reboot the PC. Click Yes.

9

SETTING UP
HOME NETWORK
SOFTWARE

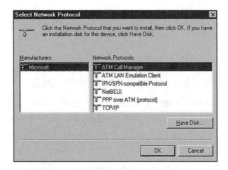

FIGURE 9.7

The Select Network Protocol box in Windows 95/98/ME.

NOTE

If you are not going to be using your home network to share an Internet connection, you can choose NetBEUI (pronounced net-*boo*-ee), which is an easy-to-use protocol designed for small Windows networks. TCP/IP requires more configuration, but it is designed to work with the Internet. NetBEUI requires practically no configuration, which is its main attraction. You can install both TCP/IP and NetBEUI if you do not know which one you would like to use at this point. If you plan to use the Internet at all on your home network, I would suggest not using NetBEUI and going strictly with TCP/IP instead.

Installing Network Protocols in Windows XP

Even though the network protocol is installed by default with your Windows XP operating system, you might want to double-check and see whether it is turned on. To do so, follow these steps:

1. Click Start, Control Panel, Network and Internet Connections, and Network Connections.

2. Click once on Local Area Network Connection. Then right-click to get a pop-up menu and click the option for Properties.

3. The Local Area Connection Properties window will pop up. Check to see whether the Internet Protocol option is checked.

4. If the Internet Protocol (TCP/IP) option is not checked, click the check box to select it, and click OK. Allow your PC to reboot if necessary.

Installing the Network Services Component in Windows

The Network Services component of Windows allows you to share resources with other PCs on the network. The primary service enabled through the Network Services component is file and printer sharing. Once again, we will review how to install this component in Windows 95/98/ME and how to ensure that it has been turned on in Windows XP.

Installing Network Services in Windows 95/98/ME

The installation of the Network Services in Windows is much like that of the Client for Microsoft Networks. It is a simple process that takes just a few steps. To install the Network Services component, follow these steps:

1. Click Start, Settings, and Control Panel, and then double-click the Network icon.

2. On the Network window click the Add button.

3. In the Select Network Component dialog box, click on Service and then click Add.

4. You will see the Select Network Service dialog box, as shown in Figure 9.8. Select File and Printer Sharing for Microsoft Networks, and click OK. Then click OK from the Network window and allow the PC to reboot.

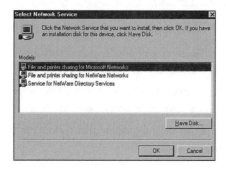

FIGURE 9.8

The Select Network Service window.

Installing Network Services in Windows XP

The network services component will likely be ready to go out of the box for you if you are operating a Windows XP machine. However, you will again want to confirm that it is turned on. To do so, simply do the following:

1. Click Start, Control Panel, and Network and Internet Connections, and right-click on the LAN or High-Speed Internet icon to get the pop-up menu.

2. Click on Properties to get the Local Area Connection Properties window.

3. You should see the File and Printer Sharing for Microsoft Windows checked under the available components. If it is not checked, check it and then click OK. Then follow the instructions to reboot the PC.

Wrap It Up

Congratulations, you've configured your PC and now are ready to network. In the next chapter we'll cover how to identify yourself on your home network and get out there in the network "neighborhood." But before we do that, let's review what you've learned in this chapter.

The operating system plays a key role in networking your PCs. Windows-based operating systems come in different formats, the newest being Windows XP. Older operating systems in Windows include Windows 95, Windows 98, and Windows Millennium Edition (ME). You don't need to have Windows to network. Other operating systems include Linux and those for the Apple Macintosh.

Many Windows-based PCs come with an option for a home network wizard. Wizards automate the process of configuring your software for a home network. Even though you might have the option of a home network wizard, you should consider following the steps outlined in this chapter to make sure you understand how a home network is set up.

In addition to network drivers, there are three major software components of a home network:

- *Network client*—The software component that allows your PC to access the resources made available by other PCs on the network.

- *Network protocol*—The component that allows your PC to communicate with other PCs on the network. The most common network protocol today is TCP/IP.

- *Network services*—The software component that makes the resources on your PC available to other PCs on the network.

Getting Around the Home Network

IN THIS CHAPTER

Preparing for a Network Stroll

You're almost ready for a stroll around the network. You've installed the hardware and drivers, you've installed the key software components for your network, and now you're ready to take a walkabout and see your network neighbors. Before you do, you must learn how to identify yourself on the network—that is, give your PC a name. Not only do you have to assign a real name such as "Bob's PC," but you also must learn how to give each PC an address, called an IP address, before the PCs can communicate. It's essentially letting your PC have a real name so that you can identify it, and a numerical network name for its identity on the network.

Giving Your PC a Name

The process of giving your PC a name by which you can identify it is easy. First, you must figure out exactly what to call it.

Believe it or not, some folks give as much thought to naming their PC as they would to naming a family pet. I would suggest naming it something not too creative, but more practical, in this manner:

- After the room it resides in—such as "Den" or "Basement."
- After the primary user of the PC—such as "Mom" or "Homer."
- After the role it takes—"Work" or "Home."

One thing that should ease your naming anxiety is that you can always change the name of your PC.

> **NOTE**
>
> One thing you should be aware of is that the PC identity is different from the names used with Windows user accounts. User accounts enable different users of the PC to create their own settings and preferences for their user sessions. User accounts also have a security aspect in that the user can maintain control over which files and folders can be accessed.

To set up your PC's identification, you'll be going back to where we left off in Chapter 9, "Setting Up Home Network Software." The process differs slightly between Windows 95/98/ME and Windows XP, so we'll review each.

Configuring Your Windows 95/98/ME Identification

To create your identification in Windows 95/98/ME, simply follow these steps:

1. Click Start, Settings, Control Panel, and double-click the Network icon.

2. When the Network window pops up, go to the Identification tab as shown in Figure 10.1.

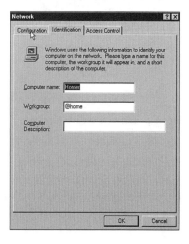

FIGURE 10.1

The Identification tab in Windows 95/98/ME.

In addition to Computer Name in the Identification tab, there is a space for Workgroup. Workgroup is another name for the grouping of PCs on your network. In larger networks such as those in business environments, there might be multiple workgroups, each with its own name by which to identify it. An example might be Finance or Marketing. In the home, however, there is no reason to have more than one workgroup.

The default workgroup name provided by Windows is Workgroup. You can simply leave this name, or provide one of your own. If you do change the name, make sure that the name is the same for every PC on your network. The workgroup name is what helps Windows identify each PC as part of a home network.

> **CAUTION**
>
> One thing to take note of is that some Internet service providers require that a certain workgroup name be used in order to receive service. AT&T's @Home cable modem Internet service is one such example. With this service, you must have the workgroup identity of @home. Check with your service provider before changing your workgroup name.

Another way to change your PC's identification name and workgroup in Windows ME is to use the home network wizard. As explained in the preceding chapter, you can use the wizard to

10

GETTING AROUND
THE HOME
NETWORK

configure your PCs for home networking. You can also use the home network wizard to update your network settings after you have previously set up the network. For example, if you decide to change the name of your PC and/or its workgroup, you can do so either through the Identification tab in the Network window or by running the home network wizard. Remember that you should have your Windows CD on hand in case you are asked for it while making changes.

To access the home network wizard in Windows Millennium Edition (ME), simply do this:

1. Double-click on My Network Places from your Windows desktop.
2. When the My Network Places window pops up, double-click on the Home Networking Wizard icon.

If you have already set up a home network in Windows and you are using the home network wizard in ME to change settings, the wizard will ask you to edit the settings on your home network. It will also ask whether you want to create a home network floppy disk for configuring other PCs on your network.

Configuring Your Windows XP Identification

As with Windows ME, you can create your PC's identification for your home network in Windows XP in two ways. One way is through the Network Setup Wizard and the other is through the Systems Configuration window in XP.

To access the Network Setup Wizard in Windows XP, follow these steps:

1. Click Start, Control Panel, and then Network and Internet Connections.
2. Under Pick a Task, click the option Set Up or Change Your Home or Small Office Network to launch the Network Setup wizard in XP.

To change the name of your PC and workgroup on a Windows XP PC, do the following:

1. Click Start, Control Panel, and then click the Performance and Maintenance category (rather than Network and Internet Connections).
2. From the Performance and Maintenance window, click the System icon, which is listed under O Pick a Control Panel Icon. This launches the Systems Properties dialog box.
3. From the Systems Properties dialog box, click on the Computer Name tab, as shown in Figure 10.2. If you have already named your PC and the workgroup, you will see these values listed in the window. Otherwise, the name of the PC and the workgroup will be blank or have default names such as Compaq PC and Mshome. Do not mistake the computer description for the full computer name.

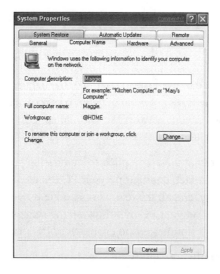

FIGURE 10.2
The Computer Name tab in the System Properties window of Windows XP.

4. To change the name and workgroup, click the Change button.

5. In the Computer Name Changes dialog box, put in the new computer name and workgroup name, as shown in Figure 10.3. Click OK and then OK again, and say Yes when asked whether you would like to reboot your PC.

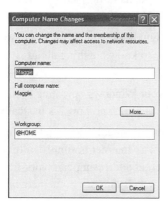

FIGURE 10.3
The Computer Name Changes dialog box in Windows XP.

TCP/IP: Internet Protocol and Your Home Network

Before you configure your network's IP addresses, remember that as explained in Chapter 9, TCP/IP is only one of many network protocols you can use on your network. NetBEUI is another network protocol you can use instead, and one that actually requires very little configuration. However, TCP/IP is the most common network protocol and is required if you want to share an Internet connection on your network, so I would suggest that you go with TCP/IP for nearly all home network installations.

Don't worry, IP addresses are not these complicated numbering schemes that require you to have a PhD in mathematics. In fact, configuring your PC to network on an IP-based network has been made incredibly easy, and all the real work is done by your operating system. You have already installed TCP/IP on your PC by following the steps in Chapter 9. Now all you need to do is go through a few simple steps to enable your PC to use TCP/IP.

Before I show you how to configure TCP/IP on your home network, I'll spend a little time explaining in more depth how IP addressing works. Don't worry, there won't be a quiz, and if you want to skip some of the more detailed information, feel free. However, I do suggest that you at least scan the following material to get a basic understanding of how IP addressing works. This will help you better understand how your network (and the Internet) works.

At the very least, read the following bulleted list to understand some of the most basic points about TCP/IP that everyone should know:

- TCP/IP is a protocol that works hand-in-hand with Ethernet and other networking technologies, such as wireless LAN and phoneline networking.
- Besides doing a quick configuration, which can be completely automated through Windows, you will not have to know anything about IP addressing. It largely works behind the scenes.
- IP addressing is built into your Windows operating system. In the preceding chapter, we installed the software to do TCP/IP, and now it's basically a matter of "turning it on."
- Although it is called "Internet Protocol," don't get confused by using IP addressing within your home network. The Internet is simply millions of computers hooked up in one big network, and if Internet addressing can work for this large a network, it certainly can help you connect the few PCs on your home network.

> **NOTE**
>
> The following section is largely for the benefit of those who want to learn a little about how IP addressing works. If you simply want to get your home network ready and running, you do not need to read this portion, but instead can skip to "How Do IP Addresses Work on My Home Network?"

The Internet Address System

TCP/IP is the address system for the Internet and most local area networks. You might be thinking of the kind of Internet addresses that you plug into your Web browser, such as www.mikewolfiscool.com. These are Web addresses that are actually called domain names, but these domain names rely on a numbering or address system that works behind the scenes.

This is true for millions of computers on the Internet. With all these computers working, there needs to be a way for each of them to communicate with one another. The way this is done is through a numbering system called IP addressing.

IP addresses look something like this:

- 209.69.75.44

or

- 131.143.1.2

The string of numbers in the preceding IP addresses consists of four sets of numbers, all separated by a decimal point. On the Internet, each Web site has a set of numbers that is different from that of all other Web sites, and on your home network, each PC has a set of numbers that differs from the next.

The maximum for each number between the decimal points is 255, and because you have four sets of numbers (as with 131.143.1.2) you have quite a few combinations to choose from—actually more than four billion! But because there is the chance that more than one PC on a network or the Internet could try to claim an IP address, some rules have been set up by a group called ICANN, a short name for the Internet Corporation for Assigned Names and Numbers. Luckily, ICANN and its predecessors designed the Internet address scheme so that you can create a home network as well as get an IP address recognized by others on the larger Internet without a problem.

The Internet Rule Makers

The Internet was designed in the late 1960s and early 1970s by academics and the U.S. government as a network to connect a few hundred computers and mainframes (really large and expensive computers). At the time of its creation, no one expected the Internet to grow as much as it did in the 1990s and beyond.

Even in the early 1980s when the methodology for IP addresses was developed, the thinking was that the Internet would always be pretty manageable and there was *no way* that they would run out of addresses. Since then things have changed dramatically, and even with the more than four billion addresses available today, there still is a threat of running out of addresses as more people and businesses get on the Internet.

Because there was a need for management of these IP addresses, ICANN was formed. Before ICANN, there was a group called InterNIC that helped to manage the Internet IP address and domain names allocation. ICANN was formed in 1998 by a bunch of academic institutions and businesses to help administrate the use of IP addresses.

Even with a group managing the assignment of IP addresses, most Internet experts believe that we need to create a new address system to increase the total number of available addresses. To this end, ICANN and other groups have already developed a new IP address system called Ipv6 (IP version 6) that extends the numbers available on IP addresses to the point at which every man, woman, child, and small dog on earth could have his or her own IP address (don't be surprised if one day this happens). The current version of the IP address system is called Ipv4. If you're wondering what happened to Ipv5, you probably are thinking a little too much about IP addressing, so let's get back to our regularly scheduled discussion.

How Do IP Addresses Work on My Home Network?

Because IP addresses are used on local networks as well as the larger Internet, designated blocks of IP addresses have been set aside for use on private networks such as your home network. This is one method that those managing the Internet have created to help ensure that IP addresses are not exhausted, because these same IP addresses can be reused within any local area network.

These are the blocks of IP addresses set aside for use in private networks:

- 10.0.0.0 to 10.255.255.255
- 172.16.0.0 to 172.31.255.255
- 192.168.0.0 to 192.168.255.55

As you can see, there are more than enough for use in your home network. If you have five home PCs networked, which is a lot for most home networks, you can use IP addresses such as these:

- PC Number 1—10.0.0.1
- PC Number 2—10.0.0.2
- PC Number 3—10.0.0.3
- PC Number 4—10.0.0.4
- PC Number 5—10.0.0.5

Pretty basic. But do you have to even go through the trouble of assigning numbers to the different PCs on the network? Read on....

Understanding DHCP

Before you configure your network to use TCP/IP, you must first have a basic understanding of *DHCP*, or *Dynamic Host Configuration Protocol*. Besides having a fancy name, DHCP serves an important function in many business and home networks in that it is the service that dynamically assigns IP addresses to the different PCs on the network. DHCP is used when a fixed IP address is not assigned to a PC (you'll learn more about assigning a fixed IP address in just a moment).

In many networks in which DHCP is used, there is what is called a DHCP server. A DHCP server can be a standalone computer, such as a server in a client/server network, or it can be a device such as a home router, as discussed in Chapter 2, "Home Network Building Blocks: What Makes Your Network Tick," and discussed at length in Chapter 14, "Internet Sharing on a Home Network." The most important thing to understand is that a DHCP server is the central controller in assigning IP addresses in a network using dynamic IP addresses.

> **TIP**
>
> A *dynamic IP address* is an IP address that is assigned to a PC because that PC does not have a fixed (also known as permanent) IP address.

When a DHCP server assigns an IP address, it looks at the PC making a request for an IP address, verifies important information such as the PC's identification and workgroup, and then does what is called "leasing" of an IP address. When a DHCP server leases an IP address, it basically assigns an IP address to the requesting PC for a period of time (such as the time a PC logs on to a workgroup until the time it logs off), and then the DHCP server reclaims the IP address.

How does DHCP work within a Windows network? If your network is a basic home network using Windows operating systems such as Windows 98/ME and XP and the PCs are configured to use a dynamic IP address, they will look for a DHCP server when logging on to the network. If they do not find a DHCP server, PCs that are configured to use dynamic IP addressing will then default to using what is called LINKLOCAL for Windows 98 and ME PCs, and what is called APIPA for Windows XP PCs. These functions are basically the same in that they assign the PCs on the network IP addresses within a range from 169.254.0.1 to 169.254.255.254 and use the subnet mask of 255.255.0.0.

10

GETTING AROUND
THE HOME
NETWORK

> **TIP**
>
> A *subnet mask* is a number assigned to all the PCs within a certain subgroup on a local area network. Whereas business networks might have many subnets, in a basic home network, you can have one. Common subnet mask numbers include 255.255.0.0 and 255.255.255.0.

Networks that are using the Internet Connection Sharing (ICS) service of Windows do not use either LOCALLINK or APIPA, but instead use the built-in DHCP server capabilities in ICS. Internet Connection Sharing is the Internet sharing service of Windows, which is available in Windows 98 Second Edition, Window ME, and Windows XP PCs.

> **TIP**
>
> If you are planning on sharing the modem of one PC and are not planning on using an Internet sharing device such as a home router or gateway, you will likely use the ICS service in Windows. You can learn more about ICS, as well as Internet sharing devices, in Chapter 14.

If you are planning on using ICS, whichever PC has the modem that you plan to share is designated as the host PC, and this PC will act as the DHCP server. When the host PC is configured using the ICS Wizard, the DHCP server function is loaded into the memory of this PC. The IP addresses assigned by a host PC using ICS range from 192.168.0.1 to 192.168.0.253, with the host PC being assigned the 192.168.0.1 address. Remember that you must keep your host PC on when using ICS for the different PCs to get an IP address from the DHCP service in the host PC.

Now that you understand how DHCP works, we'll review how to configure each IP address in the different versions of Windows.

Configuring IP Addresses in Windows 95/98/ME

When you installed the TCP/IP software component on your PC, the software automatically linked itself to the network interface card for your network. In Figure 10.4, you can see how the TCP/IP protocol has been linked to the Linksys NIC installed on the PC. Usually, the TCP/IP link for the NIC card is listed below the actual NIC card in the Configuration tab.

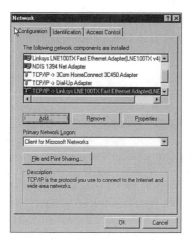

FIGURE 10.4
The TCP/IP protocol link for NIC.

To configure the IP address for a PC on the network in Windows 95/98/ME, you need to access the TCP/IP protocol icon in your Network window. To do so, follow these steps:

1. Click Start, Settings, Control Panel, and double-click the Network icon.

2. On the Configuration tab, scroll down until you see the TCP/IP icon associated with the particular network interface card you have installed.

3. Double-click on the TCP/IP icon for your NIC to get the TCP/IP Properties window. Make sure that you are on the IP Address tab as shown in Figure 10.5.

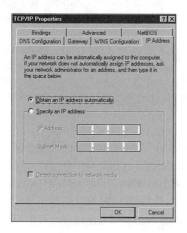

FIGURE 10.5
The IP Address tab in the TCP/IP Properties window.

10

GETTING AROUND
THE HOME
NETWORK

4. Here you want to either assign your PC an IP address that is within the range designated for local area networks (otherwise called a fixed IP address, as discussed earlier in the chapter), or have an IP address assigned automatically (a dynamic IP address).

NOTE

If you have a network with a DHCP server such as a home router, you will definitely want to choose to have your IP address assigned automatically. If you are on a home network using the Internet Connection Sharing service in Windows, your host PC will act as a DHCP server and you will want to have the client PCs (those connecting to the host PC) set up to receive their IP address automatically. If you are setting up a home network in which no PC is connected to the Internet, you can set up each Windows 98/ME or XP PC to receive its IP address automatically, and these PCs will use the built-in capabilities of what is called LINKLOCAL (for Windows 98/ME PCs) or APIPA to assign themselves an IP address when attempting to join a network. If you are using a Windows 95 PC, you will need to assign your PC a fixed IP address unless you are connected to a DHCP server such as a home router or an ICS-enabled host PC.

If you are going to have your PC have a dynamic IP address, select Obtain an IP Address Automatically.

CAUTION

Some ISPs require that you designate an IP address for your broadband modem in addition to your NIC on your network. If you have an external broadband modem that is connected to your PC using Ethernet, you will have a TCP/IP setting for this NIC, as well as the NIC on the network. Make sure that this configuration in these steps is for your NIC on the network. If you are using a broadband router or residential gateway to connect all your PCs to the Internet, you will have only one NIC for both your broadband Internet connection and your network connection.

---

5. If you want to specify your IP address, select the Specify an IP Address option. You will then need to enter an IP address that falls within the range of numbers designated for private local area networks. If you want to keep things simple, use 10.0.0.1 through 10.0.0.x, with x being the next PC on the network.

6. If you choose to specify your own IP address, you will also need to choose a subnet mask. Subnet masks are used in larger local area networks when there are different subnetworks, called subnets, that need to be interconnected. Because you need, by default,

to specify a subnet mask if you choose to specify an IP address (even though on a home network you most likely will not have more than one subnet), I suggest putting in 255.255.255.0. This is the default subnet mask for small networks such as your home network. You can use the same subnet mask ID on each PC on the network.

7. After you have chosen either Obtain an IP Address Automatically or Specify an IP Address and entered your IP address and subnet mask, click OK. Then click OK again on the Network window and click Yes when Windows asks whether you want to restart your PC.

Configuring IP Addresses in Windows XP

Before you configure your IP address in Windows XP, you should know that the default setting is to have the TCP/IP protocol as the default protocol for your network and have the IP address automatically assigned. Also, if you chose to run the home networking wizard in XP or ME, the IP addressing should have been configured for you. However, you should still go through the following steps to check whether your IP addressing is configured properly, as well as if you want to designate a specific IP address for your XP-based PC.

To access the IP configuration screen in XP, do the following:

1. Click Start, Control Panel, Network and Internet Connections, and then click the Control Panel icon of Network Connections.

2. From the Network Connections screen, right-click on the Local Area Connection icon and then click on Properties.

3. Under the General tab on the Local Area Connection Properties window, double-click on the icon for Internet Protocol (TCP/IP).

4. Under the General tab in the Internet Protocol (TCP/IP) Properties window (see Figure 10.6), choose either to Obtain an IP Address Automatically or to designate a specific IP address with the Use the Following IP Address option. If you choose to designate a specific IP address, you will also need to designate a subnet mask, which as stated previously, is used in larger networks to connect different subnetworks. I would recommend that you put 255.255.0.0. You do not need to add a Default Gateway address, because this is for larger business networks.

5. If you are going to choose the Obtain an IP Address Automatically option, and you are not using an Internet sharing device such as a home router or using Internet Connection Sharing, you will want to make sure that the Automatic Private IP Address option is checked. This is the option that enables the APIPA function in Windows XP to assign IP addresses without a designated DHCP server. To ensure that this option is enabled, click on the Alternate Configuration tab at the top of the TCP/IP Properties window. If Automatic Private IP Address is not checked, check it now.

10

GETTING AROUND
THE HOME
NETWORK

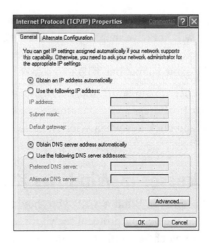

FIGURE 10.6
The Internet Protocol (TCP/IP) Properties window in Windows XP.

6. Click OK and then click OK again on the Local Area Connection Properties window. If the PC asks whether you want to restart your PC, click Yes.

Let's Explore the Neighborhood

Okay, believe it or not, you are ready to go out and explore the network. You've physically connected each PC to the others through a cable or no-new-wires–based network, loaded all the necessary drivers and network software components through the PC operating system, configured each component to work on your PC, given each PC on your network a name through the identification tab, and configured each with an IP address so that they can communicate with each other. Now, it's time to get out and explore the network neighborhood.

CAUTION

This section will introduce you to the basic methods for accessing your network. Depending on the types of operating system(s) you use, as well as the network's configuration, you might need to read the following chapter's information on file and folder sharing to get full access to each PC's resources.

Accessing the Network in Windows 95/98/ME

The main way in which many users access a PC on the network in Windows 95/98 and ME is through the Network Neighborhood or My Network Places screen. In Windows 95 and Windows 98, the network screen is called Network Neighborhood, whereas in Windows Millennium Edition the network screen is called My Network Places.

NOTE

The network screen in Windows XP is also called My Network Places, but because there are a few differences we will look at the two systems separately.

CAUTION

Because the Windows 95/98 Network Neighborhood and the My Network Places screen in Windows ME are similar, we will refer to both as the My Network Places. There are a few differences between the two in that the My Network Places screen in ME has an icon for a home network wizard, whereas in Windows 95/98 no home network wizards are available.

The My Network Places window is accessed as shown here:

1. On your desktop, double-click the icon My Network Places, shown in Figure 10.7.

FIGURE 10.7
The My Network Places icon in Windows Millennium Edition (ME).

2. When the My Network Places window opens, you will see something similar to what's shown in Figure 10.8. The first time you open it you might see just the icons for Add Network Place, Home Networking Wizard, and Entire Network. After you learn to enable file and folder sharing, you will see the different folders or drives that you want to access on the network.

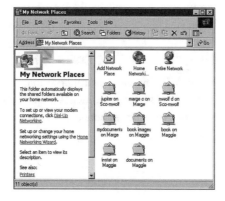

FIGURE 10.8
The My Network Places window in Windows Millennium Edition (ME).

10

GETTING AROUND THE HOME NETWORK

We'll explore how to access the different drives and folders on the network in the next chapter. However, you should be familiar with the basic ways to see the different PCs available on the network.

To access the workgroup you've created, simply do this:

1. Double-click the Entire Network icon in My Network Places. From there you should get an icon with the name of the workgroup you created. The default name in Windows is Mshome, but you can use whatever you want. Remember, to network the different PCs on your network you must use the same workgroup name.

2. From the Entire Network screen double-click the name of the workgroup icon. In Figure 10.9 the name of the workgroup in the Entire Network screen is @home. You should see an icon similar to the one in Figure 10.9 with the name of your workgroup.

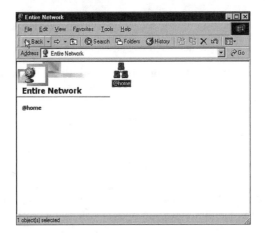

Figure 10.9
The Entire Network screen with the Workgroup icon.

3. Double-click the workgroup icon and you should see all the PCs on the network. If not, you might need to restart your PC or re-log on to the network.

Accessing the Network in Windows XP

The My Network Places screen in Windows XP is similar to that of the Network Neighborhood and My Network Places screens in older Windows operating systems, with just a few minor differences. The major difference is actually the look and feel, as is the case with many of the screens in Windows XP.

To access the My Network Places screen in Windows XP, follow these steps:

1. From your desktop, double-click the My Network Places icon. You should get a window that looks like that shown in Figure 10.10.

FIGURE 10.10
The My Network Places screen in Windows XP.

2. From the My Network Places screen, you will see the shared drives, such as those shown in Figure 10.10, which you can access by double-clicking the folder icons.

3. If you would rather view the different PCs in the workgroup as opposed to all the shared folders, you can click on the View Workgroup Computers option to the left under Network Tasks. This will show you all the PCs that are a part of the workgroup on your home network. This will take you to a screen similar to that shown in Figure 10.11.

CAUTION

Viewing and accessing other PCs on your network in Windows XP can be obstructed by the use of a function built into Windows XP called Internet Connection Firewall, especially if you are using an older operating system on a PC and trying to access a Windows XP PC. We will examine how to use a firewall in Chapter 19, "Home Network Security Planner," but if you are having trouble seeing other PCs on your network in Windows XP, you might consider disabling your Internet Connection Firewall. However, because disabling this firewall might allow external users to see your network over the Internet (if you are connected to the Internet using an always-on broadband modem), you will want to check out Chapter 19 to see how Internet security and use of firewalls can impact you.

10

GETTING AROUND
THE HOME
NETWORK

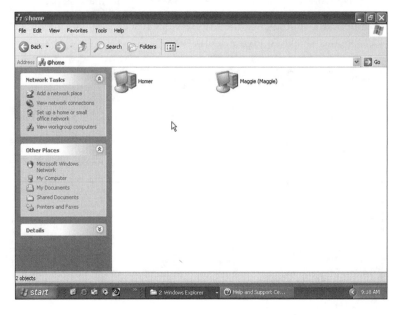

FIGURE 10.11
The Workgroup window in Windows XP.

Creating a Shortcut to Your Network

Because you will be viewing and accessing your network frequently as you read through the next few chapters, you should consider creating a shortcut to your network workgroup. This will allow you to sidestep some of the basic steps in order to get to your network and will save you time.

To create a shortcut to a home network workgroup, in Windows 95/98/ME follow these steps:

1. Double-click on the My Network Places (or Network Neighborhood) icon.

2. From My Network Places, double-click the Entire Network icon.

3. From the Entire Network window, right-click on the name of your workgroup. From the pop-up menu click on the Create Shortcut option. You will see a pop-up message that reads, "You cannot create a shortcut here. Do you want the shortcut to be placed on the desktop instead?" Click Yes.

4. You will see a shortcut on your desktop that looks like the one shown in Figure 10.12. To access your workgroup from now on, simply double-click on this icon.

FIGURE 10.12

The shortcut icon for your home network workgroup.

The best way to access a workgroup in Windows XP is to simply do this:

1. Double-click My Network Places on your desktop.
2. Click on View Workgroup Computers from the Network Tasks bar on the left side of the screen.

You now have a shortcut that will save you time in accessing the different PCs on your network.

Wrap It Up

In this chapter, you have learned how to begin exploring your network. Before you could explore your network, you learned

- How to give each PC on your network a name via the Identification tab in Windows
- How to assign your home network a workgroup name
- How IP addressing works
- How to configure each PC's IP address, either by assigning each its own or by enabling the automatic IP addressing in Windows

The exploration of a home network in Windows begins in the My Network Places and Network Neighborhood screens. In this chapter you learned, in a few basic steps, how to begin exploring the network in both Windows 95/98/ME and Windows XP through this easy-to-access screen. You also learned how to create a shortcut to your home network for quicker access to the resources on your home network.

The next chapter will show you how to really unlock your home network by enabling both file and printer sharing, two of the most important and useful functions of a home network.

10

GETTING AROUND THE HOME NETWORK

Sharing Files and Printers on a Home Network

IN THIS CHAPTER

Sharing the Good Things in Life

Probably the greatest benefit of a home network is that it enables you to share different resources with all the members of the network. No longer do you have to participate in the Sneakernet world of running floppy disks from one room to another or having to kick dad off the computer to print on his nice laserjet printer. With a home network, you can have access to all those resources from each PC in the house.

This chapter looks at how to enable and utilize the file- and printer-sharing resources in a Windows-based network. Your Windows operating system has everything necessary to begin easily sharing these resources, now that you've taken the steps in Chapter 9, "Setting Up Home Network Software," to install the file- and printer-sharing software component. Now you can activate these resources and learn to how to access them.

Turning On Sharing

In Windows 95/98/ME the software component for file and printer sharing needs to be turned on for you to begin sharing. In Windows XP the option should be turned on automatically, but we'll review how to check whether this function has been enabled.

To turn on file and printer sharing in Windows 95/98/ME, follow these steps:

1. Click Start, Settings, Control Panel, and then double-click the Network icon.

2. On the Configuration tab, click the File and Printer Sharing button.

3. You will see a File and Print Sharing window, as shown in Figure 11.1. For each PC on the network, check both boxes to enable file and printer sharing. Click OK.

NOTE

If you did not install the File and Printer Sharing component for Windows, you will need to do so before enabling this service in your Windows home network. Refer to Chapter 9 to learn how to install this component if you have not already done so.

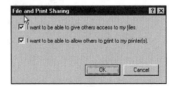

FIGURE 11.1

The File and Print Sharing window in Microsoft 95/98/ME.

4. Click OK on the Network window. Click Yes when you are asked whether it is okay to restart your PC.

To see whether file and printer sharing is enabled in Windows XP, carry out these steps:

1. Click Start, Control Panel, and then Network and Internet Connections, and click Network Connections.

2. Right-click the Local Area Connection icon.

3. In the Components Checked Are Used by This Connection area on the General tab, there should be an icon for file and printer sharing, as shown in Figure 11.2, and it should be checked. If it is not, check it and click OK. If your PC asks you to reboot, click Yes.

FIGURE 11.2
Checking the File and Printer Sharing option in Windows XP.

File Sharing in Windows

Now that you are sure that file and printer sharing has been turned on for the different PCs on your home network, you are ready to begin sharing files. Before we start, though, let's quickly review how information is structured in Windows. This is necessary because it will show you the different levels at which information can be shared across the network.

In Windows, information is stored at three levels:

- Drives
- Folders
- Files

When we talk about file sharing in general, we are referring to sharing at any of these levels. As many of you know, at the top of the information ladder are drives, which contain many folders of information and files within those folders. Drives can be your main PC hard drive or a floppy drive, a CD-ROM drive or a ZIP drive.

Folders are compilations of subfolders as well as files. Files themselves can be pure information files used by programs, such as an Excel spreadsheet, or a program itself. The following pages will show you how to share both drives and folders.

One way to get accustomed to the hierarchy of your file system is to go to the My Computer screen in Windows. To do so, double-click the My Computer icon on your Windows desktop. Here you will see the names of all the drives available to you on a given PC. All of these drives themselves can be networked, or if you do not want access to an entire drive, you can make available only certain folders on a drive or even one file, if that's all that is needed.

Levels of Access

A major consideration when you're enabling file sharing is the level of access you want to grant to each user on the network. When you designate a drive or folder to be shared on a network, you also have control over whether users on the network can simply read the file or whether they can make changes to it. You can also put password protection on drives and folders. The basic levels of access control for file sharing are given in Table 11.1.

TABLE 11.1 File Access Levels in Windows

File Access Level	Description
Full Access	This option allows any user on the network to access a drive, folder, or file and to make changes.
Read-Only Access	This allows users to have access to a drive, folder, or file but not make changes.
Depends on Password	You can designate drives, folders, and files as being accessible by a password, which you create and administer from the PC being accessed.

Deciding What to Share

You will want to give a little thought to which files you allow on the network. Giving other networked PCs access to files on a PC can be a nice benefit, but if something were to happen to a file because someone mistakenly altered it or deleted it, you could find yourself wishing you had given the matter a bit more forethought.

Most of the time, opening files on a home network is okay. But if you run a home-based business, telecommute, or bring a laptop home from work that you put on the network, you definitely want to be sure to back up certain files or designate them as read-only or not accessible on the network. And it's not only work files you should be careful with. The following is a list of files you should consider giving limited access to:

- Any private files such as a journal or letters that you do not want exposed on the network

- Program files or folders, because it could create problems if these are altered in any way

- Financial information such as Quicken or Money files, unless you want other members of the network to be able to access these files for a specific purpose

Ultimately, it is up to you which files you give full or partial access to. The built-in capabilities of Windows give you the flexibility to make those decisions.

Sharing a Drive

You can share any drive on the network, including your primary drive (usually designated as the C: drive), a backup hard drive, Zip drives, and floppy drives, as well as CD-ROM and even DVD-ROM drives. With the cost of storage going down rapidly every year, it is often the case that the newest PC in the household has the largest amount of drive space, making these PCs good candidates to act as a central storage space for large amounts of information, music files, and the like. Sharing a large drive allows a PC to act as a "de facto" server, even when you're using a non–server-based operating system such as Windows 98 or Millennium.

> **CAUTION**
>
> You might want to think twice before you enable the sharing of an entire drive. Doing so will open up all the files on your PC to others on the network, including critical system files. An accidental keystroke can mean deleting important files, resulting in a malfunctioning computer. Those with kids might want to give sharing a drive considerable thought.

Sharing a Drive in Windows 95/98/ME

To share a drive in Windows 95/98/ME, follow these steps:

1. Double-click on the My Computer icon on your Windows desktop, to get the My Computer window similar to the one shown in Figure 11.3. The My Computer screens in Windows 95 and Windows 98 look a little different from that of Windows Millennium, but they are accessed the same way.

Software Setup and Management

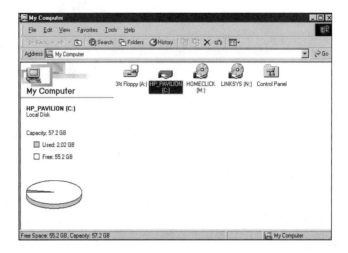

FIGURE 11.3

The My Computer screen in Windows ME.

2. In the My Computer window, right-click on the drive you want to share on the network.

3. From the pop-up menu, select Properties.

4. In the drive properties window, similar to the one shown in Figure 11.4, select the Sharing tab.

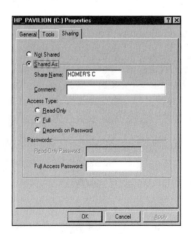

FIGURE 11.4

The Sharing tab in the drive properties window.

5. Select the Shared As option and give the drive a name. The name can be something like Den Drive C or Mom Work Drive. Whatever the name is, it should be descriptive so that everyone understands which PC it resides on and what the general purpose of the drive is.

6. Under Access Type, choose from the Read-Only, Full, or Depends on Password options.

   If you chose Depends on Password, enter two passwords, one for full access and one for read-only access. You can allow different levels of access by giving each user the appropriate password for whatever access you deem appropriate.

   If you have entered passwords, you will see a pop-up box asking you to reenter the passwords. Reenter the passwords and click OK.

7. Click OK and allow the PC to restart.

After you have carried out these steps, you will be able to access this drive from other PCs on the network. You can double-check whether you have successfully shared a drive by looking in your My Computer window. Shared drives (as well as shared folders) have a small hand under them to indicate that they are shared. Figure 11.5 shows you what this looks like.

FIGURE 11.5
A shared drive.

Sharing a Drive in Windows XP

Sharing a drive in Windows XP is similar to doing so in older versions of Windows. To enable drive sharing in XP, you can use the My Computer screen, following these steps:

1. Double-click the My Computer screen from your Windows desktop. From there, right-click on the drive you want to share to get the pop-up menu.

2. From the pop-up menu, select Sharing and Security.

3. The drive properties menu appears. Make sure that in the Drive property box, the Sharing tab is selected. Unlike with previous versions of Windows, before you are allowed to share a drive in Windows XP, you must first tell Windows that you understand the risk of sharing a root drive. When you see the message If You Understand the Risk but Still Want to Share the Root of the Drive, Click Here, click the message if you are sure you want to share an entire drive.

> **NOTE**
>
> A *root drive* (also called the root of a drive) is the highest level of the directory on a disk drive.

> **CAUTION**
>
> Sharing a root drive means that you are sharing a drive itself, and those accessing your network conceivably have control over all the directories on this drive. Because of this high level of control, Microsoft suggests not sharing a drive itself but instead sharing folders within a drive. To ensure the utmost security, you should consider sharing only those folders on the network that you want other users on your network (or anyone trying to access your PC from the Internet) to have access to.

4. In the Network Sharing and Security section, click the Share This Folder on the Network box, and then give a name to the drive as it will appear on the network, as shown in Figure 11.6.

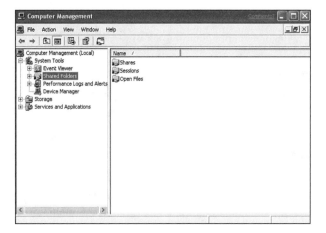

FIGURE 11.6

Sharing a drive in Windows XP.

5. Click OK to share this drive on the network.

You now can access any drive made available from other PCs on the network.

Sharing a Folder

Often you will want to share only a folder or file as opposed to sharing an entire drive on a network. You can designate a specific folder as your network folder, and put all the files you want others to access in that folder.

> **TIP**
>
> In Windows Millennium and Windows XP, if you choose to run the home network wizard, certain folders will automatically be made available on the network. In ME the folder is called My Documents and in XP it is simply called Documents. If you choose to, you can drag-and-drop files into the My Documents folder to enable sharing on the network.

To create a shared folder in Windows, you need to follow a few simple steps from the My Computer screen. As with sharing a drive, after you designate a folder as a shared folder, you can identify it as shared by the hand that appears under the folder.

> **NOTE**
>
> Folder sharing in Windows XP is slightly different from folder sharing in Windows 95/98/ME. Windows XP uses what Microsoft calls the "Simple File Sharing" model, meaning that this version does not offer the "Depends on Password" option, but instead allows for full and read-only access only.

To turn on folder sharing, follow these steps:

1. Double-click the My Computer icon from the Windows desktop.
2. In the My Computer screen, double-click on the drive you want to share a folder.
3. In the Drive window, right-click on the folder you want to share.
4. Click on the Sharing option in Windows 95/98/ME, or the Sharing and Security option in Windows XP.
5. If you are using Windows 95/98/ME, choose the Shared As option, and then assign a name to the folder that will identify it on the network.
6. If you are using Windows XP, in the Network Sharing and Security section, click the Share This Folder on the Network box. You will be asked to give the folder a name. If you want the users on the network to have read-only access, check the second box that

reads Allow Network Users to Change My Files. Otherwise, users of your network will have full access, including the ability to change and delete files, in this folder.

7. Click OK.

You should be able to see a hand under the folder in My Computer identifying that the folder is shared.

How to Access Shared Files Across the Network

In the preceding chapter, you learned how to work your way through My Network Places. Now that you've enabled file sharing in Windows, you will be able to access the resources on the different PCs on the network. You can access files or folders on your home network in various ways, whether through an application such as Word or through the My Network Places (called Network Neighborhood in Windows 95 and 98) screen in Windows. We'll take a quick look at each method and then jump into how to enable file sharing on your Windows-based network.

Using My Network Places/Network Neighborhood to Access Files on the Network

Now that you've enabled certain folders or drives as network shared, these should be viewable when you launch My Network Places. To access folders or drives in My Network Places, follow these steps:

1. Double-click the My Network Places icon from your Windows desktop. In ME or XP, you should then be able to see the shared folders available for access.

> **NOTE**
>
> Network Neighborhood will show the different PCs that are on the network. If you are using Network Neighborhood in Windows 95/98, click on the PC you want to access. You will then see the folders available to you as a PC on the network.

2. If you want to use one of the folders, double-click to see the shared subfolders.

3. If you want to access the different PCs on the network, double-click on the Entire Network icon. To see the various PCs that are networked in Windows XP, click on the View Workgroup Computers option on the left side under Network Tasks.

4. In Windows 95/98/ME, you will see the workgroup icon. If you created a shortcut to your workgroup as shown in the preceding chapter, you can use this shortcut to get to this point. Otherwise, double-click the name of the workgroup to see different PCs on the network.

Sharing Files and Printers on a Home Network

CHAPTER 11

193

11

SHARING FILES AND
PRINTERS ON A
HOME NETWORK

5. In Windows XP, after you click on View Workgroup Computers, you automatically see the rest of the PCs on the network. From here you can double-click on each PC to access the networked drives made available on that PC.

Other Ways to Access Files over the Network

You can access files on the network in a few ways. One of the most basic ways is through an application or program you are using. You simply use the same commands you would use to open a normal document, but instead of looking on your local hard drive, you look under My Network Places in the Open file command. For example, if you want to open a Word document on a drive available on one of the PCs on your network, you would do this:

1. Select the File menu at the top of the Word screen.

2. From the drop-down File menu, select Open.

3. In the Look In box, click on the down arrow and scroll down to My Network Places.

4. Click on My Network Places and you will see the different networked drives and folders available to you, as shown in Figure 11.7.

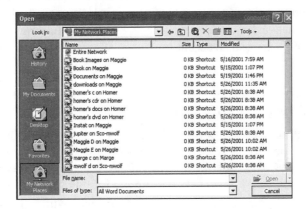

FIGURE 11.7

Opening a document on a network.

5. Double-click on the drive or folder you want to look in.

Another way to access folders or files over your home network is to use Windows Explorer or through the search command. You can find Windows Explorer as a program on your Windows 95/98 PC by clicking Start, Programs, and then clicking on Windows Explorer. In ME and XP click Start, Programs (or All Programs in XP), Accessories, and then Windows Explorer.

To use the search function in Windows, simply click Start and then Search. In Windows 95 and 98 you will see that the command used is Find rather than Search.

In Windows XP, using the Search function just as easy. To use Search in XP, do the following:

1. Click Start and then Search.
2. On the left under What Do You Want to Search For? click Computers or People.
3. Under What Are You Looking For? click A Computer on the Network.
4. You can either enter the name of the computer or simply click Search to see all the PCs on the network pop up on the right side of the Search Results window.
5. Double-click on the PC you want to access.

Printing on a Home Network

The capability to share a printer is one of the great benefits of having a home network. Although printer prices have dropped significantly in the past few years, it is still nice to be able to share a printer, even in those homes in which every PC has its own printer (see the following sidebar).

Sometimes, for example, a printer might run out of ink and you need to print that presentation before your carpool ride comes, or you might want to use dad's nice color laserjet printer instead of your old black-and-white for your school presentation. Either way, printer sharing on a network is a way to get immediate benefit from your network, and, even better, it's extremely easy to set up and use.

Printers, Printers, Everywhere

It used to be that a printer was a cherished object by all, mostly because printers were so darned expensive. A good dot-matrix printer in the 1980s would cost several hundred dollars, and when laserjet printers started to make their way on the scene, you would expect to plunk down over a thousand for one of those babies.

A new type of printer called inkjets helped change things. Although inkjet printers did not employ laser technology, they still enabled professional printing at very affordable prices. Soon almost everyone who wanted a nice printer in their home could buy one for a couple hundred dollars, and nowadays you can have an inkjet for well under a hundred dollars. In fact, you can buy a new PC and have one of these inkjet printers thrown in basically free.

And although laserjets are still much more expensive than inkjet printers, they are also coming down in price. Some of the most popular models are the all-in-one models that include a fax, printer, and copy machine.

There are two ways to share a printer over a network. One way is to give access to a local printer that is connected to a PC through a local connection such USB or parallel-port cable. Enabling the sharing of a printer this way will not impact the operation of the PC that is connected locally. The other way to share a printer on a network is to use a print server, which allows a printer to sit anywhere and does not require a local connection (such as through a parallel or USB port) to a PC. We will discuss both methods of accessing and using a printer on a network.

Telling a PC-Connected Printer to Share

Before you share a printer with other PCs, you must designate a printer as a shared printer from the PC it is connected to.

To enable a PC-connected printer to share in Windows 95/98/ME, follow these steps:

1. Click Start, Settings, and then click on the Printers command.
2. In the Printers window, select the printer you want to share on the network.
3. Right-click the printer icon of the printer you want to share, and select the Sharing command.
4. A printer Properties window such as that shown in Figure 11.8 will pop up. Select the Shared As option and give your printer a name.

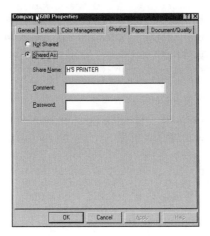

FIGURE 11.8

Sharing a local printer on the home network.

5. If you want to use password protection for the laptop, enter a password. As with all passwords, be sure to record it in a safe place.
6. Click OK.

To enable a PC-connected printer to share in Windows XP, follow these steps:

1. Click Start, then Control Panel, and then the Printers and Other Hardware category.

2. Click on the Printer and Faxes icon.

3. Right-click on the printer you want to share on the network, and click the Sharing option.

4. Choose the Share This Printer option, and put the name of the printer in the Share Name field.

5. Click OK.

After you follow these steps, the printer on your PC will be open for use by different PCs on the network. Now all you need to do is turn on printer sharing to this printer from the other PCs on the network, and you will be ready to print to your heart's desire.

Installing a Network Printer

Now that you've told your printer that it will be accessible by other PCs on the network, you can "install" the printer on any PC you choose, anywhere on the network. Installing a network printer is not that different from installing the printer locally.

> **NOTE**
>
> The difference between a *local printer* and a *network printer* is simply whether the printer you are using is connected to a PC or whether it is on the network (connected to another PC or connected through a print server). Any printer that is directly attached to your PC with a printer cable is a local printer, but if a PC is accessing a printer through a network connection, it is a network printer.

You use the same installation wizard to install a network printer that you use if you are installing the printer as a local printer, with just a few minor differences. The installation of a network printer varies a little from Windows 95/98/ME to Windows XP, so we will review each version's installation individually. First, let's look at the older versions of Windows.

To install a network printer in Windows 95/98/ME, follow these steps:

1. Click Start, Settings, and then Printers.

2. From the Printers window, double-click the Add Printer icon to get the Add Printer Wizard box to pop up, as shown in Figure 11.9. Click the Next button.

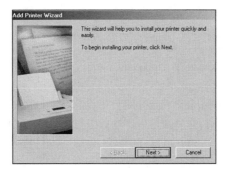

FIGURE 11.9

The Add New Printer Wizard.

3. When the Wizard asks how the printer is attached to the PC, choose the Network Printer option.

4. The Wizard asks you to type the network path or click the Browse button to view available network printers. Click the Browse button to get the Browse for Printer window, as shown in Figure 11.10.

FIGURE 11.10

The Browse for Printer window.

5. In the Browse for Printer window, double-click on the Entire Network icon and then double-click on the workgroup icon, such as the @home workgroup shown in Figure 11.10.

6. You will be able to see the PCs that have printers designated for sharing on the network. Choose the PC with the printer you want to share, and double-click the PC icon. Then choose the printer attached to the PC and click OK.

7. In the Add Printer Wizard screen you will also be asked whether you want to share MS-DOS–based programs. If you have older programs on a PC such as older word processors, click Yes and then click Next. If you do not have any DOS-based programs, stay with the default selection of No and click Next.

8. You might be asked whether you want to use the existing driver for this printer. Choose to keep the existing driver and click Next. If your PC does not have the driver, it will copy the driver from the PC that is locally attached to the printer and copy to the PC from which you are attempting to access the networked printer. In some cases, you might be asked to specify that you "Have Disk" in order to copy the drivers directly to the PC requesting to access the network drive.

9. Give the network printer a name to be identified as on the network, such as Homer's Printer, and click Next.

10. You might be asked whether you want to print a test page after the printer is installed. Click Yes and then Finish. You will likely see a pop-up message similar to that shown in Figure 11.11 indicating that you have successfully installed a network printer. If your printer did not print successfully, click No and work through the printer troubleshooter.

Figure 11.11

A successful network printer installation.

Installing a network printer in Windows XP is not drastically different from doing so in older versions of Windows. The printer installation wizard is also used.

To install a network printer in Windows XP, follow these steps:

1. Click Start, Control Panel, and then Printers and Other Hardware.

2. Click the Add a Printer command to launch the XP Add Printer Wizard. Click Next to get to the Local or Network Printer window.

3. You have a choice between Local Printer and Network Printer. Choose the Network Printer option.

4. You can either name the printer path or browse for the printer. Choose Browse and click Next.

Sharing Files and Printers on a Home Network

CHAPTER 11

199

11

SHARING FILES AND
PRINTERS ON A
HOME NETWORK

5. In the Browse for Printer window, double-click on the PC that has the printer you want to connect to, and then click on the printer and click Next.

6. Windows tells you whether you have the drivers installed for the local PC. Click OK if your PC indicates that it is going to look for the drivers.

7. You are asked which printer manufacturer and model you are using; or if you have an installation disk, you can click the Have Disk option and have the drivers copied directly to the local PC.

8. You are asked whether you want to designate this printer as the default printer. Choose Yes or No and click Next.

9. You should get a message indicating that you have successfully completed the Add New Printer Wizard. Click Finish to begin using your new network printer.

After you have installed a network printer, you should be able to print from this printer as if it were connected to the PC you are working from through a printer cable. The only difference will be that it is going through whatever network connection you have instead of a local printer port.

Using a Print Server

The other way to share a printer is to use a print server. A print server is a piece of hardware that allows you to access the printer over a network, but unlike a printer that is shared by a locally connected PC, a print server allows a printer to sit anywhere it would like and not have a local connection to any PC on the network. The advantage of this method is that you can set up a printer in space-constrained or centrally located areas of the house without having a PC next to it. Print servers essentially free the printer from the PC itself.

TIP

Some devices such as home routers that enable the sharing of an Internet connection also incorporate built-in print servers. This means you could not only connect different PCs into one of these devices to share an Internet connection, but also directly connect a printer to allow for printer sharing. You should read the product information carefully when buying a combination product such as this to be fully certain that it does have these capabilities, as well as to find out how the product works.

When setting up a printer server, you treat it as if it were a PC on a network. So if you have an Ethernet network, you can connect the print server directly into the Ethernet hub. You will also need to configure the print server from a PC that you designate as the administrator PC. The print server is assigned its own IP address like any of the PCs on the network, and this is how it is identified when a print job is sent its way.

You will still need to configure each PC on the network with the printer drivers, much as you would when setting up a network printer without the use of a print server. The configuration and setup of a print server for use on each PC is different depending on the manufacturer, so if you choose to install a print server, review the manufacturer's instructions carefully.

Yeah, but Do I Need One?

Print servers might not be necessary in a home network environment, but if you are setting up a small office or home office network, you might want to consider the use of a print server. Print servers can also allow you to connect multiple PCs to a network, so if you need more than one printer in a specific location in your home or small office, a print server might be the way to go.

Another reason print servers have stayed primarily in the office network is price. However, as with most types of network equipment, prices have come down dramatically in recent years; print servers can be had for less than $100 today. Some manufacturers of affordable print servers are included in Table 11.2. Some, such as the HP JetDirect 70x Home Print Server, can be used with phoneline-based networks.

TABLE 11.2 Print Server Manufacturers

Manufacturer	Web Site
Linksys	www.linksys.com
Netgear	www.netgear.com
SOHOware	www.sohoware.com
Intel	www.intel.com/network/smallbiz
Hewlett Packard	www.hp.com

Managing a Network Printer

A printer that is part of the network is not very different from one that is local. Various configuration options are open to the user of a printer on the network. Because there are various printer manufacturers, there are also various printer property options, so things might vary from model to model. The best way to get familiar with your printer options is to peruse the printer's Properties dialog box.

Some of the options you will be able to configure on the network printer include the following:

- *Paper orientation*—This allows you to change between portrait and landscape orientation.

- *Document quality*—You can lower the resolution of the print. If you are configuring for a child's PC, you might want a lower print quality than for a PC that is used primarily for work.

- *Color management*—If you have a color printer, you can choose to print in color or black and white.

- *Printer port*—This is something that is important to understand in case the local PC that is connected to the printer ever changes or you move the printer to another PC on the network.

In the case of changing a printer port, you will want to be able to change the network path (which is the port in the case of a network printer) through the Properties dialog box. To access the printer's Properties dialog box to change the network path or configure any of the other properties for the network printer, follow the steps given next.

To access the printer properties in Windows 95/98/ME, do the following:

1. Click Start, Settings, and then Printers.

2. From the Printers window, as shown in Figure 11.12, you will see the printer you have installed as a network printer. If you chose this as your primary printer, it will have a check next to it to indicate that it is the default printer. Right-click on the default printer and from the pop-up menu choose Properties.

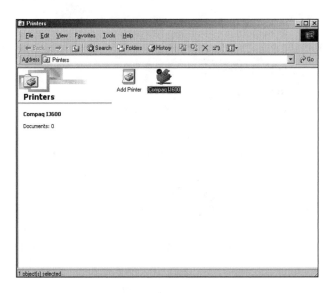

FIGURE 11.12
The Printers window.

3. The printer's Properties dialog box will offer several tabs to choose from. The Details tab gives you the option to change the printer/network port. As shown in Figure 11.13, the printer port on a network printer is the network path. If the printer is the locally connected printer, the printer path will likely be LPT1, the traditional printer port.

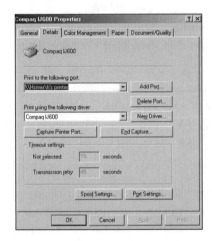

FIGURE 11.13

Printer properties.

To access the printer's Properties dialog box in Windows XP, follow these steps:

1. Click Start, Control Panel, and then Printers and Other Hardware.

2. Click the View Installed Printers task.

3. From the Printers and Faxes window, right-click on the printer whose properties you want to access. From the pop-up menu select Properties.

Remember that the properties can be different for each printer. Also, remember that you are not limited to one network printer, but you can have different printers available to you over the network.

You will want to have one printer designated as your default printer, meaning that it will be the one you print to unless you indicate otherwise. When printing from an application such as a word processor or spreadsheet, you can choose from among the different printers by clicking the Print command and then clicking on the down arrow under Printer Name.

When you have more than one printer available to you over the network (including the locally connected printer), you can change a printer to act as the default printer by simply following these steps:

1. Open the Printer window (or Printers and Faxes as in Windows XP) as shown previously.

2. Right-click on the printer you want to designate as the default printer, and click Set as Default Printer.

Network Printer Troubleshooting

Printers are sometimes temperamental beings, and they can be even more so when attached to a network. From something as simple as a paper jam to corrupted drivers, you might find yourself doing a little troubleshooting if you have problems printing over the network.

Remember that when you need to troubleshoot a printer, you want to determine whether the problem is local or a network problem. If you can print from the local PC (the PC attached directly to the printer without the use of the network), your problem is likely a network problem. If you cannot print from the local PC, you likely have a printer problem specific to the local PC connection, or the printer itself might be malfunctioning.

The following are some potential things to check for if you are having problems printing on a home network:

- Disconnected or damaged printer cable
- Disconnected or damaged network cable
- Printer turned off
- Printer jammed
- Corrupted printer drivers
- Network path to printer has changed
- Printer malfunctioning or needs maintenance such as new toner

As is the case with any equipment, drivers can sometimes be corrupted. If you cannot determine the reason for a malfunctioning or nonresponsive network printer, you might want to reinstall the printer, either locally or on the network. If the printer works from the local PC, you can reinstall the printer from the networked PC that is trying to access the printer by following the steps outlined earlier in this chapter. You will first want to uninstall the printer by going to the Printers window and deleting the network printer. You do this by right-clicking on the printer icon and choosing the Delete option.

Wrap It Up

This chapter showed you how to use two of the most important functions on your network, file and printer sharing.

In the first part of the chapter on file sharing, you learned the following:

- You must enable each PC to share on the network.
- You can share both drives and folders on the network.
- There are three levels of network access for both drives and folders: full, read-only, and password protected access.
- There are various ways to access shared files on a network, including the use of My Network Places, via My Computer, or directly through an application.

In the second half of this chapter you learned the following about printer sharing on a network:

- You must designate a printer as shared before other printers can access it over a network.
- Installation of a network printer can be done easily through the Add Printer Wizard in Windows.
- Use of a print server can allow you to place a printer anywhere you want on a network without being in close proximity to a PC.
- You can configure network printer properties for each PC on the network through the printer's Properties dialog box.

Networking with Macs

IN THIS CHAPTER

Macs: The Apple of Your Network Eye?

There are a few basic questions in life to which nearly everyone has a clear answer: Are you a Yankee or Red Sox fan? Cat person or dog person? PC or Mac user?

As you probably know by now, over the past 25 or so years the world has divided itself into three distinct camps: You are a Mac, UNIX, or Windows devotee, often just tolerating the others. Although new operating systems such as Linux are gaining popularity within the home, most home users still use Windows-based computers (referred to as PCs) or a Mac. And in some households and small businesses, both PCs and Macs coexist and actually are networked together.

This chapter is devoted to those cat people of the computer world, the Mac user (and to those who live with cat people). We will take a look at the basics of Mac networking, as well as how to create a Mac-and-PC based network. We will also look at enabling essential networking services such as file sharing and Internet connection sharing. To get started, let's look at some basics to help you get started on your Mac network.

Mac Hardware ABCs

Unlike their PC counterparts, Macs have a rather long shelf life. People and businesses alike tend to keep older Mac systems in service longer than they do their PCs. In this chapter, we will discuss networking with Macs old and new. All PowerMacs are based on the PowerPC chip, as opposed to PCs, which are based on Intel's Pentium architecture. For the purposes of our discussion here, and in order to include new and legacy systems, we will divide all Macs into three classes. First and foremost, the iMac, G3, and G4 are the newest among the Macs available today. The second tier of Macs, which were made between 1997 and 1999, includes the 60x-class PowerPCs (this includes the 601, 603, 603e, 604, and 604e type CPUs). The third tier of Macs discussed here is basically everything else that came before, including the first-generation PowerPCs (the 6100 to the 9600) to the famous tiny, all-in-one 030-based Mac SE. None of the machines in the second and third tier of Macs have lost their usefulness, and most can be networked quite productively alongside their iMac, G3, G4, and Intel-based counterparts. The vast majority of PowerMacs have integrated Ethernet, although a few models do not. Because most *do* have Ethernet capabilities, using either an AAUI-15 port that requires a separately purchased transceiver or an RJ-45 port (like a large phone jack), the following list consists of only those models that lack Ethernet:

- 5200/75 LC
- 5300/100 LC
- 6200/75
- 6300 (all)
- 20th Anniversary Macintosh

If, on the other hand, you own an iMac or G3/4 PowerMac, you already have built-in Ethernet. Some earlier iMac versions (typically called Revisions among Mac users) are limited to 10 megabit per second (Mbps) Ethernet, but most have 10Mbps and 100Mbps capabilities. Some G3/4 systems even have what is called Gigabit Ethernet. Although this might seem somewhat over the top right now, they are quite fast when connected to other Gigabit systems.

If you are a mobile user, you should know that most PowerBooks *do not* come equipped with Ethernet. In fact, the list of PowerBooks is about as long as the preceding list, as you can see here:

- 520, 520c
- 540, 540c
- DuoDock II/Plus (AAUI-15, requires a transceiver)
- iBook (all)
- G3 PowerBook ("Kanga")
- G3 PowerBook ("Wall Street," "Lombard," and "Pismo")
- G4 PowerBook

There might be some confusion over the G3 designation. Although most Mac power users know how to identify individual iMac, iBook, and G3/4 models by codename, not everyone can. The difference is rather easy to tell. The "Kanga" series, the original G3 PowerBook, was all black. The "Wall Street," "Lombard," and "Pismo" G3 PowerBooks are still black but have a wide, curvy gray stripe across the top inset with a large white Apple logo.

12

NETWORKING WITH MACS

NOTE

A quick word on MacOS X and networking. First of all, don't let the UNIX name scare you. MacOS X is all Mac and then some. Setting up a MacOS X system for networking is very easy, and the Networking component is almost identical to the old TCP/IP. Of course, because most people are new to the latest offering from Cupertino, I'll cover all the details later in this chapter.

Mac Networking ABCs

Macs are famous for their ease of use. In fact, the original windows-based interface was not a product of Microsoft, but instead was a creation of Apple Computer (which allegedly got the idea for Xerox's famed Palo Alto Research PARC). Networking with a Mac is no exception; it is quite easy to connect several Macs together.

There used to be differences in networking with Macs, one of the biggest being its original networking protocol, LocalTalk. LocalTalk was *the* communications protocol in the vast majority of pre-PowerMac Macs until Ethernet was slowly introduced. When LocalTalk was first introduced, its transmission rate of 28Kbps seemed adequate, the same speed as older 28.8 dial-up modems (ca. 1996). With the widespread use of Ethernet networks today , the speed of LocalTalk, as you would suspect, seems rather poky.

Macs do, however, use a service called AppleTalk to provide simple file and printer sharing to all Macintosh networks. AppleTalk is actually a protocol specifically designed for enabling file and printer sharing, and it works easily with Ethernet networking protocols (nerds say "*over* Ethernet," as in "AppleTalk runs over Ethernet"). An Ethernet-based network using AppleTalk uses a combined (or layered) protocol called EtherTalk.

You can create a LocalTalk-only network, or combine both LocalTalk and Ethernet-based connections on one network using a special bridge; but unless you're hampered by hardware limitations, there's no reason why you shouldn't be using TCP/IP over Ethernet. We'll talk about TCP/IP shortly. After that, we'll talk a bit about what it takes to support LocalTalk in the days of DSL, cable modems, and Ethernet in the home.

First, let's take a quick look at your computer.

Giving Your Mac a Look

In addition to basic network protocols that are native to Macs (Ethernet, LocalTalk, and AppleTalk), you should also know a little about the makeup of your Mac. By understanding what your Mac is (and isn't) equipped to do, you will better understand how to set up a Mac-based network.

The first thing you should note is what model your Mac is. As stated previously, if you have a pre-PowerMac model, you will likely use the LocalTalk protocol for communication on your network, while using AppleTalk to enable printer and file sharing. These older models all have one or more serial ports, which look like those shown in Figure 12.1. Serial ports are the main way older Macs connect to one another using the LocalTalk protocol, over serial cables.

If, however, you are using any of the Ethernet-capable Macintosh models, you will want to take advantage of its far greater speed. Of course, Ethernet is not useful for networking only. If you are located in a region that has facilities for broadband Internet access, Ethernet will invariably play a large role in your ability to access it.

Digital Subscriber Line (DSL) and cable Internet access both use Ethernet ports to pass the network data in to and out of your computer. In fact, the function of accessing the Internet via broadband access is much like being another computer on a very, very large network. In this fashion, simple networking and broadband access are almost identical in configuration.

FIGURE 12.1
Mac serial ports.

> **TIP**
>
> All recent Macs have internal PCI expansion slots where you can add an Ethernet connection if you do not already have one. Pre-PowerMac models use what are called NuBus slots for expansion. You will want to refer to your Mac's documentation to see which types of expansion slots you have.

Your Mac might also have an external expansion slot called an AAUI port. An AAUI port can be used for networking by using what is called a transceiver. These devices allow you to connect to an Ethernet network.

Some Macintosh models don't have the standard RJ-45 Ethernet port and instead provide what is called an AAUI (Apple Attachment Unit Interface) port. This port was designed to allow one interface to use various connectors. The concept never really took off, however, and you'll generally be able to find only RJ-45 transceivers, little plugs that adapt the AAUI port to a standard RJ-45 port. Some Macintosh models actually come with both an AAUI and an RJ-45 port, though only one will work at a time. The AAUI port is shown in Figure 12.2.

FIGURE 12.2
An AAUI port on a Mac.

Setting Up a Basic Mac-to-Mac Network

Now that you are familiar with the basic ports and know which models include built-in Ethernet ports and which network using primarily a serial or an AAUI port, we will look at how to set up a basic Mac network. Depending on which kinds of Macs you are using, you will use either LocalTalk or TCP/IP as the primary network protocol. To be perfectly clear,

LocalTalk works over serial connections, whereas TCP/IP, the language of the Internet, works over Ethernet, facilitated by either an RJ-45 port or an AAUI port adapted to Ethernet using a transceiver. Let's first take a look at an Ethernet network, and then we will examine setting up a LocalTalk network. A little later we will also look at creating a LocalTalk-to-Ethernet bridge for those who want to connect an older Mac with one of the newer, Ethernet-equipped Macs.

NOTE

MacOS X is no different when it comes to networking hardware. To configure TCP/IP to connect to another Mac, click on the desktop to activate the Finder, click on the Apple menu, and select the System Preferences item. Then, click the Network item once. Unless you've been here before, it will start in the TCP/IP tab with the External Modem selected as the connection device. Change the Configure menu to Built-in Ethernet, and change the options to the same specifications as in OpenTransport's TCP/IP control panel.

Creating an Ethernet Peer-to-Peer Network

Simple in both method and implementation, connecting an Ethernet network is much like connecting a telephone to a wall jack. There are, however, some differences. First, you will need a few things. Following is a list suitable for a two-machine peer-to-peer network:

- One length of Category 3 or Category 5 "crossover" Ethernet cable
- MacTCP or OpenTransport installed on both machines
- AppleTalk installed on both machines
- One or two AAUI Ethernet transceivers (as required)

Ethernet cables come in various forms, the most common of which is Category 5 UTP cabling, with an RJ-45 jack. RJ-45 jacks look like an oversized phone plug. You could also use an older Category 3 cable, which is designed to work without error on 10Mbps networks. Older PowerMac models are limited to 10Mbps unless you add a third-party Ethernet card, so it's of no real import. On the other hand, all iMacs, iBooks, and G3/4 portables and desktops are capable of 10/100Mbps operation. Some are even capable of 1000Mbps operation.

Connecting the two could not be easier. Simply locate the RJ-45 or AAUI RJ-45 transceiver port and plug in the cable. So-called "crossover" cables are special in that on one end the SEND and RECEIVE wires are swapped. To finish getting connected, see the "Configuring Your Mac Network" section, later in this chapter. Figure 12.3 shows the two-node peer-to-peer arrangement.

FIGURE 12.3
A simple two-node peer-to-peer arrangement.

Creating an Ethernet Multinode Network

Creating an Ethernet multinode network is less complicated than it sounds. A computer, in networking terms, is sometimes referred to as a node. So when we speak of a multinode network, we are simply talking about a set of three or more connected computers. The model discussed previously would not work here, so we introduce the hub.

A hub is a simple device that merely pushes information around to any connected computer. Things connect in much the same way as in our earlier two-computer example, but here the hub acts as an intermediary, as illustrated in Figure 12.4.

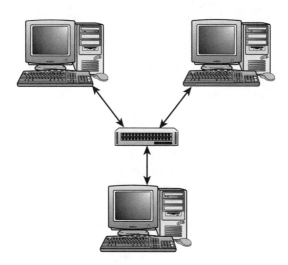

FIGURE 12.4
A simple three-computer topology connected by a hub.

In this arrangement, called a topology, you are required to use "Straight Through" Ethernet cabling and cannot use the crossover cable from the earlier example. The hub takes care of getting the right information to the right place. Hubs are quite cheap these days. You can find a five- to eight-port hub (that means you can connect five devices to it) at your local computer store for $40 to $75.

> **NOTE**
>
> It is well beyond the scope of this chapter to discuss LAN configuration, which includes a server, a hub/switch/router, and one or more nodes. For more information on network relationships, see Chapter 3, "Network Relationships: Network Types and Topologies," to understand how larger networks use servers.

Bridging LocalTalk to Ethernet

Although you might want to consider upgrading your older Macs to Ethernet (if you can find a cheap NuBus or PDS card), you might still want to link older Macs that currently are equipped only to do LocalTalk networking with an Ethernet network. To do so, your best bet is to use a LocalTalk-to-Ethernet bridge.

> **NOTE**
>
> NuBus cards are not cheap. They would be if they were still in common use today, but it has been several years since NuBus ruled the Macintosh expansion market. PDS (Processor Direct Slot) is an even more interesting creature. Although it was originally designed to allow the processor to be upgraded, several third-party peripheral makers and even Apple made other use of these slots. Common examples are video cards and SCSI device adapters.

These bridges are available for purchase from companies like Asante. Asante's AsanteTalk bridge is available at www.asante.com (type AsanteTalk into the Search field at the upper-right side of the home page). A hardware bridge such as AsanteTalk, pictured in Figure 12.5, usually can connect an Ethernet-based Mac or hub and up to eight LocalTalk Macs or printers. This is not, however, an inexpensive solution. Expect to pay $120 or more, depending on whom you purchase it from. Asante will likely be the least expensive source.

FIGURE 12.5

AsanteTalk hardware bridge for linking Ethernet and LocalTalk.

After you have your bridge device, you can construct a network connecting the LocalTalk- and Ethernet-based PCs by following these steps:

1. Connect the bridge to the LocalTalk network. If you are connecting only one device, you can connect the LocalTalk Mac or printer directly to the bridge. If you are connecting a multiple-device LocalTalk network, you might need a separate adapter.

2. Connect the bridge to the Ethernet hub. If there is only one Ethernet-based Mac, you can directly connect to the bridge using an Ethernet cable.

3. After you turn on your Macs and bridge, they should be able to find each other on the network. Your LocalTalk and Ethernet network should look like that shown in Figure 12.6.

12

NETWORKING
WITH MACS

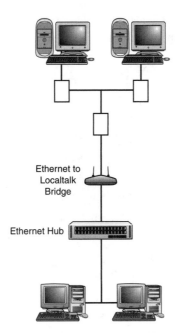

FIGURE 12.6

A LocalTalk and Ethernet home network.

Creating a LocalTalk Network

Creating a LocalTalk network varies slightly depending on whether you want to create a two-Mac network or a network with more than two Macs.

If you are creating a basic two-Mac network, the only the additional equipment you will need to connect the two computers is a Mac serial cable. These cables are available through any computer or electronics store that supports Macs.

To set up a two-Mac network, simply do this:

1. Turn off both Macs.
2. Connect one end of the serial cable into the serial ports (often the same as the printer port on a Mac) of both Macs.
3. Restart both Macs, because you are ready to start the software configuration.

To set up three or more Macs on a LocalTalk network, you will need to set up a daisy-chain network. The typical daisy-chain network would include three Macs and LocalTalk adapters connected by normal phone wiring, often called PhoneNet.

After you have the necessary LocalTalk adapters (a three-pack of adapters can be purchased from a company called Farallon at `www.farallon.com/products/localtalk/phonenet.html` for about $50) and phone cabling, you can construct your network in a few basic steps. To set up your LocalTalk network, follow these steps:

1. Attach a phoneline into the open port of a LocalTalk adapter.
2. Plug the connector on the adapter into the serial port of your Mac. (If you have a printer already attached, feel free to use the modem port.)
3. For each Mac, you should connect to another LocalTalk adapter. Each adapter has two ports so that they can connect to one Mac on each side in daisy-chain fashion.
4. For the last Mac on each side of the daisy-chain, make sure that a plastic terminator, which comes with each adapter, is in the port that is not in use.

When you're finished, your LocalTalk network will look like that shown in Figure 12.7.

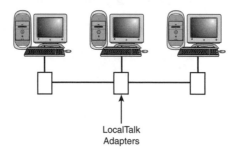

LocalTalk
Adapters

FIGURE 12.7

A Mac LocalTalk network.

Configuring Your Mac Network

After you have physically connected all the Macs in your network, you will need to configure the software, much as you would in a PC home network. We will take a look at how to configure your network using both TCP/IP and AppleTalk. Although AppleTalk will allow you to enable basic services such as file and printer sharing without having to use TCP/IP, you will need to use TCP/IP if you are to connect and share a broadband connection. Luckily, AppleTalk and TCP/IP can be run in tandem, so you can enjoy the simplicity of AppleTalk and all the services and applications that accompany TCP/IP.

Configuring TCP/IP on a Mac Network

TCP/IP, the language of the Internet, makes it possible to surf the Web, download software and files, and send email. You will also find that a Mac network using TCP/IP is really no different from any other network using TCP/IP, and allows you to communicate with other networks such as those using Windows or Linux as their primary operating system.

> **NOTE**
>
> System 7.5 and later use OpenTransport for TCP/IP connectivity, but it comes only with System 7.6. If you have System 7.5.x and would like to use OpenTransport, you must install it. The irony is that the easiest way to get it is by downloading it from Apple's FTP server. If you're already connected to the Internet, go to `ftp://ftp.apple.com/ Apple_Support_Area/Apple_Software_Updates/English-North_American/Macintosh/ Networking-Communications/Open_Transport`, and download the file named `OT_1.1.2-Net_Install.sea.bin`. (Tip: Try just loading `ftp.apple.com` first and then clicking on each link. There's nothing worse than typing all that mess and having a typo.)

To configure your Mac to use TCP/IP with OpenTransport, follow these steps:

1. Click the Apple menu and then Control Panels, and select the TCP/IP Control Panel. You will see something similar to that shown in Figure 12.8.

2. From the File menu, choose Configurations.

3. Choose the default configuration, which will likely be for your Internet connection. Then click on Duplicate and change the name of the setting to something like "Mac Network."

4. Click on this new configuration and then click the Make Active button. Click Done.

5. Back in the TCP/IP window, choose the method in which you are networked in the Connect Via pull-down list.

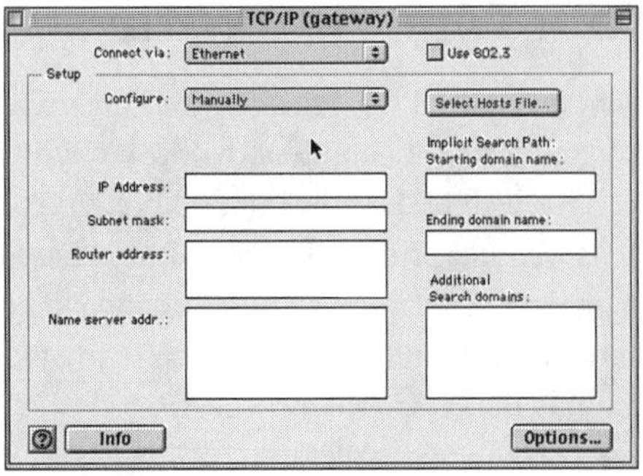

FIGURE 12.8
The TCP/IP Control Panel.

6. Unless you are connected to a home router or some other device with a DHCP server that will assign an IP address automatically, you need to enter an IP address for each computer on the network. A good place to start is at 192.168.0.1, going up from there.

NOTE

IP addressing in Macs works just as in any other network. You will want to choose a private IP address set aside for LAN-based networks. To learn more about choosing an IP address (or to refresh your memory), see Chapter 10, "Getting Around the Home Network."

---

7. Use subnet mask 255.255.255.0 and click Close.

To configure your Mac running MacOS X (these steps are current as of MacOS X 10.0.4), follow these steps:

1. Click on the Apple menu, select System Preferences, and click the Network pane item. You will see something similar to that shown in Figure 12.9.

2. From the Location menu, create a new location or use the default, Automatic.

3. From the Configure menu, select the Built-in Ethernet item. The options in the TCP/IP tab will change.

4. Unless you are connected to a home router or some other device with a DHCP server that will assign an IP address automatically, you need to enter an IP address for each computer on the network. A good place to start is from 192.168.0.1, going up from there. If you have already configured an older Mac from the previous set of instructions, you would use an IP address something like 192.168.0.2, or 192.168.0.3, or higher.

5. Use subnet mask 255.255.255.0 and click Close.

FIGURE 12.9
TCP/IP as seen in MacOS X.

Now you should be able to connect your Macs on an IP-based network. This is the major step you need to accomplish before you can share an Internet connection. After you have configured your Mac for IP addressing, you can share an Internet connection much as you can with a PC-based network.

As with a PC network, you will want to choose between a software and a hardware Internet sharing solution. The hardware solutions are the same as those explained in detail in Chapter 14, "Internet Sharing on a Home Network." Software solutions are specific to Mac-based solutions, because they are designed to run on a Mac operating system. Table 12.1 lists different software Internet sharing solutions.

TABLE 12.1 Internet Sharing Software for Mac Networks

Company/Software	Web Address
Vicomsoft/Surfdoubler	www.vicomsoft.com
Asante/Friendlyshare	www.asante.com
Sustainable Softworks/IP Netrouter	www.sustworks.com
Stalker Software/PortShare Pro	www.stalker.com

Configuring AppleTalk Services

One of the more important components of Mac network software is the Chooser. The Chooser is the area in which you control basic AppleTalk functions. You can find the Chooser by going to your Apple menu, where you will then be able to activate AppleTalk by simply choosing to change the toggle from Inactive to Active.

MacOS X does not have a Chooser, but instead uses a more flexible Go menu in the Finder. Keep in mind that this menu is not available in the Classic Environment (MacOS 9.x emulation for legacy applications), so you'll have to switch to the MacOS X desktop to reach it.

After you make a remote share active, you can access it by opening the Go menu and selecting the Connect to Server item at the bottom of the list (tip: CMD-K will also open this dialog box). You can try to locate the share automatically or by entering an IP address (for example, 192.168.0.5) and waiting for the share to appear.

After it does appear, the remaining screens are almost identical to the ones from OT's TCP/IP control panel. Note, however, that you will not be able to use Microsoft's Universal Authentication Method (UAM) system with MacOS X. There's no version available as of this writing.

> **NOTE**
>
> A good number of Macintosh-compatible printers require AppleTalk in order to work, but there are some conflicts with AppleTalk printing and the Internet, especially under Systems 7.5 through 8.1. If you have this problem, the fix is easy. First, set up your printer and get it working, which will involve turning on AppleTalk. Restart your Mac and then configure your Internet connection. Try to never turn off AppleTalk and all should work fine. If not, contact Apple support or support for your printer manufacturer.

After activating AppleTalk through the Chooser, you need to specify the type of network you are using through the AppleTalk control panel. After you open the AppleTalk control panel (as shown in Figure 12.10), choose whether you are using an Ethernet or a LocalTalk network (which is called a printer port network, because LocalTalk uses the Mac's serial port, which also doubles as a printer port).

FIGURE 12.10

The AppleTalk control panel showing Ethernet.

After you activate AppleTalk and specify the network type through the AppleTalk control panel, you can configure your Mac network for both file and printer sharing. The steps to activate both differ slightly depending on the Mac operating system you are using, but overall, the steps are similar across the different versions. To activate file sharing on a Mac, follow these steps:

1. Click the Apple menu and then Control Panels, and open the file sharing control panel (also called the sharing setup control panel on some Macs).
2. Fill out the fields to give your Mac a network identity, as well as a password.
3. From the file sharing control panel, turn on File Sharing. Click Start on the File Sharing icon.
4. After you turn on file sharing, click Close on the control panel.
5. From Control Panels, click on the Users and Groups control panel and double-click on the Guests button. Then choose the option Allow Guest to Connect. Close the Users and Groups control panel.
6. To enable the sharing of a hard drive or folder, go to the desktop of your Mac and choose which you would like to share. Choose the drive or folder, and from the File menu click on the Sharing option.
7. From the Sharing menu, click on Share This Item and Its Contents.

After you set up a Mac to share a folder or a disk, you must do the same thing on the other Macs on the network as well. To do so, you need to go to each Mac on the network and set up file sharing by enabling AppleShare through Chooser. To do this simply follow these steps:

1. Open Chooser and select AppleShare.
2. On the right side of AppleShare, choose the disk or folder you want to access. Choose it and then click OK.
3. A logon screen will pop up. Choose Guest and then you will be able to access the drive from this Mac.

Connecting Mac and PC Home Networks

With today's environment of exploding options for both PCs and Macs, many homes have both types of computers. And although you might think that the two worlds never mix, with a software solution and a network, you can soon begin to access Mac-based computers from a PC and vice versa.

There are basically two ways to connect the two platforms in a network. You can choose to use a software package called DAVE, from Thursby Software Systems (www.thursby.com), which allows you to connect your Mac to a PC/Windows-based network to access files and printers. You can also allow a PC/Windows system to access resources on a Mac network using a software package called PC MacLAN, from Miramar Systems (www.miramar.com).

Even though you will be able to connect the two different platforms on a network, this does not mean that you will be able to use all file types on the other platform. Program files are not compatible, for example, if the program was written for one operating system. Some files such as data or text files (for example, Word or Excel files) are readable by both types of operating systems because vendors such as Microsoft often have applications for both platforms.

Wrap It Up

As you learned in this chapter, you can easily add Macintosh clients to your home network, and all local area networks for that matter. You have learned the following:

- Macintosh clients can exist on networks like Windows machines
- Macintosh clients can coexist on networks with Windows clients
- How to connect Macintosh computers together
- The ease of connecting Macintosh computers to others through a hub
- The ease of configuring the MacOS and MacOS X for connecting to various other computers

You also learned that not all Macs are built with the capability to connect to an Ethernet network. You did, however, learn that AppleTalk, though not particularly fast, is a cheap and easy way to quickly connect Macs. Most Mac owners already have a cable (hint: a printer cable will work) that they can use for a simple network.

Finally, and most importantly, you learned that Macs can share the Internet just like Windows machines. Files can also be shared between MacOS and Windows-based systems, as long as the appropriate editor or viewer software is present.

Understanding and Sharing Internet Connections

PART
IV

IN THIS PART

Getting Online the High-Speed Way

IN THIS CHAPTER

Getting online with a high-speed connection is not always a guaranteed proposition. In fact, dial-up modems still account for most Internet subscriptions, because many people haven't been able to get high-speed access to their home or work. Although many Internet service providers (ISP) are scrambling to get their services to everyone who wants them, the simple fact is that many consumers are not within reach of where the technology has been deployed.

But this situation is quickly changing. The number of broadband subscribers is growing at an amazing rate, as consumers everywhere are getting cable modems, DSL, or even newer technologies, such as satellite and fixed wireless Internet access.

What do all these terms mean and how can you tell the difference? This chapter reviews the broadband Internet technologies and discusses which one is right for you. It looks at how each one works, what the advantages are of each, and how you can go about getting services. The reason we have a whole chapter dedicated to broadband is that it's a very important part of your network. Sharing a broadband connection is one of the main reasons people get home networks in the first place. See the following note if you need to be convinced about the value of high-speed Internet connections.

> **NOTE**
>
> You might be thinking, *Why is the move to broadband a good thing? My dial-up connection seems to be just fine for me.* If you are skeptical about the value of a high-speed connection, you will quickly change your tune after trying high-speed for a while. In fact, when it comes to Internet connections, faster is, quite simply, better. The availability of rich content such as music and video is much more enjoyable when you are using a high-speed connection, and even when you are just surfing your latest favorite sites, you don't have to wait around while pages load slowly, as you do with a dial-up connection.
>
> And when it comes to sharing an Internet connection over a home network, broadband is much better because there is more bandwidth to share. With a dial-up connection, you will see a pretty quick drop-off in performance after you split the connection to more than one user.

In the next chapter we'll take a look at how to set up your home network so that you can share your high-speed Internet connection using a simple broadband modem with the capabilities built into your operating system. We'll also look at special pieces of networking equipment that allow you to easily share your broadband connection among multiple computers.

What Is Broadband?

The term *broadband* is everywhere these days. Telephone and communications providers bombard us with the word *broadband*, which in today's hip-to-be-square environment has taken on a bit of cache. But what exactly does broadband mean?

The interesting thing about broadband is that there is no agreed-upon, universal definition other than that it means higher-speed communications. From there, the definitions of the actual speed of what makes up broadband communication are all over the map. Some say it is defined by T-1 speeds, which is 1.5Mbps.

> **NOTE**
>
> A *T-1* is a high-speed digital communications link. T-1s are used by businesses, universities, and even sometimes individuals to send voice or data traffic. Communication service providers such as your local phone company will lease T-1 links to businesses so that these companies can have a high-speed link to voice or data networks such as the Internet.

Some people say that broadband speeds start at T-3 speeds, which is a higher-speed link than a T-1, one that operates at 45Mbps. Others say broadband is any digital communication that moves at speeds higher than 56K analog modems. For our purposes we'll define broadband as any communication link that moves at speeds higher than 128Kbps, which is the speed of an ISDN line.

> **NOTE**
>
> *ISDN*, which stands for Integrated Services Digital Network, is a digital communications technology that operates at 128Kbps. ISDN is complicated technology that for the most part has not been widely used in homes (with the exception of countries such as Japan), and will likely become less common as newer technologies such as DSL and cable modems become widely available.

13

GETTING ONLINE
THE HIGH-SPEED
WAY

Here Today, Here Tomorrow: The Past, Present, and Future of the Dial-Up Modem

So you've learned a little about broadband modems, but what about dial-up? A dial-up modem communicates digital information in nondigital format—in other words, analog. When a modem communicates a signal, it chooses the appropriate tone that corresponds to either a one or a zero, because these are the basis of digital communications. The tones are then translated by the receiving modem back into pure digital format—ones and zeroes—to be processed by the PC on the other end of the call.

Analog modems can communicate at speeds ranging up to 56 kilobits per second, or 56Kbps. This might seem slow when you're thinking about technologies such as Fast Ethernet screaming along at 100Mbps, but it's really quite zippy when you're comparing it to the early days of the modem, back when mainframes used to communicate at 300 bits per second. In fact, 300bps was the standard speed for modems from the 1960s all the way through the early 1980s. This was fine back then, because most of the communication was e-mail and other text-based communications.

But as more people had personal computers and decided to communicate using a modem, it became apparent that faster speeds would be needed. Before long, modem speeds jumped to 1200 bits per second, then to 2400, and before long things were moving at a phenomenal 9600 bits per second.

Today's analog modems can communicate at speeds up to 56Kbps. This is almost 200 times as fast as the original 300bps modems used in what can now be called the modem Ice Age. If you are dialing into an ISP today using a modem purchased within the past couple of years, it is likely a 56Kbps (or 56K for short) modem.

With all this speed, this is all we would ever need, right? Wrong. In fact, analog modem technology is seen as downright poky, even at 56K speeds, as new technologies such as DSL and cable modem make their way into new homes. If you are lucky enough to have one of these broadband technologies, you know that you'll never go back to analog modem technology, at least until you move to a neighborhood without a speedy broadband connection (D'oh!). Because there are still many places that do not have broadband, you can be sure that good old dial-up connections are not going away anytime soon.

Aside from speed, there are a few other differences that distinguish broadband technology from analog modems:

- *Broadband technology is digital.* Instead of having to translate PC information into analog format, broadband is digital from end to end, and this allows for much more efficient communications.

- *Broadband technology is always-on.* This means that instead of your having to go through a dial-up routine every time you want to send an e-mail or connect to the Internet, your connection is constant. This is good in that you can stream continuous content such as music without having to dial up using a phoneline.

- *Not everyone can get broadband.* Your access to broadband depends on where you live and whether or not a broadband service provider currently offers service in your area.

Broadband is more expensive than dial-up connections, but this will change over time as more people get broadband. The service providers who offer broadband have spent hundreds of millions of dollars upgrading and preparing their network for high-speed Internet, and as with any new service, they will charge a premium.

Types of Broadband

Although broadband refers to any type of access to the Internet that operates at speeds higher than 128Kbps, this does not mean that all broadband technologies are the same. The main types of broadband today are DSL and cable modem, although other lesser-known technologies, such as satellite and fixed wireless, are making some progress in certain parts of the country.

DSL

DSL stands for Digital Subscriber Line. Digital Subscriber Line technology takes advantage of the existing phone wiring that is installed between your home and the telephone company's central office.

NOTE

Central office is the term for the phone company's local facility where large telephone switches connect all the calls (and DSL links) to each other locally and over long distances. Most neighborhoods have a central office within a few-mile radius.

DSL can use the same copper pair of wiring that is used for phone calls by taking advantage of a wider range of frequencies than plain old telephone service (or POTS, which phone-company technicians refer to as traditional voice calls). Traditional POTS service occupies the frequency range of 0 to 3,400 hertz. The copper phone wires can handle much higher frequencies than this, up into the millions of hertz. This allows service providers to offer services such as DSL on some of the unused frequency spectrum.

This special utilization of the different frequencies available on existing phone wiring allows for much higher speeds. The highest-speed dial-up modem moves at a paltry 56 kilobits per second; DSL can move at speeds up to 8Mbps, and even higher for newer, more experimental types of DSL. The most common type of DSL for home users moves at 1.5Mbps, nearly 30 times the speed of a 56K modem.

Another unique characteristic about DSL is that it is distance sensitive. This means that any subscriber receiving DSL services must be within a certain distance from the phone company's central office. The normal understood distance limitation from the central office is approximately 18,000 feet. Although this might seem like plenty, it actually means that 20% of the population in the United States cannot expect to ever receive DSL service because they simply live too far away from the central office.

In addition to distance limitations, there are a few other technical hurdles for DSL. DSL relies on having a clear path from the central office to your home over a pair of copper wires. However, the presence of what are called loading coils—which ironically are present to amplify the voice call and increase the distance it can be sent—impair the capability to send DSL signals.

Another hurdle is what is called a bridge tap. Bridge taps are extensions of additional copper pairs off the copper pair between the central office and your home. Links with bridge taps are not able to offer DSL service.

The last technical hurdle is fiber optics. Increasingly the phone company is using fiber-optic cabling close to your home for transmitting voice calls. Those links that have fiber-optic cabling might not be able to offer DSL service because DSL is a transmission technology designed to work over copper wiring.

DSL Equipment

What makes DSL work? As with any type of broadband equipment, there is special equipment for the home side (called client side) as well as for the phone company's central office. The home-side equipment is what is called a DSL modem or router. DSL modems can be internal or external to the PC, and they usually come to you through your service provider when you order DSL. The installation of the DSL modem can be done by a technician or by the customer, depending on what processes the DSL provider has in place. Self-installation also depends on the technology—DSL is a finicky technology to get working correctly and often requires a technician to spend a few hours (or more!) at your home to get things up and running.

The DSL equipment in the central office is called a DSLAM (pronounced dee-slam, short for what's called a DSL Access Multiplexer). The DSLAM's job is to take the DSL and voice signals from the subscriber's copper pair wiring, split them, and then send each signal to the appropriate network. Voice traffic goes on to the phone company's traditional voice network, and the DSL traffic is routed to an ISP, which sends the signals onto the Internet. If your phone company is your ISP (instead of an alternative ISP such as AOL), the traffic will likely be sent directly to the Internet.

In Figure 13.1 you'll see how the DSL modem sends traffic to the phone company's central office alongside normal voice traffic, and how the DSLAM then splits the two and sends them to the appropriate wide area network.

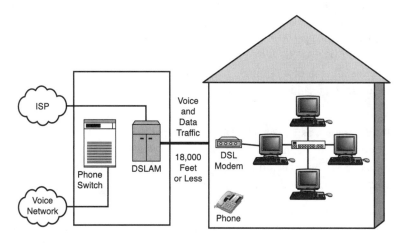

FIGURE 13.1

DSL equipment at home and the central office.

Choose Your DSL

Believe it or not, not only are there multiple types of broadband technologies, but even within a certain broadband technology there can be more than one type. This is certainly the case with DSL.

The type of DSL that is used most commonly by home users is called ADSL, which stands for Asymmetrical DSL. Asymmetrical means that speeds are not equal each way, but instead your speeds coming downstream are faster than those moving upstream.

NOTE

Downstream is a term used by broadband enthusiasts to mean the speed at which you receive data over your high-speed connection, whereas *upstream* means how fast you can send data.

ADSL allows you to receive data four times faster than you can send it. Although this disparity might seem strange, it is actually smart because broadband providers know from monitoring usage of customers that people do a lot more receiving of data than actual sending of data. Think about your typical Web surfing experience—you probably do a lot of clicking and reading, but you are probably not sending a whole lot of data upstream. This asymmetric operation allows for broadband service providers to conserve available bandwidth on the system by allocating more of it to downstream usage.

Not all ADSL is the same. There are two types of ADSL in wide use today: Full-rate ADSL and G.Lite ADSL. Full-rate ADSL is the faster of the two, able to reach speeds of 8Mbps downstream and 1.5Mbps upstream if the subscriber is within 12,000 feet of the central office. The downside of Full-rate ADSL is that the technology is more expensive and that it also usually requires the installation of a "splitter," which divides the voice and data traffic at your home. This means that a technician must come to your home, which means more time and cost.

G.Lite ADSL (also known as Universal ADSL) is cheaper than other types of DSL because it is designed specifically for the home user. It allows for speeds up to 1.5Mbps downstream, and upstream speeds of 384Kbps. The downside with G.Lite ADSL is that you'll have to settle for the lower speeds, although 1.5Mbps is pretty darn fast for most of us!

Other types of DSL technology exist, but mainly for business subscribers and for future uses such as video over DSL. Two DSL technologies commonly used for business are HDSL (High Bit-Rate DSL) and SDSL (Symmetric DSL). Both are symmetric, which means that they can send data at the same speed both upstream and downstream. This is important for businesses that send lots of information as part of their daily operation. A newer DSL that is still being developed is called VDSL (Very High Bit-Rate DSL). VDSL can really hum, sending data downstream at speeds up to 52Mbps. The problem with VDSL is that it doesn't go very far, because customers must be within 1,000 and 4,500 feet of the central office. Some people envision VDSL as a future home-DSL technology that will enable your phone company to deliver not only Internet but video services as well.

Your Phone Company as Your Cable Company (and Vice Versa)?

Your phone company is not content to simply sell its users voice and Internet service. Most large phone companies have grander plans, with many hoping to someday become your entertainment services company as well. Some already sell video services over DSL technology today. Qwest (formerly US West) has thousands of subscribers to its video service, which uses an early form of VDSL, in Phoenix, Arizona. This is the largest example, but there are other phone companies selling video over DSL today. Some are selling video and Internet service in large apartment buildings where they can send the signals over the in-building copper wiring from the basement.

What are your cable companies doing about this competition? Trying to sell you phone services, of course! Many large cable companies are trying to become your one-stop shop for communication, Internet, and video, all over their traditional lines that send you ESPN and the Regis Philbin Channel. In fact, AT&T—otherwise known as Ma Bell—is the largest cable service provider today and has plans to offer voice service to most of its customers someday.

What's next, your electric company becoming your Internet service company? Don't be surprised!

NOTE

Which technology should you choose? The good news for the DSL customer is that most of the time you don't have to choose between DSL technologies, because most of the time the decision has already been made for you. DSL providers usually offer a certain type of technology for their customers, and provide the customer with the appropriate DSL modem that works with their service.

13

How to Find a DSL Provider

Someday—and with certain providers today this is already the case—you will be able to buy your own DSL modem at a store and take it home and install it. But before buying a DSL modem, you will want to talk to the service provider and make sure that you are buying equipment approved for operation with the provider's DSL service.

In some cases you might actually receive DSL from more than one service provider. This might seem strange because you usually have only one local phone company, but the government has made it law that the phone company must share its copper wires with other providers so that they can provide DSL service. One way to determine who provides DSL service in your area (or whether you can even receive DSL service at all) is to use a DSL lookup service. You can find one at www.2wire.com/dsllookup/finddsl.asp. Here you simply plug in your area code, and you will find out which providers are available in your area and what the monthly DSL subscription rate is.

There are other DSL lookup services on the Web in addition to this one. www.dslreports.com is a good site to not only look for DSL by zip code, but also check out reports from other subscribers in your area on the quality of service from each provider.

Cable Internet Service

If you haven't already gotten a flyer advertising high-speed Internet service with your cable TV bill, you probably will get one soon. Most cable companies realized a while ago that this thing called the Internet was going to be big, and with their high-speed lines to about four out of five households in the U.S. (the penetration varies in other countries), they would be able to use the excess capacity on their lines to provide blazing-fast Internet access. And blazing fast it is—for $40 or so a month you can receive up to 30Mbps (sometimes faster!) speeds.

Although providing cable Internet hasn't been a totally smooth road, most of the larger cable providers also offer broadband Internet service to at least some of their customers, and hope to soon make that all of their customers.

How Does Cable Internet Service Work?

At first it might seem strange, receiving your Internet service over your cable TV lines. But in reality, the line that extends from the cable company's head end to your home is a very high-capacity one that is normally very underutilized.

> **NOTE**
>
> A *cable head end* is where the cable provider's service originates, for both its traditional television services and its Internet services. For its traditional TV service, the head end is equipped with satellite dishes to receive the signals, which then are sent to subscribers over the high-speed cable lines. The head end is also equipped with high-speed Internet-access connection equipment, as well as servers that monitor Internet subscriber usage and information.

The overall bandwidth available through your cable connection is about 550MHz, which would technically allow you to receive more than 1,000 channels of digital cable television. The typical signal for an analog television channel is given approximately 6MHz (or six million cycles per second) of spectrum. This same 6MHz spectrum can accommodate 10 channels of digital television.

With Internet service, the cable service provider allocates the same 6MHz spectrum to downstream Internet data. Upstream data, which is data you send rather than receive, is allocated 2MHz of frequency spectrum.

The connections for both TV and Internet are made over coax cabling. This cabling is similar to that discussed in the section "Network Cabling (or Lack Thereof)" in Chapter 2, "Home Network Building Blocks: What Makes Your Network Tick," and it is a very high-speed cabling that can carry high quantities of data. The coax cabling extends from the customer's home to the cable head end.

More recently, cable service providers are using what is called hybrid fiber coax (HFC), which is a combination of both coax and fiber. In networks with HFC, the coax extends from the customer's home into a central node within the neighborhood. This is where the signal is then changed from an electrical one to an optical one (this change from electricity to light is called optoelectronic conversion) and then sent (at the speed of light) to the cable head end, where the signals are then sent on to the Internet. In the case of a customer receiving an Internet signal, all this is done in reverse, with the customer receiving the signal.

Cable Internet Equipment

Cable Internet service is like DSL in that it requires a piece of equipment both at the home side and within the cable provider's network. The home device is called (what else) a cable modem, which allows the home user to take high-speed connections from the coaxial cable and then connect, usually through an Ethernet connection, to a PC or some form of Internet sharing equipment (see Chapter 14, "Internet Sharing on a Home Network," for more on sharing broadband service). As is the case with DSL, you will likely receive a cable modem through your provider when you order cable Internet service, and the installation of the device will happen when a technician comes to your home and turns on the device. Efforts are underway within the cable industry to allow users to buy their cable modems at retail stores and then install them themselves, and although you can buy your own cable modem in certain areas of the country, these efforts will take time.

13

CableLabs: Making Things Work Together

An industry organization by the name of CableLabs has made it their mission to enable broadband cable Internet service to be used by as many people as possible. They do so by serving as the standards body for the cable industry for new services. Without CableLabs, everyone within the cable industry would likely use similar but different technologies for Internet services. This would mean that if you were an equipment manufacturer, you would have to create a different piece of equipment for each company, and the chance would be low that the pieces of equipment would work with one another. See the problem? Trying to sell cable modems at a local store would be nearly impossible—the store would have to stock different types of equipment in each location, because cable providers differ by locality.

To ensure that the whole cable industry worked together, CableLabs created what is called DOCSIS (short for Data Over Cable Service Interface—don't worry, you won't have to remember it). Manufacturers of cable Internet equipment such as cable modems must make sure that their product is DOCSIS certified by CableLabs, or risk shame and banishment from the cable modem community (or, worse, low sales).

CableLabs is also looking to create other standards for other types of services. Remember, as phone companies look to become your Internet and television service provider, cable companies want to provide phone services. To this end, CableLabs has created a standard called PacketCable, which will allow cable providers to provide phone services, and another initiative called CableHome, which is aimed to allow your cable company to provide services to those customers who have home networks. Home networks—that's you!

At the cable head end side, the cable provider has what is called a cable modem termination system (CMTS) that takes in all the traffic from a group of customers and then sends it along to an Internet service provider. Often the ISP will work closely with the cable provider and have servers at the cable head end to monitor and manage the Internet services. Figure 13.2 shows a cable Internet network. Each home that receives cable Internet service is equipped with a cable modem, which sends and receives signals to the CMTS located at the cable head end.

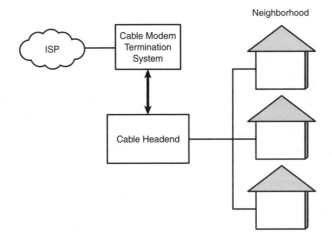

FIGURE 13.2
A cable provider network for TV and Internet services.

Choosing a Cable Internet Service Provider

Choosing a provider for your cable Internet service is pretty easy: Just find out who your cable TV provider is and whether they offer Internet service, and you're ready to go. The problem with cable Internet service is not so much figuring out who your provider is, but the fact that they might not offer Internet service in your area. As with DSL, the cable providers must do a lot of work to make sure that Internet service is offered in each neighborhood, and this work takes time. However, today cable Internet is offered in many neighborhoods, and you likely just need to call your local cable provider and ask whether they offer service to your address yet.

A Word on Cable ISPs

The world of cable Internet differs from DSL and other technologies in that there are only a couple of major ISPs to choose from. The smaller number came about because when the cable companies realized that they could offer Internet services, they helped form ISPs that would specialize in offering service for cable Internet.

The two largest cable Internet ISPs are @Home and Road Runner. These ISPs work closely with the local cable company to provide Internet service where the cable company has coax cabling running to the homes. The cable company usually installs the cable modem and gets the customer situated for service, and when the customer is up and running they are using the ISP's connection to the Internet. You will usually get your bill for broadband service on your cable bill, although this is not always the case because in some locations the cable provider hasn't gotten their systems working together to the point where they send a single bill.

@Home and Road Runner, though the largest, are not the only cable ISPs. Two other cable ISPs are High Speed Access Corporation and ISP Channel.

If you have some form of Internet access, you can check for the availability of cable Internet service at www.cable-modem.net.

Satellite Internet Access

If you cannot receive DSL or cable Internet access, do not fret. If you live anywhere with access to the southern sky, you should be able to receive broadband Internet. How, you ask? Through satellite technology!

With new advances in satellite technology, broadband Internet service is within reach of nearly everyone. This is great, because many people live in more remote areas where their phone or cable company has determined that it is not feasible to make broadband Internet accessible. Although this might seem unfair, it is a sound business decision because it costs a lot of money to create broadband networks, and companies can realistically expect to make money only in areas such as large cities where they will get a lot of subscribers. But with satellite Internet access, none of that matters, because these providers can reach nearly everyone.

How Does Satellite Internet Work?

The term *satellite* in itself conjures up intrigue and scientific wonder. The idea of metal objects in orbit around the earth has captured the imagination of many since the Soviets first launched the first satellite—the Sputnik—in 1957.

Since then, thousands of satellites have been launched into space by governments and businesses, and today many of the services provided by satellites touch nearly everyone in some way (many without our even knowing!). One of the newer technologies is the availability of high-speed Internet access.

If you are a customer of satellite Internet services, you are usually equipped with a small dish that is placed atop your roof, a satellite modem (or two sometimes—one for sending and one for receiving signals), and cabling that connects your dish to your in-home modem.

Providing high-speed Internet access via satellite is tricky because most satellite systems were designed to distribute high-speed signals to the appropriate audience, not receive them. Because of this, many of the early satellite Internet services also require the use of a normal dial-up modem (that's right, of the 56Kbps variety) to send signals. This is changing quickly, however; most of the satellite Internet providers either have developed two-way services or are frantically developing this technology.

Figure 13.3 shows a diagram of a satellite Internet access network. This diagram is of a two-way satellite Internet service, in which you can both send and receive signals through your modem and dish. The signal from the dish is sent to the satellite orbiting the earth, which then sends the signal to the satellite ISP hub. The satellite ISP hub is similar to the DSL central office or cable head end in that it takes the signal from thousands of subscribers and then connects it to the larger Internet.

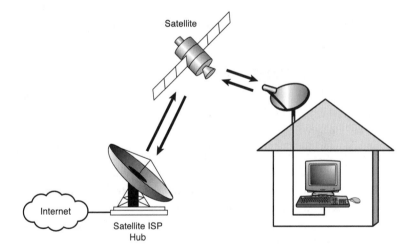

FIGURE 13.3

A satellite Internet network.

Most satellite Internet services allow you to receive signals at speeds of 400–500Kbps, not as fast as cable or DSL, but plenty fast compared to dial-up.

Choosing a Satellite Internet Service Provider

Unlike with DSL or cable Internet service, you don't have to live within a certain city or geographical location that has been targeted for service by one of the service providers. The unique thing about satellite Internet service is that you can live almost anywhere and subscribe to the service. So when you hear people complaining that they can't get broadband where they live, tell them to check out satellite Internet (or to buy this book so that I can tell them!).

One of the other differences with satellite Internet is that you can choose from any of the service providers, because any one of them should have access to where you live. You can usually order direct from the service provider, or choose from a retail partner that offers the hardware and the capability to sign up for the service in the store. Because most satellite service providers also provide television services, you might be able to get TV service through the same provider. Table 13.1 lists the providers who currently offer satellite Internet service or have announced their intentions to do so.

TABLE 13.1   Satellite Internet Service Providers

Satellite Service Provider	Web Address	Service Available
Starband	www.starband.com	Today
DirecPC	www.direcpc.com	Today
Teledesic	www.teledesic.com	2005
Tachyon.net	www.tachyon.net	Today (Note: Tachyon offers high-speed access to businesses, but if you need broadband Internet and cannot get service elsewhere, you could consider their services.)

Fixed Wireless Internet Access

One of the latest technologies to become available to home users—and probably the least understood technology by most consumers—is that of fixed wireless Internet. Fixed wireless is a technology that utilizes wireless technology to transmit to local antennas on the roof of your house. This means that you get your signal from local antennas, as opposed to a satellite system that transmits from space.

The availability of fixed wireless is less than that of the other broadband technologies, because it has only started to garner attention in the past few years. However, the buildout of fixed wireless broadband networks has gathered a lot of momentum, and service providers are moving quickly to deploy in different cities around the United States.

How Does Fixed Wireless Internet Work?

Fixed wireless uses wireless signals from local transceivers (kind of like a large wireless LAN). Each home that receives fixed wireless service is equipped with an antenna that is placed on the roof. The antenna is connected to a modem that resides in the home, usually next to your PC. The antenna and modem are connected using some form of cabling. The whole setup is installed by the fixed wireless service provider.

Before any of the installation takes place, the fixed wireless provider will first make a trip to your home to make sure that you can receive this service. Unlike satellite Internet service, fixed wireless service is limited by what is called line-of-sight restrictions. This means that the antenna on your roof must have a clear path of communication to the local transmission tower.

The Cure for Line-of-Sight Restrictions?

Fixed wireless systems are limited to serve only those subscribers with an unimpeded path from the local transmission tower. This means that when the antenna sends a signal to the tower, if lots of foliage or buildings are in the way (such as in a downtown area), chances are that the signal won't make it.

However, the large networking company Cisco has discovered a technology with the really complicated name of Vector Orthogonal Frequency Division Multiplexing (VOFDM). Don't worry, you don't have to know anything about VOFDM other than that it allows fixed wireless systems to communicate through areas that don't have a clear line-of-sight.

Transmission towers are placed within certain reach of what are called Network Operation Centers (NOCs). The transmission towers relay the signal from your home to the NOCs, where the signal is then sent onto the Internet. The fixed wireless NOC is similar to a cable head end for cable Internet, or a central office used for DSL Internet.

Figure 13.4 shows a fixed wireless Internet system. The transmission from the house to the transmission tower is a radio link that depends on line-of-sight, and then the signal is carried to the NOC and then to the Internet. Speeds for fixed wireless systems are comparable to those for cable Internet. Sprint Broadband Direct, the largest fixed wireless service provider, advertises speeds of 5Mbps downstream and up to 256Kbps upstream.

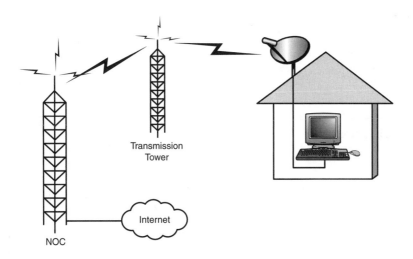

Transmission
Tower

Internet

NOC

FIGURE 13.4

A fixed wireless Internet system.

Choosing a Fixed Wireless Internet Provider

Of the four major broadband service technologies discussed in this chapter, fixed wireless is the least widely available. However, this situation might change over time because the main appeal of the technology is that it is relatively cheap to install and deploy for companies looking to provide broadband Internet service. The mere fact that a fixed wireless system does not require expensive upgrades to cabling (either copper or coaxial) or launching of satellites (not exactly a cheap endeavor) makes it probably the easiest type of service to get off the ground (excuse the pun).

So although fixed wireless is not widely available today, that might quickly change. The handful of service providers today, included in Table 13.2, might soon change to a multitude of service providers, such as is the case with DSL service. Most fixed wireless providers have lookup services on their Web pages for you to see whether service is offered in your area. Remember, however, that even if service is available in your area, a technician will still need to come to your home and see whether there is a clear line-of-sight to your particular location. Some service providers do have creative workarounds such as high-rise antennas, but you will also have to consider whether you want this long, funny-looking antenna on your roof.

TABLE 13.2 Fixed Wireless Service Providers

Fixed Wireless Service Provider	Web Site	Availability
Sprint Broadband	www.sprintbroadband.com	Largest fixed wireless provider, with coverage in more than 90 cities
AT&T Digital Broadband	www.iatt.com	Growing rapidly, available in California, Texas, Alaska, and Nevada in 2001
MCI Worldcom	www.mci.com	Is planning to offer fixed wireless services, but has not announced where

Choosing Between Broadband Services

After reading this chapter, you should realize that the broadband revolution is within reach not only of those lucky few who happen to live in silicon valley. No, many large companies have been investing millions and millions of dollars to make sure that you can have access to some form of high-speed connection as well, so that you and those on your home network can access the Internet at lightning speeds.

Still, not everyone has access to broadband today. The likelihood of getting broadband increases for you if you live in a large city. However, considering that satellite broadband services should be available to anyone, anywhere, the truth is that technically you should be able to get off that poky dial-up connection faster than you think.

Each broadband technology does have certain advantages. In Table 13.3 you can compare each technology by speeds, cost, and other characteristics. But remember, if you can get one of the technologies, I would suggest that you do it, because broadband is worlds different from basic dial-up service, especially if you are sharing an Internet connection over a home network.

TABLE 13.3 Comparison of Different Broadband Technologies

Broadband Technology	Speeds	Cost	Other Info
Digital Subscriber Line (DSL)	From 256Kbps to 8Mbps depending on distance to central office and type of service	$19.95 up to $100 depending on speed and technology	DSL gives you a dedicated connection, meaning that you don't have to share bandwidth with your neighbors

TABLE 13.3   Continued

Broadband Technology	Speeds	Cost	Other Info
Cable Internet	From 1Mbps to 30Mbps, depending on how many users are in your neighborhood	$29.95 up to $49.95, depending on whether you lease your modem or buy it	Cable Internet can usually be packaged with your TV service; often easier to get than DSL
Satellite Internet	400–500Kbps	$19.95 to $39.95	The most widely available; maymight be the best option for those living in remote areas
Fixed Wireless Internet	Up to 5Mbps	$34.95 to $49.95	Newest technology, rapidly expanding availability

Broadband and Your Home Network

Broadband is a nice luxury to have, but those who have it will claim that it is not a luxury at all, but a necessity. To those who have broadband access that is distributed over a home network, it is an *absolute necessity*, right up there with oxygen, food, and shelter.

There are many ways to set up all the different PCs on a home network to access the broadband connection. This is a great way to take advantage of the ample bandwidth available, as well as distribute the cost of the broadband connection among multiple users. If you want to do it the low-cost way, you can choose to use Internet connection sharing software, which either is included as part of your Windows operating system (Windows 98, ME, and XP) or is a separate piece of software such as Winproxy.

Or you can use a separate piece of Internet sharing hardware such as a home router or residential gateway. What are the advantages and costs of each? Don't worry, I'll explain each to you and how to go about setting up broadband sharing in Chapter 14. That way you can really take advantage of your new broadband connection that you learned about in this chapter!

Wrap It Up

Broadband is quickly moving from a technology that was available only to a lucky few to one that is going to be required by anyone who has a couple of computers and a desire to move faster than the comparatively slow speeds of dial-up Internet modems. This chapter showed you the types of broadband technology and explained how to go about getting the technology. Here are some things to remember as you go about investigating broadband for yourself:

- There are four basic choices for anyone considering broadband technology: DSL, cable, satellite, and fixed wireless.
- DSL is sent over your existing phone wiring, and it can usually be bought as part of a service package from your phone service provider. DSL service is limited by distance availability.
- Cable Internet is sent over the same cables on which you get your cable TV service. Normally your cable TV service provider will act as your cable Internet service provider.
- Satellite Internet is the most widely available of all the services and is the best choice for those who live in rural areas.
- Fixed wireless Internet is the newest of the technologies; it relies on radio transmissions from an antenna on your roof to a local transmission tower.

If you are considering sharing an Internet connection over a home network, you should strongly consider getting a broadband connection. Options for sharing your broadband connection are discussed in Chapter 14.

Internet Sharing on a Home Network

IN THIS CHAPTER

The world of the Internet is an exciting one. Those who have had the opportunity to use the Internet, whether at work, school, or home, know that it offers a whole new world of information and communication at your fingertips. So with all the possibilities that the Internet and broadband present, wouldn't you want to share your Internet connection? Of course you would!

The preceding chapter looked at the world of broadband and the different options for getting on the Internet. This chapter explores the different ways for sharing both a broadband and a dial-up modem (because 80% of the online world is still using dial-up, and there's no doubt that dial-up Internet access will continue to account for most connections for years to come).

Some of you might be wondering what exactly I mean by *Internet sharing*. Internet sharing is the simultaneous use of one Internet connection by more than one PC within a home. So while you might be checking out the latest on your favorite musician in one room, your roommate or spouse can be checking out what the weather will be like tomorrow on the weather site, all using the same modem and Internet connection. The magic of the home network is that you can share this connection and be in different areas of the home and doing completely separate activities on the Internet.

Although it might be obvious on a home network:

- The most important reason is economic. Why pay for multiple Internet accounts when you can share one? This is especially true with broadband, which can cost from $30 to $100 a month.
- It helps cure the "Internet Log Jam"—that time of day when multiple people in your house want to get on the Internet but only one connection is available.
- The low cost of PCs today makes it feasible for people to have multiples PCs, and with more PCs why not share an Internet connection?
- A home network connecting to a broadband connection creates new ways to enjoy the Internet. For example, with the capability to stream music around the home, the Internet-enabled home network can be your whole-home music system. No longer do you need to sit huddled over your PC, wherever it might be sitting, but instead you can be anywhere in the home and listen to audio music streamed into your home and over the home network.

These are just a few reasons why you'd want to use a home network to share your Internet connection. But let's quit talking about why you should share and get to the good stuff—how to go about actually doing it!

Internet Sharing: Hard or Soft?

The sharing of an Internet connection can be done in two ways:

- Internet sharing software
- Internet sharing hardware

We'll go over both of these methods, each of which has distinct advantages. The main advantage of using software is that the capabilities for sharing Internet access are built into your Windows operating system, making the cost of adding an Internet connection to new PCs essentially nothing. All Windows operating systems from Windows 98 Second Edition on have built-in capabilities to share Internet access. If you are using an older OS, you can download some freeware that allows you to share your Internet connection.

TIP

If you are using a Windows PC and are using an operating system older than Windows 98, you should seriously consider upgrading. The newer versions of Windows and are much easier to network because Microsoft has built in new Internet sharing, and the newer operating systems have a better chance of working with the different types of equipment you may choose to use on your home network.

Internet sharing hardware, which is a specific piece of equipment that works with your Internet modem to simultaneously share a connection over the network to multiple PCs, is great because it affords the following benefits when compared to using software only:

- You have a dedicated device such as a home router or residential gateway that can be connected directly to the modem and that allows you to then place the different PCs in any room you'd like. The device shares the connection using one or more types of local area networking, such as Ethernet, wireless, HPNA, or powerline.
- The hub or switch technology is often built into the hardware, allowing you to use it as your connection station for multiple PCs.
- The hardware allows you to share one IP address among multiple PCs for accessing the Internet.
- Internet sharing hardware usually has some level of built-in security protection, which is necessary with always-on broadband.
- You don't need to have one of your PCs always on, acting as the central point for accessing the Internet.

14

INTERNET SHARING
ON A HOME
NETWORK

Clearly it is up to you to make the choice. We will take a look at the options and how to set up your network using both a software and a hardware option so that you can decide which is best for you.

Choosing Between Hardware and Software

Maybe the most important factor in deciding whether to use software or hardware is whether you have a broadband connection. If you do have a broadband Internet connection (DSL, cable, satellite, or fixed wireless), you should strongly consider using Internet sharing hardware. This is because broadband is always on, and if you have a piece of Internet sharing hardware such as a home router, you will have the extra security you need and you do not have to rely on one PC to be the main connection point to the Internet. Also, many home routers have built-in hubs or switches, so you can directly connect PCs into the router to network as well as share an Internet connection.

If you have a dial-up Internet account, chances are you are dialing up with a PC equipped with a dial-up modem, which makes it necessary to have this PC as the central access point for your home network's Internet access. If this is the case, you will want to use the Internet sharing software that is available in your operating system or, if you are using an older operating system, use one of the available programs that enable Internet Connection Sharing.

If you do decide that Internet sharing hardware such as a home router or gateway is right for you, you will need to buy one. The good news is that these products are low-cost (a home router with a built-in four-port hub can be purchased for less than $100) and are available at any computer or electronics store. We'll even suggest the name of a few manufacturers of these products to make your job easier.

Using Internet Sharing Hardware

Before we show you how to set your network to share an Internet connection using hardware, we'll take a quick look at the options available. This section explains the basic concepts that will allow you to decide whether hardware is right for you.

The basic function of Internet sharing hardware is to allow multiple PCs to connect to a network. The basic type of home networking hardware is called a home router or gateway. These devices work with a broadband modem (and over time will eventually be combined with a modem) to then connect to the different PCs on the network.

The difference between a home gateway and a home router is minimal to the end user, and for all practical purposes they should be considered the same thing. Those within the networking industry have some particular definitions for each, but the important thing to remember is that each allows you to connect multiple PCs to the Internet. From here forward we will refer to

Internet sharing hardware as a home router, but if you are interested in reading more about home gateways, read the following sidebar.

> ## Home Network Future: The Home Gateway
>
> Over the past few years, many large companies have started to discuss a new category of device that, if you asked them, will change all our lives. This device is called a home gateway.
>
> The concept is that as more and more people subscribe to broadband, the capability to deliver new and exciting services into the home will multiply, all enabled by this magical device called a home gateway (or residential gateway, depending on whom you are talking to).
>
> What does a home gateway do? Well, according to these people, it will eventually do everything. It will be the device that will allow you to subscribe to streaming audio and video services, get cheap voice services over your broadband connection, and even allow you to let your refrigerator manufacturer check on the health of the big white box and see whether there is a need for any maintenance or upgrades.
>
> If this seems ambitious, it is. The idea of an all-in-one device that connects the Internet with your networked home (not just your PCs, but your TV, stereo, home systems, and so on) is the holy grail of many companies in the technology industry. But the idea of the home gateway is still somewhat vague, and it is hard to go to a store and pick up one of these products. Instead, the earliest home gateways are called home routers, which allow you to basically share your Internet connection, usually a broadband connection, with multiple PCs.
>
> An industry group called the Open Services Gateway Initiative (OSGI) has been formed to help define how services will be delivered to you in the future over your home gateway. Ways to deliver services ranging from entertainment, voice, gaming, home control, security, and more are being defined. Although the ordinary home networker will never need to know much about OSGI, you might someday get a gateway that is OSGI-approved that allows you to subscribe to all sorts of services. You can read more about OSGI at www.osgi.org.

How Home Routers Work

Figure 14.1 shows a home network using a home router. The home router is a device that attaches directly to the broadband modem, usually with an Ethernet connection. New home routers are coming to market that also allow you to connect to multiple PCs using wireless, powerline, and phoneline technology.

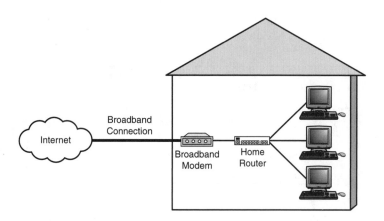

FIGURE 14.1

Sharing a broadband connection with a home router.

The function of the home router is to allow all the PCs on the home network to access the Internet, while looking like just one PC to the Internet. In other words, it allows you to share one Internet IP address across all the PCs on your network.

You might be curious as to why you shouldn't just hook up a hub or switch to your broadband modem directly, and share your Internet connection that way. This is because a home router and a hub/switch differ in that a router has the extra intelligence to be able to bridge the local area network, or home LAN, and another network such as the Internet. The router looks at the actual messages being sent over the network, and it can decide whether the message is for another PC on the network or whether it is designated for the Internet.

The function that the router performs which allows for the sharing of the IP address is called Network Address Translation, or NAT. NAT, as defined previously, allows the router to present one IP address to the larger Internet. So when a PC on the home network requests to see an Internet page, the Internet sees the same IP address no matter which PC on your home network is making the request. This is the basic capability of a router that allows you to share the Internet connection over the home network.

Why do you need to use NAT? Most ISPs assign one IP address per subscriber. If you do not use a piece of hardware or software to perform Network Address Translation, the ISP would see two or more PCs requesting an IP address. They would then ask you to pay for another subscription, if this is their policy.

> **NOTE**
>
> Some ISPs have a policy that each subscriber pay for a separate IP address if more than one subscriber is accessing the Internet. However, with the growing reality that most consumers will use some form of Internet sharing software or hardware, many ISPs are beginning to adjust their policies and accept such installations. If you feel you should cross your I's and dot your T's, check your subscriber agreement to see your ISP's policy on multiple subscribers.

Another key function of your home router or gateway is what is called Dynamic Host Configuration Protocol, or DHCP. DHCP is a service performed by your home router (or other routers and special servers on larger networks) that automatically assigns an IP address to each PC on the network. So instead of each PC being given a fixed IP address, each PC that requests access to a network gets a dynamic IP address.

As you learned in Chapter 10, "Getting Around the Home Network," you can have IP addresses assigned dynamically by a home router or through the capabilities built into the Windows operating system, or you can use a DHCP server, such as a home router. In most home networks in which a home router is installed, each PC on the network will use the router to have an IP address assigned rather than using the IP addressing capabilities of Windows or using a fixed IP address.

A Word About Internet Security

One of the other benefits of using a home router is security. Although we will go in depth into home Internet security in Chapter 18, "Home Network Security Overview," it is important to mention that any user of broadband Internet is at risk of having someone improperly access their private information if proper precautions are not taken.

With an always-on connection, it is impossible to be around your PC 24 hours a day, and even if you were, there would be a chance that someone could be accessing your PC "behind the scenes." One of the dangers of enabling TCP/IP and file sharing in Windows is that someone from outside your home network can fool your network into thinking that he should have access to everything on the network.

Luckily, with a few precautions you can be almost entirely safe (although you can never be 100% safe from a security breach) from some form of attack. Software-based protection is one method of security we will examine later, in Chapter 19, "Home Network Security Planner." There are also hardware-based solutions such as

14

home routers. Home routers' use of Network Address Translation, or NAT, enables some inherent level of protection because it makes it more difficult for external users to see the PCs behind the home router operating on the Internet.

Whatever you decide to do, you should give serious consideration to some level of Internet security. To learn more about Internet and home network security, see both Chapter 18 and Chapter 19.

Buying a Home Router

If you do decide that you want to use a home router, the first thing to do is buy one. Thanks to advances in technology, the cost of a basic home router has come down quickly. A good home router that allows you to connect up to four PCs on a network using Ethernet technology can be found for under $100. Wireless routers or gateways can be found for around $300. In Table 14.1 you will see a list of manufacturers of home routers, as well as names of selected products. Remember that product names change frequently, so you will want to check the Web sites for the latest product info.

TABLE 14.1 Home Router Manufacturers

Manufacturer	Product	Web site
Linksys	BEFSR41—EtherFast 4-Port Cable/DSL Router	www.linksys.com
SOHOware	Broadguard Cable/DSL Router	www.sohoware.com
Netgear	RT314 Cable/DSL Router	www.netgear.com
D-Link	DI-714 Wireless Router	www.dlink.com
3Com	3Com Home Wireless Gateway	www.3com.com

Installing a Home Router

Connecting a home network to a home router is pretty simple. The following discussion will assume that you are using an Ethernet network, but the same basic methods to connect can be used to describe a wireless, phoneline, or powerline router.

For the sake of our discussion, we will assume that you have a four-port Ethernet home router, so you can connect up to four PCs in addition to the broadband modem. In addition to having home network ports to connect the PCs, the home router will have what is usually called a WAN (sometimes labeled DSL/Cable) port, which allows you to connect to the broadband modem. Newer models of these home routers might have a USB connection.

The first thing you will want to do is physically connect the home router to the broadband modem. To do so, follow the basic instructions given next. You will also want to carefully review the user manual for the home router to make sure you are following any specific instructions from the manufacturer regarding its specific product.

To physically install a home router, follow these steps:

1. Make sure that the power is off to both the home router and the broadband modem.

2. Connect the network cabling into the RJ-45 jack of the home router labeled WAN or Cable/DSL. The back of the home router will look something like that shown in Figure 14.2.

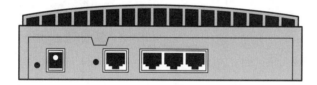

FIGURE 14.2

A home router.

3. Plug the other end of the cable into the cable modem.

4. If the cable or DSL modem is not yet connected to the Internet connection (the connection providing the actual Internet link, usually coming from the wall), connect the cord to the broadband modem.

5. Connect the different PCs on the network into the home router. Remember, a home router with built-in hub or switch capability can replace the hub or switch in your Ethernet network. See Figure 14.3 for a diagram of what this step should look like.

6. Plug the power cable into the home router and then into the wall.

7. Turn on the power to the home router and then the broadband modem.

Your home router should be physically installed now. You are ready to configure the home router from a PC using the instructions given next.

14

INTERNET SHARING ON A HOME NETWORK

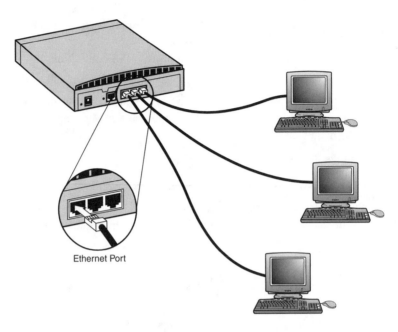

Ethernet Port

FIGURE 14.3
Connecting the PCs on a home network to a home router.

Configuring a Home Router

Depending on which manufacturer and product you have purchased, the setup utility will vary. I suggest that you read through the installation instructions given later in this section and then take a look at any installation information provided with your home router to familiarize yourself with the specific instructions for your product.

You can configure your home router from any of the PCs that are connected into the device. Most home routers today use some form of Web configuration utility, meaning that you configure through a Web browser. This might seem strange, but in reality it is a very easy way of doing things. You will likely be instructed to type an IP address provided by the home router manufacturer into your Web browser to get the Web configuration utility. The IP address is that of the home router on the network. When you type the router's IP address, the Web browser reads the information provided by a small Web server embedded in your home router and launches the configuration utility screen. After the home router is configured with an IP address, it then assigns different IP addresses for internal use using its DHCP capabilities. The address appears to the external world (the Internet) as one address because of the router's NAT capability.

NOTE

Web server is a term for any computer or other device that provides a Web page or Web information when you access its Web address (such as www.sams.com) or IP address (such as 192.168.1.1) through a standard Web browser. A Web server can be a big computer such as those working at sites like Yahoo, or it can be a small embedded one such as the one in a home router.

The following discussion will walk you through the installation of a home router from Linksys. Because Linksys's home router uses a Web configuration utility, all setup is done through a standard Web browser.

Some routers might be configured through a regular software installation. If this is the case, you will want to read carefully the instructions provided by the manufacturer to guide you through the installation process.

The rest of the configuration of the home router with Web-based configuration should go as shown here:

1. After typing the IP address of the home router, you are asked for a User Name (sometimes called an Administrator ID) and password. Most configuration utilities come with a default password and ID provided by the manufacturer, so check your product's manual and installation instructions.

2. In the Linksys Web configuration utility, you first see the Setup tab. Other options are included that we will review later. The Setup tab should look something like that shown in Figure 14.4. Notice that the utility is accessed through a normal Web browser with the IP address typed in the address bar.

3. The first two fields in the configuration utility ask for a Host Name and Domain Name. The reason for these fields is that some Internet service providers (such as cable Internet provider AT&T@Home) require them to access your Internet service. You will need to check with your provider to see whether you are required to use a specific hostname (sometimes called computer name) and domain name.

4. The next two fields are for the LAN IP address. These fields will likely be populated already with the default information from the home router manufacturer. In most cases, you will want to go with the default information. The LAN IP address is the address that identifies your home router on the network, and it should be the same number you typed into your Web browser to access the configuration utility.

14

INTERNET SHARING ON A HOME NETWORK

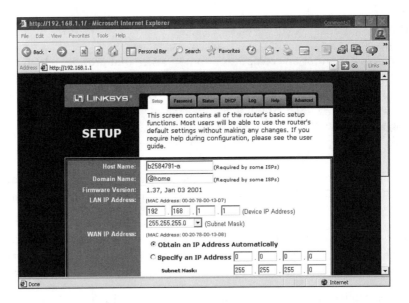

FIGURE 14.4

The Web configuration utility for a home router.

5. The next two fields are for the WAN IP address. The WAN IP address is the address used to identify your broadband modem on the Internet; it allows access to information over the Internet. Choose between Obtain an IP Address Automatically and Specify an IP Address.

CAUTION

Choosing between a fixed and a dynamic IP address is very important. You will need to determine whether your ISP gives you a new IP address each time you use your Internet account or whether it has assigned you a permanent (also called fixed) IP address. You can tell this by looking at the information provided to you by your ISP or by looking at your broadband modem. Often providers write the IP address on the bottom of the modem. If you do not find it, you can call your ISP and ask whether they use dynamic IP addressing (the term for assigning a new address each time) or a fixed IP address. Most providers use dynamic IP addressing.

---

6. The next few fields are under Login. You have the choice between two forms of login authentication: PPPoE and Disable. You should choose to disable unless your ISP uses PPPoE. PPPoE is a form of login authentication used by some DSL ISPs. You should check with your ISP to see whether they use PPPoE. If you use a cable modem, you will likely want to choose the Disable option.

7. Under the User Name and Password field, you can enter a name and password for access to the router configuration utility. If you think there is the possibility of an unauthorized person accessing your router configuration utility, you should choose a name and password that are known to you only. You can also choose to go with the default password provided by the home router manufacturer. Linksys routers have a default password of "admin" and leave the User Name space blank.

8. Click the Apply button for all your configuration settings to take effect.

9. Click on the DHCP tab at the top of the configuration utility. Click the Enable option for the DHCP Server field. The DHCP server gives each PC on your network an IP address automatically. The DHCP screen will look like that shown in Figure 14.5.

NOTE

PCs on a home network that have been configured to obtain an IP address automatically do so by first looking for a DHCP server such as your home router. If they cannot find one, they use the built-in IP addressing in Windows. This means that if you turn on the DHCP server for a home network that has already been enabled to obtain IP addresses automatically, each PC will look to the router first to get its address rather than going through Windows. You will want to make sure that for each PC that will be using the DHCP server capabilities of the home router, you have configured to receive IP addresses automatically. Refer to Chapter 10 for a review on how to configure IP addresses, as well as to the following information on how to configure your PCs for automatic IP addressing.

---

10. Also enter the number of users on the network (number of PCs) in the Number of DHCP Users field. Click Apply and then click Continue.

11. Reset your broadband modem by turning it on and off. Then restart your PC to allow it to get the proper information for operation from the router.

Your home router should now be ready to enable Internet sharing for different PCs on the network. Your PC should now be able to obtain an IP address from the home router using the embedded DHCP server if it has been configured for automatic IP addressing.

If you haven't already done so, you will want to enable each PC on the network to receive an IP address automatically, to take advantage of the built-in IP address capability of the router's DHCP server. You should have done this already by following the steps in Chapter 10, but in case you didn't, you simply need to follow the instructions given next.

14

INTERNET SHARING ON A HOME NETWORK

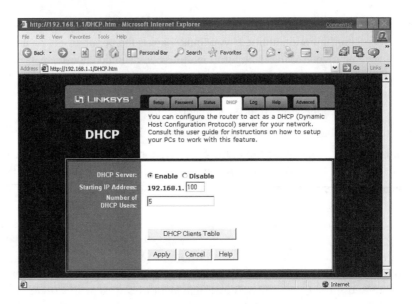

FIGURE 14.5

The DHCP screen on a home router configuration utility.

To enable automatic IP addressing in Windows 95/98/ME, follow these steps:

1. Click Start, Control Panel, and then double-click the Network icon.

2. In the Network window, double-click the TCP/IP component installed for your NIC. This should read something like TCP/IP > 3Com 3C450 Adapter. If you do not see the TCP/IP component installed, see Chapter 9, "Setting Up Home Network Software," for how to install this component, which is necessary to do any form of Internet sharing on a Windows PC.

3. In the TCP/IP properties window, click on the IP Address tab. Make sure that the Obtain an IP Address Automatically option is checked; if not, check it. Then click OK. When Windows asks to restart your PC, click Yes.

4. Carry out this procedure for every PC on the network that will be sharing the Internet connection through your home router.

With Windows XP you simply need to double-check whether the Obtain an IP Address Automatically option is turned on, which it should be because that is the default for this operating system.

To double-check whether automatic IP addressing is turned on in Windows XP, simply do this:

1. Click Start, Control Panel, Network and Internet Connections, and then Network Connections.

2. In the Network Connections window, right-click on the Local Area Connection icon and click Properties.

3. In the Local Area Connections window, double-click the Internet Protocol (TCP/IP) icon on the General tab to get to the Internet Protocol (TCP/IP) Properties window.

4. Make sure that the Obtain an IP Address Automatically option is chosen. If not, click this option and then click OK. Click OK again. When asked to restart your PC, click Yes.

You should now know how to set up Internet sharing with a basic home router. Again, Internet sharing hardware varies slightly in capabilities from manufacturer to manufacturer, but most of today's products are pretty simple to use and can be purchased very affordably. Remember that you can often substitute a hub or switch, or even a wireless access point, with a home router because these products often come with these capabilities built-in. You will want to read each product's information carefully before purchasing, however, so that you know exactly what you are buying.

Using Internet Connection Sharing Software

Although having a piece of Internet sharing hardware such as a home router or gateway is a nice and easy way to connect multiple PCs to the Internet, you can just as easily share an Internet connection using software. In fact, things are made even easier by the fact that Windows 98 Second Edition and newer versions of Windows have the capability to share an Internet connection—called Internet Connection Sharing (ICS)—built-in. If you have older versions of Windows or simply want to use some other form of software, you can get free or very cheap software products to allow you to share an Internet connection. Although we will look at the different types of software available to share an Internet connection (for those of you who have operating systems older than Windows 98 SE), we will first examine how to use the built-in capabilities of Windows using ICS.

Introduction to Internet Connection Sharing in Windows

ICS is a service that is built into the Windows operating system. It allows you to take one PC, called the host, and offer its Internet connection to other PCs on the network. These PCs that are using the host's Internet connection are referred to as clients. You can share a broadband connection such as that of a cable or DSL modem, or share a basic dial-up modem. In either case, the host computer acts as the primary interface to the Internet and then directs the communication requests from the LAN to and from the Internet. The host PC using ICS also acts as the DHCP server, assigning IP addresses to the different PCs on the network.

14

INTERNET SHARING
ON A HOME
NETWORK

> **Caution**
>
> If you are going to use the host PC using ICS to assign IP addresses to the different
> PCs on the network, you will need the host PC to be turned on for the different PCs
> to communicate on the network. This is because in a network using ICS, the host PC
> becomes the default DHCP server and essentially enables other PCs to communicate
> by "leasing" them their IP addresses.

Because the host PC acts as the intermediary between the different PCs on the network and the Internet, it is functioning as what is called a proxy server. A proxy server is essentially a PC or any device that separates a direct connection between two networks. In the case of using ICS, it is the proxy server between your home LAN and the Internet. This is important from a security perspective, because a proxy server acts as a guard between the two networks. Only the IP address of the host computer, and not the addresses of the other PCs on the network, is visible to the larger Internet. In this regard, ICS and other software-based proxy servers act like home router hardware.

> **Caution**
>
> Internet security is a much larger topic than will be discussed here. If you are connect-
> ing a network to the Internet, especially an always-on connection such as that of a
> broadband modem, you should read about how to set up Internet security for your
> network in Chapter 18 and Chapter 19.

With ICS, you can allow the PCs on the network to act as if they were directly connected to the Internet. They will be able to use Internet-based utilities such as e-mail, and a Web browser such as Netscape Navigator and Internet Explorer. If you are using certain programs on a client PC on the network such as an Internet-based game, you might need to configure the PC to allow for incoming requests for information from the Internet.

Installing Internet Connection Sharing in Windows

Depending on which version of Windows you are using, you might need to install the ICS component into Windows before you run ICS. Windows 98 SE and Windows ME do not come with ICS preinstalled. With Windows XP, ICS is installed by default. Before you follow the steps given next, be sure to put your Windows install disk into your CD-ROM drive, because your PC might ask for it to get the necessary components.

To install ICS on a Windows 98 SE and ME PC, follow these steps:

1. Click Start, Settings, Control Panel, and double-click Add/Remove Programs.
2. In the Add/Remove Programs Properties dialog box, click on the Windows Setup tab.
3. Make sure that the box for Communications is checked (most likely it is). Click on the Communications line (while not unchecking the box) and then click the Details button below.
4. In the Communications Details dialog box, check the box next to Internet Connection Sharing. Click OK and OK again.

Enabling Internet Connection Sharing in Windows

The preceding steps will launch the Internet Connection Wizard in Windows 98 or the Home Networking Wizard in Windows ME. Internet Connection Sharing will be installed by default in Windows XP. After you run through the steps to install ICS in Windows 98/ME, you can use the Internet Connection Wizard (in 98) or the Home Networking Wizard (in ME) to enable ICS. In Windows XP, you simply need to launch the Network Setup Wizard by clicking Start, Control Panel, Network and Internet Connections, and then clicking Set Up or Change Your Home or Small Office Network.

Although you will want to install ICS and run the wizard to enable it on every PC, you first should make sure that ICS is installed and enabled on the host PC. The host PC is, once again, the PC that is directly connected to the Internet.

Depending on whether you are using Windows 98 SE, ME, or XP, the steps will vary slightly. Also, you will make certain choices depending on whether you are connecting using a dial-up modem or through a broadband modem from the host PC.

If you are using a broadband modem, you will be using two NICs (unless you are connected via a USB connection directly to the modem). One NIC will be your connection to the broadband modem, and the other will be your connection to the network. If you are using a dial-up connection, the PC you designate as the host will need to have only one NIC, which will be the connection to the home network. When sharing a broadband connection from a host PC, you will need to specify, when setting up Internet Connection Sharing, which NIC is for the broadband modem.

14

INTERNET SHARING
ON A HOME
NETWORK

Setting Up the Internet Connection Sharing Host PC

Again, the host PC is the one on the home network that is directly connected to the Internet. The rest of the PCs on the network (the clients) will access the Internet through the host PC after ICS is enabled. Let's look at how to enable ICS for a host PC using different versions of Windows.

To set up a Windows 98 SE PC as the host PC, follow these steps:

1. Make sure that the Internet Connection Sharing Wizard has been launched from the previous steps. From the start screen click Next.

2. Choose the appropriate NIC that is connected to the broadband modem, or if you are using a dial-up modem, choose that as your primary connection. Then click Next.

3. Insert a floppy disk, which will be used to configure any client PCs on the network that are sharing the Internet connection from the host machine. Any PC using an operating system older than Windows ME will need a setup disk to use ICS. Make sure that you use a formatted disk. Click Next after inserting the disk.

4. The wizard tells you to remove the disk; do so, click OK and then Finish.

5. Click Yes when asked whether to restart the PC.

To set up a Windows ME PC as the host PC, follow these steps:

1. Make sure that your Home Network Wizard has been launched from the previous steps. If it has not, double-click the My Network Places icon on your Windows desktop and then double-click the Home Network Wizard icon in the My Network Places window.

2. From the welcome screen, click Next and then click Edit Home Network Settings on This PC.

3. You are asked whether you want to connect to the Internet through another PC or through a direct connection to your ISP, as shown in Figure 14.6. Choose the direct connection and then choose the device with which you will connect to the Internet (either a NIC to your broadband modem or a dial-up modem). Click Next.

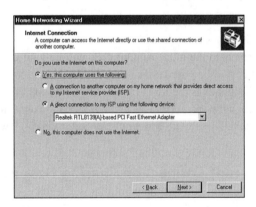

FIGURE 14.6

Sharing an Internet connection in Windows ME.

4. You are asked whether you want other PCs on the network to connect to the Internet through this computer. Click Yes and then choose the NIC that is connected to the network (it will be the NIC connected into an Ethernet hub/switch if you use an Ethernet network).

5. You are asked to give your PC a unique name and a workgroup name. Be sure to use the same name and workgroup that previously identified the PC. If you have not given the PC a name and workgroup yet, give a name to the PC that will uniquely identify it on the network, and be sure to use the same workgroup name for each PC on the network.

CAUTION

Remember that some broadband ISPs require that you use a specific name and workgroup name for the PC connecting directly to the Internet. Check with your ISP to see whether you are required to give your PC a specific name and workgroup ID. The other PCs connecting through the host PC will use the same workgroup name to connect to the host PC, but will not be required to use the same PC name.

6. Click through to the part where you are asked whether you want to create a home network setup disk. If you are networking Windows 98 or 95 PCs, you need to use a home network setup disk. If you are using Windows ME or XP, you do not need to create a setup disk because you can simply configure the client PCs using the home networking wizard.

7. Click Next and then click Finish. When asked whether to restart your PC, click Yes.

To enable a Windows XP PC as the host PC, follow these steps:

1. Launch the Network Setup Wizard by clicking Start, Control Panel, Network and Internet Connections, and then clicking Set Up or Change Your Home or Small Office Network.

2. Click Next twice until you get to the screen that asks you to select a connection method. Select the option that indicates that this PC connects directly to the Internet (the host PC) and other PCs will connect through this PC.

3. Click Next.

4. If you have a broadband modem connected through Ethernet, select the NIC connected to the modem when asked to select the Internet connection, as shown in Figure 14.7. If you are using a dial-up modem, select the modem as your connection.

14

INTERNET SHARING ON A HOME NETWORK

FIGURE 14.7

Choosing your Internet connection in the Windows XP Network Setup Wizard.

5. You are asked for a computer name. Give your PC the name you have previously used to connect it to the network. Click Next.

6. The Name Your Network prompt appears. Put in the name of the workgroup you are using. If you set up a workgroup in Chapter 10, you will want to use the same workgroup name. The default name for a workgroup in Windows is MSHOME, which is fine to use if you do not already have a workgroup name.

7. Click Next and you get a summary of the settings. If all the information looks correct, click Next and follow the instructions. Say Yes when you are asked whether to restart your PC.

If you are using a broadband connection, you can also set up Internet Connection Sharing in Windows XP through the local area network Properties window.

To activate ICS manually through Windows XP, do this:

1. Click Start, Control Panel, Network and Internet Connections, and then Network Connections.

2. On the NIC that connects to the broadband modem, right-click and select Properties.

3. Click on the Advanced tab.

4. In the Internet Connection Sharing box (below the Internet Connection Firewall), check the box that says Allow Other Network Users to Connect Through This Computer's Internet Connection.

Setting Up an Internet Connection Sharing Client PC

After you set up the PC that will be sharing the Internet connection as the host PC, you will want to set up the different PCs that will be accessing the Internet as clients using Internet Connection Sharing in Windows. The steps vary slightly depending on the operating system you are using, so we will look at each.

Before you set up each client PC using the home network or Internet connection wizards, you will want to make sure that each PC is configured to obtain an IP address automatically. As you read in Chapter 10, you will need to have the IP protocol installed and configured on each PC to use Internet sharing in Windows. You more than likely have already configured Windows to assign an IP address automatically, but in case you haven't, you will want to read Chapter 10's sections on IP addressing titled "Configuring IP Addresses in Windows 95/98/ME" and "Configuring IP Addresses in Windows XP" to learn how to do so.

With both Windows 98 and ME, the home network wizard automatically enables the host PC to act as the DHCP server by embedding this capability in its memory. With the client PCs, you will want to go through the steps in Chapter 10 if you previously configured the PCs to used fixed (nondynamic) IP addresses.

After you set up a client PC to access the Internet using ICS, you should be able to access the Internet at any time by launching a browser on the client PC. This will tell the host PC to dial in to the ISP if it is using a dial-up modem, or will directly connect to the Internet over a broadband modem.

Setting Up a Windows 98 PC as an ICS Client

If you set up a Windows 98 or ME PC as the host PC, you were asked during the process of setting up the host to install a floppy disk to create a home networking disk for the client computers. You will need that disk now.

1. Insert the floppy disk into the client PC.

2. Click Run and then click Browse. If you used Windows 98 SE as the host PC, browse the A: drive and look for a file that looks like A:\icsclset.exe. If you used Windows ME as the host PC, the file will look like A:\setup.exe. Double-click on this executable file and then follow the instructions through the wizard to configure the PC.

3. Click Yes when asked whether to restart the PC.

After you run the home network setup disk on the client, you should be able to access the Internet on the client PC through the host PC's modem. You should be able to access the

14

INTERNET SHARING
ON A HOME
NETWORK

Internet through a dial-up or broadband modem by clicking on your browser. You will want to make sure that the host PC is turned on when attempting to access the Internet through a client PC.

Setting Up a Windows ME PC as an ICS Client

Unlike with Windows 98, when setting up a Windows ME PC as a client, you will not need a home networking setup disk, but instead will just run the Home Networking Wizard.

1. Launch the Home Network Wizard through the My Network Places screen.

2. Click Next and then check that you want to change or edit your home network settings. Click Next.

3. In the Internet Connection portion, click Yes This Computer Uses a Connection to Another Computer on My Home Network. Click Next.

4. Give your PC a name and a workgroup name. Use the same name you have previously used if you have already set up your home network. If not, be sure to use the same work-group name as that of the host PC.

5. Click No when asked whether you want to create a home network setup disk. Click Next and then Finish. When asked whether you would like to restart the PC, click Yes.

Setting Up a Windows XP PC as an ICS Client

When setting up a Windows XP PC as the client, you will use the Network Setup Wizard:

1. To launch the Network Setup Wizard, double-click on the My Network Places icon on your Windows desktop, and on the left side of the My Network Places window, click Set Up a Home or Small Office Network.

2. Click Next to get to the third screen of the wizard, and then choose the option labeled This Computer Connects to the Internet Through Another Computer on My Network or Through a Residential Gateway. Click Next.

3. You are asked to choose the connection to your network. You are given the option to let Windows choose the connection or to choose yourself. If you have more than one NIC on your PC, click the Let Me Choose option. Otherwise, click the option that allows Windows to choose and click Next.

4. You need to give your PC a name. Enter the name of your PC as you want it to be identi-fied on the network. If you have already set up your network in Windows, give it the name you used previously. Click Next.

5. You are asked to name your network. Use the same workgroup name as you did when setting up your host PC.

6. Click until you have the Finish option. When asked whether you want to restart your PC, click Yes.

Other Internet Sharing Software

You've now seen how to share your Internet connection using the built-in capabilities of Windows. If you are set on using a software-based solution, I strongly recommend using the built-in capabilities of Windows. However, there are also good standalone software packages that enable you to share an Internet connection.

Table 14.2 lists some software vendors who make Internet sharing software. You will find the name of the product as well as a Web address where you can find out more about the product. Much of the Internet sharing software available today is freeware, meaning that you can download it free. One place to go on the Web for downloads of freeware is www.cnet.com, which offers many kinds of software packages. There you can get free downloads of such Internet sharing programs as WinProxy, one of the most popular.

TABLE 14.2   Internet Sharing Software

Software Vendor	Product	Web Address
Avirt	Avirt SOHO	www.avirt.com
Ositis	WinPproxy	www.ositis.com
Sygate	Sygate Home Network	www.sygate.com
Tiny Software	WinRoute Lite	www.tinysoftware.com
Vicomsoft	Internet Gateway	www.vicomsoft
Wingate	Wingate Home	www.wingate.com

Some of the Internet sharing software shown in Table 14.2 offers benefits you might not get when using the built-in capabilities of Windows ICS. For example, WinRoute Lite from Tiny Software offers a built-in firewall. As you will find out in Chapter 19, firewalls protect your PC and network from unwelcome intruders trying to access your PC over the Internet.

Sygate's Home Network software also includes a built-in firewall, as well as a capability the company has named OneNIC. OneNIC enables the user to share a broadband Internet connection using just one NIC, rather than the normally required two (you require only one if you are using a home router).

Other software that would enable Internet sharing would be for non-Windows–based PCs. Vicomsoft makes a product that enables Internet sharing on Apple's Macintosh operating system.

14

INTERNET SHARING
ON A HOME
NETWORK

Wrap It Up

In this chapter you learned how to share your Internet connection with multiple PCs over a home network. Internet sharing using a home network can be done using either a hardware solution or a software solution. Each of these solutions has its own unique benefits.

Internet sharing hardware is often called a home router or gateway. Here are some important things to remember about home routers:

- They usually connect to a broadband modem and the different PCs on the network.
- The home router often incorporates a built-in hub or switch (or access point for wireless), allowing you to replace this piece of networking equipment and enable Internet sharing at the same time.
- Home routers enable the sharing of one IP address among multiple PCs and provide some level of inherent security.
- Home router setup and configuration is pretty simple, and is often done through a browser-based configuration utility.

Internet sharing software is available as a service in newer Windows operating systems, or through separate software packages. The Windows-based Internet sharing service is called Internet Connection Sharing, or ICS. ICS is available in Windows 98 Second Edition, Windows Millennium, and Windows XP.

Other software packages for Internet sharing are widely available on the Internet. Many of these packages are freeware, which means that the products can be downloaded and installed free.

Unleash the Network

IN THIS PART

Home Networks and
Entertainment: Audio, Video,
and Gaming

IN THIS CHAPTER

Time to Have Fun

Although networks are seen by many people as serious and important things, not to be trivialized by something like having fun (these people typically wear starched shirts and are named something like Thaddeus), you are about to find that networks can make your life much more, well, fun. The network is a great distribution platform for audio and video content, as well as a way to connect those who want to go head-to-head in a video game. This chapter explores making your network a home entertainment network.

Although we could spend days and days (and chapters and chapters) explaining how to wire your home for whole-home video and audio, I am here to tell you that we won't. There are plenty of books on whole-home A/V (audio/visual), and I suggest that if you want to zap DVD content over coaxial cable to each room and set up multiple zones in your home to rock out to Menudo, then you should check out one of these books. But if you instead want to find out how to begin to leverage your home network for entertainment—the same kind we've spend the past 12 chapters talking about and setting up—then you've come to the right place.

This chapter looks at the ways you can begin to distribute audio, video, and gaming from one networked PC to another. We will also look at ways to use a networked PC as a server for both video and audio content, as well as ways to connect your DVD drive to a TV.

Let's first take a look at audio distribution using your home network.

Home Networked Audio

The capability to send digital music around your home using a home network is a reality today. Whether it's the MP3 audio we talked about in earlier chapters or streaming audio directly from the Internet, the capability to listen to music or other content from anywhere in the home is one of the newest and most popular applications of home network technology.

We'll explore two basic home audio networks:

- *PC to PC*—Sending audio files around the home using a home network
- *PC to Stereo/Audio Receiver*—Sending audio files to a stereo or a networked audio receiver using a home network

Before we do that, let's look quickly at how to make your PC an audio server by using MP3 software.

A Ripping Good Time: Creating MP3 Files

One of the best ways to create a digital "jukebox" out of your PC is to take the music that is currently on CDs or even on the Internet and store it on your PC's hard drive. This can be done easily and quickly with software and a CD-ROM drive.

CAUTION

The music industry has been actively fighting free distribution of copyrighted content over music-swapping services such as Napster. It is up to the individual whether to use a music-swapping service, but you should educate yourself about the possible legal consequences. Taking your own CDs and then putting the music on your PC in MP3 format is perfectly legal, however, as long you do not redistribute the content to others outside of your household.

Software that creates MP3 files from other file formats (such as those on a CD) are called "rippers." Rippers allow you to basically translate one file format to another. Many kinds of rippers (including the first two in the following list) are available from www.download.com. These are some of the more popular ones:

- MusicMatch Jukebox
- Easy CD-DA Extractor
- Real Networks RealJukebox

After loading a ripper program onto your hard drive, you can simply start the program and follow the instructions for converting files to MP3 format. I suggest putting all your music files such as the MP3 files in their own hard-drive directory so that you can access them easily when you are ready to listen to the music on the network.

After you have ripped and saved some music files, you will want to be able to listen to them. This is done easily through an audio player. With audio players, you can listen to not only MP3 files, but other file formats as well.

Table 15.1 lists available players for MP3 and other digital audio files. You should know that MP3 is not the only file format for digital audio, only the most popular for digital music distribution from a PC. Most rippers, such as the ones listed previously, can also act as digital audio players. If you want to learn more about digital audio and streaming media, go to www.streamingmedia.com.

NOTE

Streaming media is the term for the distribution of media content (audio, video) over the Internet in a constant "stream" as opposed to a full download. You can listen or play a file and have the file come to you in bits, rather than getting the whole file at once. When you play an MP3 across a home network, it is essentially streaming over the network in bits and pieces (or packets), rather than in one large chunky file.

TABLE 15.1   Digital Audio Player Software

Player	Web Address
RealPlayer	www.real.com
Microsoft Windows Media Player	www.microsoft.com
Winamp	www.winamp.com
Sonique Media Player	www.sonique.lycos.com
Apple QuickTime	www.apple.com

PC-to-PC Home Audio Networks

If you are curious about where you can share digital music files, here's the answer: wherever you have a networked PC. The basic home network, with some basic software, is all you need to get started. Before we show you how to connect your PCs in a home audio network, let's take a quick look at the basic software requirements for a home audio network.

All you need to do is simply access the drive with the stored digital music files on it with an audio player, and then import the files for play. When you import audio files, you do not need to actually place these files locally on a PC's hard drive. Instead, the process of importing files is that of listing all the relevant file info, such as the title of the song and the size of the file.

The process of importing, also called opening or adding files, to your audio player is very easy. We'll walk you through importing some MP3 files in an audio player called Winamp, a free audio player available at www.winamp.com. We will look at playing MP3 files that are located on a hard drive on a PC somewhere on the network other than the PC you will be playing the music from.

After Winamp is installed on a PC, this is all you do:

1. Go to the bottom of the player and click Add Dir, short for add directory. This allows you to play all files in a certain directory.

2. In the Open Directory dialog box, scroll down to My Network Places (or Network Neighborhood in Windows 95/98), as shown in Figure 15.1. Double-click on My Network Places.

3. Choose the PC and then the directory you would like to open. After you click OK, all the music files stored in this directory will stay resident in the player's memory.

4. Click the Play button and enjoy the music.

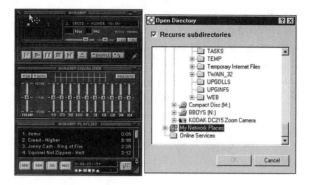

FIGURE 15.1
Importing music files over a network.

Again, it is often helpful to locate all your music such as MP3 files in one directory on one PC. Another way you can organize your music is through playlists. All the popular audio players allow you to group your favorites into playlists, and when you play these, the player will access the different music files on the network within the playlist.

PC-to-Stereo/Audio Receiver Home Audio Networks

Whole sets of new devices have emerged to allow you to distribute audio over your home network to your stereo system or just about anywhere you want without using a PC as an audio receiver. These new networked audio receivers can use Ethernet, phoneline, wireless, or even powerline networking as the medium to transport signals around the home. Figure 15.2 shows how a networked audio receiver fits within a home network.

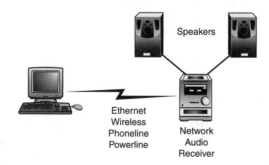

Speakers

Ethernet
Wireless
Phoneline
Powerline

Network
Audio
Receiver

FIGURE 15.2
A network audio receiver on a home network.

Depending on what type of receiver you are using, particularly with a wireless network audio device, you might need a special transmitter device that connects to your PC. Some receivers may just use the network interface card you have installed. You will certainly need whatever type of technology is specific to the audio receiver. For example, if your audio receiver is phoneline based, you need a phoneline NIC to communicate with this device. Most networked receivers include a NIC or whatever transmitting device is necessary to communicate with the receiver.

Table 15.2 lists networked audio products that will allow you to distribute different audio files around your home network.

TABLE 15.2 Digital Audio Receivers for Home Networks

Company/Product	Network Technology/Other	Web Address
S3/Rio Receiver	Phoneline & Ethernet (powerline will be supported in future)/Supports MP3 and Windows Media Player formats	www.riohome.com
Dell/Digital Audio Receiver	Phoneline & Ethernet/ Supports MP3 and Windows Media Player formats	www.dell.com
Compaq/iPaq Music Center	Phoneline & Ethernet/ Has hard drive for storing music/Can connect to stereo, TV, LP Player	www.compaq.com
X10/MP3 Anywhere	Wireless/Uses transmitter unit from PC to send to any stereo unit by connecting to receiver unit	www.x10.com

Home Networked Video

What about video over a home network? Believe it or not, you can share video files around the home, much like you can your audio files. However, because video files are much larger than audio files, the capability to send video files such as those from a DVD player on your PC to another PC might be limited to the speed of your home network. For example, if you have a wireless home network that operates at 10Mbps, this will likely not be fast enough to send a DVD signal over the network. Because 10Mbps is the theoretical speed and the actual speed is more likely in the 5Mbps to 7Mbps range (and even lower if you are transmitting through walls), the video quality is likely to be even lower.

Because of the higher demands of video, creating a whole-home video network that distributes TV-quality-video can require the installation of a structured wiring system. The capability to play video from a source such as a DVD, a VCR, and cable TV to other viewing screens relies on high-quality video wiring such as RG-6 coaxial cable, which is part of a structured wiring system. You can refer to Chapter 8, "Other Networking Technologies: Phoneline, Powerline, and Structured Wiring Ethernet," to learn more about having a structured wiring system installed in your home.

Some products, such as one called Avcast (from a company called Broadband Home), allow you to use your existing coax cable installed for cable TV to distribute your video, audio, and even data around the home. You can share a DVD or VCR, as well as your cable set-top box, through the existing coaxial cable in your home by installing their components. Figure 15.3 shows how an Avcast network works. You can find out more about Avcast at www.avcast.com.

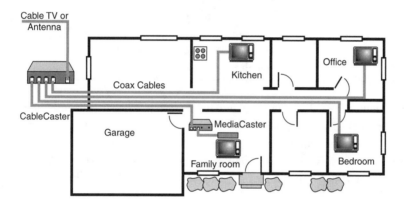

FIGURE 15.3

An Avcast video home network.

You can send video over an Ethernet network, even if the quality is not as high as you are used to seeing when you watch TV from your couch. If you do have a DVD player on one of your PCs or simply want to access video files stored on your hard drive, you should be able to access that PC from other PCs after you have installed video player software. Various video player software is available today, often coming with your hardware such as a new DVD drive. You will need to check whether you can install the software on networked PCs for playing a DVD or other type of drive over the network.

You can also create a distribution network for standalone video sources (DVD or VCR) to distribute to other TVs in the house, without having to install new whole-home video wiring, using some of the newer technologies. Some of these products use wireless technology, and some even use home phonelines. Table 15.3 lists some of the products available to extend your video source to other rooms in the house, even without the use of a PC-based home network.

TABLE 15.3   Non-PC Video Distribution Products Using No-New-Wire Networks

Company/Product	Technology/Description	Web Address
X-10/DVD Anywhere	Wireless/Sends video wirelessly from any video source around the home	www.x10.com
Terk/WaveMaster 20	Wireless/Sends video wirelessly from any video source around the home	www.terk.com
Terk/LeapFrog Home Network System	Phoneline/Sends video using existing in-home phonelines from any source to any TV	www.terk.com
SercoNet (products available soon)	Can send video, PC, and other network traffic over existing phonelines at high speeds	www.serconet.co.il

Clearly, many options are available for video distribution in a house. Because of the rapid changes in home networking technology, there will be many more new products forthcoming in the next few years that will allow you to send video streams around the home. Also, existing technologies such as IEEE 1394 will advance to become a home networking distribution of video and other high-value content. For more information on IEEE 1394, see the following sidebar.

Firewire: Extending the Multimedia Network

What is firewire? Firewire is the consumer name for a technology called IEEE 1394. You might remember the IEEE moniker from our discussions of Ethernet technology, which is also called IEEE 802.13. Both are standards developed by the IEEE, but they have very different goals.

Ethernet, as you know, was designed primarily for networking PCs. IEEE 1394, which we will refer to as Firewire, is a high-speed connection technology specifically geared toward distribution of multimedia. Firewire is really big among consumer electronics companies, which have all begun to put Firewire ports on their latest gadgets such as video players and TVs. PCs are also beginning to get Firewire connections, and with Microsoft's strong support of Firewire, Windows XP has the best Firewire support yet. It's no wonder that all these companies have latched onto this standard, because it allows you to send multimedia content at speeds up to 400Mbps, with new speeds of up to 1600Mbps in the future. That's 1.6 *gigabits*!

So is Firewire a home network technology? It is fast becoming so, especially now that the folks in the IEEE have developed new technology that allows for Firewire to be transferred over longer distances. Originally Firewire was developed by Apple Computer, and when it was developed, it was built to go distances of four meters. In a whole-home network, four meters is not enough, so the new standard called IEEE 1394b allows for longer distances.

Still, Firewire requires a special cabling, so even when new versions of the technology are available, you will still need to put 1394 cable around the home, if you want to send Firewire signals over longer distances. Nevertheless, keep an eye out in the future for Firewire becoming a big part of multimedia home networks.

Gaming on a Home Network

One of the best reasons to install a home network is to participate in multiplayer gaming. Going head-to-head with someone else on your network, or even on the Internet, is extremely fun and could end up as one of the top uses of your home network.

Here's all you need in order to play a game over a home network:

- A network-compatible game—most games indicate on the purchase package or on the download description whether they can be played over a network
- Joysticks or other gaming hardware you desire; most games can be played with a keyboard and a mouse
- Support of networking protocols for a specific game
- Adequate PCs to support whatever game you decide to play

Perhaps the most important requirements are the last two. Because different games are authored by different people using different systems, you might need to have not only TCP/IP supported, but also IPX/SPX and NetBEUI. These are protocols included with each Windows operating system; installing network protocols is reviewed in Chapter 9, "Setting Up Home Network Software." In recent years, most games developed for multiplayer gaming have supported TCP/IP because it is the dominant networking protocol.

You also need to make sure that each PC on the network can support the games. Games are probably one of the most taxing uses of a PC, and some older PCs have trouble with some of the newer games. You want to make sure that your PC has the required hardware and software as outlined on the box or, if you downloaded the game, within the specifications on the download site.

15

HOME NETWORKS AND ENTERTAINMENT

Installing a piece of network gaming software is simple. You need to install the game on each PC on which you want to play. This is because the game processing happens locally on each PC, while information regarding your opponent (and vice versa) travels over the network.

When you play a networked game, you will usually need to designate a host. The host is the person/PC who initiates the game, and after a game is initiated, other players can join. Most games ask you at startup whether you will be playing solo or with others. When you choose to play a network game that has already been hosted, you can just click Join Existing Game and you'll be ready to go.

Let the Games Begin

Okay, so you want to begin gaming but you're not sure where to actually get a game? Don't worry, there are plenty of free, downloadable games on the Internet, as well as even a basic game available in some versions of Windows you can use. You can also check any purchased game you already own and see whether it has a network option, as well as go to any software store and browse the wide variety of games that are network compatible.

To check out the Internet for some free downloadable games, check out www.download.com. You can also go to gaming portal www.gamespot.com for a wide array of downloadable game demos, as well as information about network gaming in general.

Let's Play Acies

We'll take a look at a basic program by the name of Acies, which is a network-enabled chess and checkers game that can be downloaded free. Acies can be downloaded at www.download.com or www.easyfreeware.com.

Acies is a great game to get started with in network gaming because it is easy to install, and it is a game that can be used by almost anyone in the family. Many network games have some level of violent content, so if you have young children in your house, a game like Acies is a good choice.

After downloading Acies to your PC, you can install it by simply going to My Computer and finding the directory it was saved in. Double-click on the setup file and let Acies walk you through installation. You need to install Acies on any PC on the network that you want to play the game on.

After Acies is installed on each PC that will be participating, you can start play simply by following these steps:

1. Click Start, then Programs, and then click the Acies icon.
2. A pop-up screen asks whether you want to be the host or a guest, as shown in Figure 15.4.

FIGURE 15.4

Choosing to be the host or a guest in a networked game.

3. Click Host and then put in your name next to Nick (short for Nickname). Click Listen.

4. A hosting-game message pops up, indicating that the host PC is listening for a guest to connect at a given network/IP address.

5. On the guest PC, click on the Acies icon as indicated previously, and when asked, choose to play as a guest. When asked, enter both your name and the name of the host.

6. Click the Connect button, and you will see the game board launch with the name of you and your opponent, as shown in Figure 15.5. You can choose to play either chess or checkers.

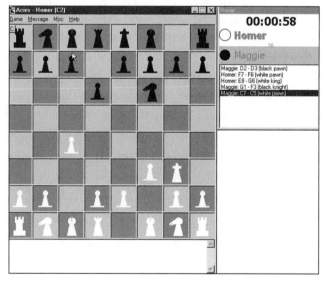

FIGURE 15.5

Playing chess over a home network.

Acies is only the beginning of the fun you can have with networked games. There are games for all types, ranging from strategy games to flight simulators to battle and arcade games. Card games are extremely popular as well, and one of the games included in Windows 95/98 and

ME (but not XP) for network gaming is Hearts. You can play Hearts against one or more opponents on a network, simply by choosing to play a multiplayer game when starting your Hearts session. Playing Hearts can be another good way to get started with network gaming.

Another extremely popular genre of multiplayer games is the shoot-em-up kind, such as Doom, Quake, and Descent. These games are very realistic and can deliver hours of heart-pounding excitement. You should be aware that because these games are so realistic, they aren't advisable for young children.

Wrap It Up

Home networking is much more than simply passing data from one PC to another. A home network can be an entertainment infrastructure, allowing you to distribute audio and video around the home to and from any PC, as well as to non-PC entertainment components such as your stereo and television. Network gaming is also a great way to take advantage of the connections you have among PCs, allowing you (or someone in your home) to earn bragging rights about who is the king of the latest shoot-em-up.

Digital audio distribution is extremely popular among home network users. You can send MP3 or other music files from one PC to another using basic audio-player software. You can also use some of the newer network products to send digital audio files from your PC to any stereo in the house using phoneline, wireless, and Ethernet technology.

You can use your home network to send video streams to different PCs on the home network. Some new home network products also allow you to send video signals from different sources around the home on existing coax cabling. You can also use other products that utilize wireless and phoneline technology.

Many games today are enabled for network gaming. Network games usually require one PC to act as a host and others to join the game session as guests. Many free network-enabled games are available on the Internet, and Windows 95/98 and ME include a network-enabled card game called Hearts.

Using Non-PC Devices on the Home Network

IN THIS CHAPTER

It's Not Just PCs Anymore

For years, industry pundits have been calling for the end of the PC era, saying that new gadgets in various shapes and sizes would take over and the PC would soon be a thing of the past. Visions of PC museums popped up, where people would walk through halls lined with beige boxes and keyboards, all the while snapping pictures and waxing sentimental.

Well, don't plan your day trip to this little museum just yet. It's clear that the personal computer is not going away soon, and chances are it will be here for a long time to come. But what does that mean for these new gadgets, and what exactly were these things anyway? Were they able to connect to a home network?

The truth of the matter is that non-PC devices have been connected to networks for some time. Specialized devices targeted to complete a specialized set of functions have been in use in business networks and warehouses, and now are beginning to make their way into homes. These specialized devices often communicate wirelessly, through powerlines, or even through standard Ethernet connections.

So What Is a Non-PC Device Anyway?

Following are some examples of non-PC devices that have existed in the business environment:

- Print servers
- Networked storage devices
- Bar-code readers
- Networked machinery such as industrial equipment
- Personal digital assistants, or PDAs
- Networked phones

You might not be surprised at some of these devices, because many of us have become aware of handheld PDAs that connect to our PCs and allow us to organize our day (my wife would wander around in circles, bumping into walls, without hers). With the popularity of home networks surging and the thing we call convergence in full force, we are beginning to see new types of devices other than PCs begin to enter the home, many targeted for home users. Some of these new devices are called Internet appliances.

Internet appliances can range from what are called Web pads (small handheld screens you can use to surf the Web) to Internet alarm clocks (small clock radios that are connected to the Internet for music and news updates). Some of these devices might have a built-in dial-up modem, or might connect to a home network using a wireless connection. Although those devices that don't directly connect to your PC might not be part of a home network (but

Using Non-PC Devices on the Home Network

CHAPTER 16

283

16

USING NON-PC
DEVICES ON THE
HOME NETWORK

instead call directly with their own modem to the Internet), they can still be a nice complement to a PC-based home network.

> **NOTE**
>
> *Internet appliances* are any non-PC devices that connect to the Internet directly or through the home network for the purpose of communicating both internally and on the Internet.

In this chapter, we will examine non-PC devices that can be used as part of your home network. We will explore the different kinds of non-PC devices and then look at a few examples of products you might consider using to make your network more valuable.

Although there are all sorts of devices that will eventually communicate with one another, we will focus specifically on three categories of non-PC devices:

- Network storage devices
- Internet appliances
- PDAs (such as Palm and Pocket PC devices)

Let's start by taking a look at network storage devices.

> **TIP**
>
> For a look at connecting your home systems and appliances to your home network, check out Chapter 21, "Smart Home: Home Automation Networks."

Network Storage Devices: Your Network Filing Cabinet

The capability to store information is very important on any network, whether a large office network, a Web server, or a home network. The cost of storage—what we would normally call hard drives—has gone down significantly in recent years, and now we more than likely buy PCs with hard drives in the tens (and soon hundreds) of gigabytes, rather than just lowly old megabytes (or even, if you've been around for a while, kilobytes).

And now storage is no longer confined to hard drives in a PC. In fact, hard drives themselves can be attached directly to a network. Admittedly, not a lot of people today have what is called network attached storage, or NAS, in their home, but this might change very soon.

NOTE

Network attached storage, or *NAS*, is basically networked hard drives. These devices act as servers, except that they are not generally part of a standalone computer. NAS devices are generally used in business environments, although, as you will see, NAS devices are beginning to make their way into the home.

You're probably asking yourself why you would want to use a NAS device in your home such as that shown in Figure 16.1, as opposed to just taking advantage of a hard drive in a PC, or even other removable media such as a Zip drive that can be attached to your PC. Well, some of the differentiating features of a NAS device are listed here:

- The devices can be directly networked, because most have an Ethernet port for directly connecting to a hub or switch.
- Most have nice management features such as embedded Web servers.
- The actual storage space on these devices is much higher than that of a Zip or writable CD-ROM drive. Most start at 20 gigabytes and go up from there.
- Unlike a PC's hard drive (but like a Zip drive) these devices are very portable, most weighing only a few pounds.
- If you want to create a home server or even a Web server, these devices can be a good way to get started.

FIGURE 16.1
A network attached storage device.

Setting up a NAS device is extremely simple. Because these devices have network connections built in, they look like another PC to the network. You will likely be able to get an IP address assigned to your NAS device automatically, or configure one through the setup screen with your NAS software.

The one downside of NAS devices is that they are not exactly cheap. Although storage costs overall have come down, you are still paying for the large amounts of storage included, as well as the embedded intelligence of these devices. The smallest NAS devices, which usually have

Using Non-PC Devices on the Home Network

CHAPTER 16

285

16

USING NON-PC
DEVICES ON THE
HOME NETWORK

at least 20 gigabytes of storage space, start at around $500. This price will go down over time, especially as more products for the home are brought to market. This compares with about $100 for a good USB Zip drive. Table 16.1 highlights the names and prices of network attached storage products.

TABLE 16.1 Network Attached Storage Products

Company	Product/Starting Price	Web Address
Linksys	EtherFast Instant GigaDrive/$499	www.linksys.com
Netgear	Netgear Network Disk Drive/$499	www.netgear.com
Cobalt	Qube 3 Server Appliance/$999 (this product is designed to be a Web server)	www.cobalt.com
Snap Appliances	Snap 1000/$499	www.snapappliances.com

The bottom line in deciding whether a NAS device is right for you depends on what you plan to do with your network and whether you want to pay extra for the convenience and functionality of such a product. The $500 or so dollars required to get a basic network storage device should be weighed against what you get. If you want to create an internal intranet site or even create your own Web site, one of these products might be a good idea. If you are simply looking to back up a hard drive, you might consider a cheaper alternative such as a Zip or a writable CD-ROM drive.

> **TIP**
>
> For even larger storage, Iomega, the manufacturer of ZIP drives, also makes Jaz drives, which use removable disks of one or two gigabytes of storage. A Jaz drive, like Zip drives and many of the CD-RW and DVD-RW drives, can connect to your PC through a USB or parallel port and can be configured to share over a network. Jaz drives start at about $250.

Internet Appliances: The Internet Moves Out of the PC

What are these things called Internet appliances? Although the term *Internet appliance* might have you thinking about Web-surfing dishwashers (believe it or not, some companies are thinking about such things), the true purpose of Internet appliances is to let people get on the

Internet and perform functions such as Web surfing, sending e-mail and performing instant messaging, all without using a PC. The idea is that PCs are complex devices (What? No!!) and that not everyone will want to use a PC to enjoy the benefits of the Internet. Whether or not you believe this to be true, a whole bunch of companies do and are rushing products to market that fall into the Internet appliance category.

Should you use an Internet appliance? Well, if one of the following statements is true, you might consider using such a device in lieu of a standalone PC:

- You, or a person in your family, is intimidated by using a PC but wants to access the Internet.

- You want to use a small and portable device to access the Internet (even lugging around a laptop connected to a network can be burdensome), and you're interested in the really convenient small Web-surfing devices.

- You want a specific function that can be performed by an Internet appliance that you can't really get in a PC (for example, an Internet alarm clock—yes, there *are* Internet alarm clocks).

- You want to have the latest technological gizmos and would like to use some of the new Internet appliances to wow and impress your friends.

As you can see, there are a few categories of Internet appliances. Table 16.2 lists types of Internet appliances, as well as companies and their products that fit in the specific category.

TABLE 16.2   Internet Appliances and Who Makes Them

Internet Appliance Category	Description	Company/Product
Web pads	Wireless devices with touch screens that let you surf the Web anywhere in your home	Intel/Web Tablet; Honeywell/WebPAD; Ericsson/Cordless Web Screen; Qubit/Orbit Web Tablet
Internet terminals	Appliances that connect to the Internet and have their own keyboards but are smaller than PCs; some of these allow you to surf and send emaile-mail using your TV	Microsoft/WebTV; AOL-TimeWarner/AOLTV; Compaq/iPAQ; Intel/dot.Station; Sony/eVilla

TABLE 16.2 Continued

Internet Appliance Category	Description	Company/Product
Internet-connected smart devices	Small devices in the home that take advantage of a built-in Internet connection, such as an Internet alarm clock or picture frame	Lavazza e-espressopoint (a networked coffee maker); Simple Devices/SimpleClock (Internet alarm clock); Kodak/Smart Picture Frame
E-mail stations	Low-cost (between $100 and $200) devices that allow you to do e-mail through their own modem or through a network connection	Cidco/Mailstation, Landel/MailBug, Sharp/TelMail TM-20. Simpliance/e-MailBox

This table shows you that there is no shortage of new and interesting devices that can take advantage of an Internet connection. These products vary widely in price, and you should carefully review them before purchasing one. Also, you should ask yourself whether you really need one (okay, so no one really needs an Internet alarm clock, but it might make for good water-cooler talk).

Next we take a closer look at an Internet appliance called a Web pad from the microprocessor giant Intel. This quick examination is intended to give you an idea of how an Internet appliance works.

A Closer Look: Web Tablet

Intel's Web tablet is a neat product—set to be delivered by the company sometime in 2001 or early 2002—that allows users to surf the Web anywhere around the home using a wireless LAN connection to their PC. The PC acts as a server for the Internet connection, and the Web tablet acts as a wireless receiving terminal.

As you can see in Figure 16.2, a Web tablet is a small and portable device that communicates to a PC through a wireless NIC. The product itself can be set up to use the modem built into the PC, or it can use the PC's connection to a LAN and then access a modem elsewhere on the network.

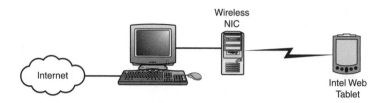

FIGURE 16.2
A Web tablet on a home network.

Depending on what your existing network is, you might need to also buy a wireless NIC to communicate with the Web pad. If you do not have a wireless NIC, such as Intel's AnyPoint Home RF NIC, you will need to buy one.

> **CAUTION**
>
> With the first version of the Intel Web tablet, you need to use an Intel AnyPoint wireless NIC. These products use the Home RF standard as the wireless LAN technology. In the future, Intel will have Wi-Fi wireless LAN NICs and Web tablets, so you will need to be sure to check the labels of each carefully.

The software provided allows the PC to act as a server for the Web tablet. The software takes the PC's Internet connection, whether a local modem or a connection through a home network, and then routes any incoming or outgoing information to and from the Web pad.

Web pads can be set up using basic installation software provided with the product. As you can see in Figure 16.3, Intel's product has a wizard that helps you configure the PC's connection for the Internet. The Web pad is designed to automatically search for a connection when it is turned on for the first time. When a connection is made from the Web pad, you will be able to configure the Web pad for your particular preferences, as well as set up different user profiles for members of your family.

The Intel Web pad is only one example of the products that are fast becoming available to the general public. Other companies such as Compaq, Sony, Ericsson, and MainStreetNetworks are also delivering neat products that allow you to surf the Internet anywhere in your home. And as you saw in Table 16.2, there are plenty of other types of Internet appliances that can be connected to your network.

Using Non-PC Devices on the Home Network

CHAPTER 16

289

16

USING NON-PC
DEVICES ON THE
HOME NETWORK

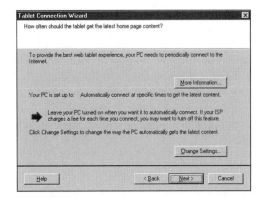

FIGURE 16.3
The Web pad configuration screen.

PDAs: The Handheld Gets Connected

The handheld assistant market has exploded over the past few years. At first, both business executives and technology enthusiasts discovered the convenience of having all their personal information at their fingertips in these powerful devices that can fit in a pocket. As prices came down and the number of models proliferated, personal digital assistants, or PDAs, were soon being used by much more than the early-adopter crowd, and now you can see everyone from students to stay-at-home parents tapping away at these devices.

Personal digital assistants were designed to connect to your PC and allow you to take important information such as contacts and calendars, as well as files such as Word documents, on the road with you. The latest models include the capability to play music, such as MP3 files, and record your voice. And, with the capability to add expansion slots to many of the models, you can even allow your PDA to connect to your PC from anywhere on a network.

PDAs are generally available in two types:

- Those based on the Palm platform
- Those based on Microsoft's Pocket PC platform (originally called Windows CE)

Both types have their devoted followers, and there are some differences between the two. However, for our purposes, you should know that both can be connected to a home network.

The conventional way for a PDA to connect to a PC is through a cradle or a cable to allow for what is called syncing.

> **NOTE**
>
> *Syncing* is the process of connecting your PC with your PDA to allow for communication of important information. When you sync a PC and a PDA, the PDA gets the latest information from the PC such as contacts and calendar information, while any information that you entered into your PDA is relayed and updated to the PC. You can also send files such as word processor or spreadsheet documents to some models of PDAs.

Another way a PDA may connect is through an ad hoc connection to another PDA. PDAs can create ad hoc connections, essentially small networks, for exchanging data such as business-card information. Even models based on the Palm and Pocket PC platforms can exchange information. These ad hoc connections have traditionally connected using infrared, which is a small beam of light that has limited range. Newer connections are using wireless technology such as Bluetooth, or even Wi-Fi wireless LAN connections and Ethernet connections.

Figure 16.4 shows a wireless LAN card designed for a PDA model called the Visor (made by HandSpring), which are PDAs designed to operate on the Palm operating system. This card would allow you to connect directly to any PC that is connected to a wireless LAN through an access point. This particular wireless LAN card, called the Xircom Wireless Ethernet Module, can connect to any Wi-Fi access point.

> **TIP**
>
> To learn more about home wireless LANs, check out Chapter 7, "The Wonderful World of Wireless Networking."

FIGURE 16.4

A wireless LAN NIC for a Visor PDA.

Do I Want to Network My PDA?

Before you consider networking your PDA, you should ask whether you will get additional benefits from this type of connection. Because most PDAs come with cradles or cords to allow for syncing with your PC, you do not need to equip your PDA with a network card to connect it and update its information. The PDA will simply sync up with the PC through its local connection—either a cable or a cradle—and then be ready to use, whether you're in your home, away at work, or on the road.

Connections to other PDAs are also made easy via the built-in infrared capabilities of most PDAs. Like remote controls (and most laptop PCs), PDAs have the capability to signal at low speeds using the little infrared communication port on board.

Here are some things to ask yourself when considering whether to use a network connection:

- Do I want to be able to have my PDA communicate from anywhere on the network? A PDA Ethernet or wireless LAN card will allow the PDA to sync up from remote locations.

- Do I want to be able to connect to another PDA equipped with a network card?

- Will I want to take advantage of future applications that might be available through my PDA network connection, such as instant messaging or Web browsing?

As with many new technologies, you can expect new features to continue to emerge for your PDA, and networking applications are one of the areas that are expected to be ripe for future uses.

You can equip your PDA with a modem today and access e-mail and do limited Web browsing on many of today's PDAs. These modems are available through expansion modules, much like network cards. Some PDAs, like the Palm VII, come equipped with a wireless modem to communicate to the Internet.

With all the promise of networking PDAs, there are still some reasons for caution. Because the enabling of networking for PDAs (beyond basic syncing with a PC) is still very much in the early stages, here are some potential problems you should be aware of when considering networking your handheld organizer:

- One of the biggest limitations of PDAs is their battery life. Using a networking card, such as a wireless LAN card, can be very draining on a PDA's battery and might require that you recharge your battery more frequently than you like.

- The memory and processor of PDAs are much more limited than those of your PC, so networking and accessing the Internet will likely not be as fast and convenient as they are on a PC.

- Networking with PDAs is still in its developmental stages, and no common standard technology is defined at this point. You likely will not find it as easy to network and communicate with other PDAs and PCs on a network for years to come.

Wrap It Up

Networking is no longer just about PCs. The capability to connect all sorts of devices in your home network is a reality today, and new and exciting devices will emerge in coming years to help you get more out of your network.

These are the three major categories of non-PC devices you can connect to your network:

- Network attached storage devices
- Internet appliances
- Personal digital assistants, or PDAs

Network attached storage, or NAS, allows you to add a large storage drive on your network without it being attached directly to any PC. NAS devices usually have Ethernet connections, can be configured with their own IP address, and can serve as home network servers as well as Web servers.

Internet appliances are an emerging category of devices that can access the Internet either directly or often through a home network. Internet appliances come in different forms, including Web pads, e-mail stations, Internet-connected smart devices, and Web terminals.

Personal digital assistants, or PDAs, are popular devices that many people use as handheld organizers and productivity tools. These devices have always been designed to synchronize their information with PCs, but new capabilities, such as network synchronization and ad hoc networking with other PDAs using Bluetooth technology, are rapidly emerging.

Communicating on Your Home Network

IN THIS CHAPTER

Time to Communicate

The capability to communicate in your home with the different members of the household is increased greatly with a home network. No longer are you forced to live in a world of posting yellow sticky notes, and yelling your spouse's or children's name when it's time to eat dinner (although, I suspect, this type of behavior will never go the way of the typewriter). Now you can utilize your home network to communicate both inside your home and to others on the Internet.

The capability to communicate inside your home means not only through messaging, but through the use of your voice as well. Using a home network for voice communications is easy, and we'll show you not only how to turn your home network into a whole-home intercom system, but also how to make voice calls over the Internet using your home network.

First, let's take a look at messaging.

Messaging on a Home Network

One of the most popular applications of the Internet over the past few years has been instant messaging. The capability to send a message in real-time to a friend online, as well as to be notified when one of your friends has logged on and is ready to begin exchanging messages, has found a huge following. Not only do students and bored office workers find this application fun, but others such as seniors and those away from loved ones who want to feel that instant connection have used instant messaging at one time or another.

One of the great things about instant messaging is that not only can you use it across the Internet, but you can also use it to communicate with someone on your home network. Running a messaging client program on any PC on the network is extremely easy and, best of all, free, so you should surely take advantage of some of the downloadable software programs for messaging that I will show you.

One widely used messaging service, called ICQ, is available today free through the Internet. ICQ, which reads "I Seek You," is extremely popular, with more than 100 million subscribers to their free messaging service. Because ICQ is free and very easy to use, it is a great messaging program to set up and use, both for Internet messaging and for communicating with someone on your home network.

> **NOTE**
>
> Using ICQ in your home network requires an Internet connection. Sending messages within a home network without an Internet connection is also possible using a program called Microsoft NetMeeting, which we will take a look at in the section "Voice Communications on a Home Network," because NetMeeting also enables voice communication (that is, a home intercom system).

Installing and Using ICQ as a Home Network Messaging System

Before you use ICQ, you must first download it, which requires an Internet connection. After you are online, go to www.icq.com and download the ICQ program. The latest version of ICQ is 5MB, which will take a while if you have a dial-up modem. If you have a cable or DSL modem, you can download the program in a couple of minutes.

After you have downloaded a free copy of ICQ, you are ready to begin installation. Because you have a home network, you will be required to download the program only once, but you will need to install the program on each PC on your network in order to use ICQ.

To begin installation, simply double-click on the file you have downloaded (or copied from another PC) and follow the commands. The process will go like this:

1. From your Windows desktop, double-click on the My Computer icon.
2. Choose the drive you have saved the program to. In this case, I saved the ICQ2000b.exe file to my C: drive, in the Downloads folder.
3. Double-click the ICQ file, which has a name similar to ICQ2000b.exe, to begin the installation process.
4. When the ICQ setup screen pops up, you are told which directory the program is choosing to install the program to. If you like the installation directory, click Next, or choose a new directory and then click Next.
5. Follow the instructions to begin the full installation of the program. If you are asked to reboot your PC to begin the ICQ messaging service, click OK.
6. After the installation is complete, you will begin the installation process. Figure 17.1 shows the ICQ Registration window. You need to choose the appropriate connection. If you are connecting using a dial-up connection, even if you are on a home network, you should choose this option because this helps ICQ understand your Internet connection type.

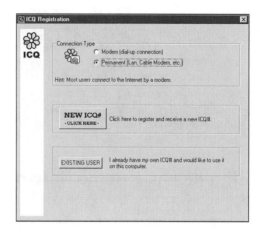

FIGURE 17.1

The ICQ messaging registration screen.

7. Click the New ICQ# icon to be assigned an ID with which you can communicate. This is important in that you will need a separate ICQ number for each member of the home network who wants to participate in a messaging session. You should ensure that all users on the home network receive their own ICQ number that they can use to sign on when they want to send and receive messages.

CAUTION

You should be very aware that it is the individual users on your home network that get an ICQ#, and not the different PCs on the network. Because ICQ chat can be used for chatting not only over a home network, but also over the Internet, individual ICQ users within a household will often have their own personal chat partners—such as schoolmates or friends—that they want to have access only to themselves. Oftentimes, this is more important on the receiving end of an ICQ instant message; imagine the horror of a school-age daughter when she realizes that her dad received an instant message intended for her from one of her friends about how the friend thinks that so-and-so in fifth period history class thinks they're "hot stuff." Talk about miscommunication!

---

8. To be sure that no user of the home network is using another's ICQ either accidentally or purposely (younger brothers are notorious for such behavior) for reasons described in the preceding Caution, you will want to be sure that each ICQ is password protected. When asked during registration for a password, make sure that you enter one and write it down.

After you are finished, you are assigned your ICQ# and are ready to begin messaging. A pop-up screen like that shown in Figure 17.2 appears.

FIGURE 17.2

The ICQ messaging screen.

9. To begin chatting, simply click on the Add/Invite Users bar. You will get the Add/Invite Users screen that asks you to search by e-mail, nickname, or ICQ number. I suggest that you make note of everyone's ICQ number, and then you can simply enter the ICQ number when you want to initiate a chat session.

After you begin to use ICQ, you will find that the interface is very intuitive and easy to use. As shown in Figure 17.3, a messaging-session screen pops up when you initiate a conversation. From here, you simply enter your message, press Enter, and wait for someone on your home network or the Internet to respond.

FIGURE 17.3

The ICQ Message Session screen.

Being able to send a message in real-time to someone inside your network, as well as over the Internet, is both fun and extremely useful. Imagine you are playing a multiplayer game with someone in another room (or another country, for that matter) and you want to warn them about the Samurai warrior sneaking up behind them. Sending them a message is one quick way to do it. Messaging is also a great way to keep in touch with others around the home. Just think: No more shouting, "It's time to go to bed!"

ICQ is only one of many instant messaging systems. Other messaging systems include those shown in Table 17.1.

TABLE 17.1   Instant Messaging Sites

Messenger Service	Web Address
AOL Instant Messenger	`www.aol.com/aim`
Excite Messenger	`http://messenger.excite.com/`
MSN Messenger	`http://messenger.msn.com/`
Yahoo Messenger	`http://messenger.yahoo.com/`

Because these are Internet-based messaging systems, you need to have an Internet connection turned on when you are using these systems. However, if you would like to use a messaging system that doesn't require an Internet connection, you might want to consider LanTalk Pro. LanTalk Pro is a great instant messaging program specifically designed for an office or home network. This program can be downloaded free; if you like it, you will need to pay the company only $16 for its use. The program allows you to set up messaging on each PC in your home network, even if you don't have an Internet connection.

LanTalk Pro can be found at `www.lantalk.net`. From there you will find the program as well as instructions on how to install and use it for your home network messaging system.

Voice Communications on a Home Network

There's nothing like a human voice. From the scratchy phone calls of decades ago to today's anywhere-and-anytime wireless phones, people love to communicate with another person with their voice. And with your home network, things are no different. You can now talk using the built-in capabilities of your home network and Windows software.

One of the neatest applications of a home network is the capability to set up a network intercom system. Think about it, over the home intercom system, you can tell Timmy to clean his room, tell Sue that her ride to work is here, or talk smack with your brother in the next room as you thump his character in your network game.

Of course, to set up a home intercom, you need both a microphone and a set of speakers for each PC. Most PCs today come equipped with speakers, and many have microphones built into the monitors. If you do not have a microphone, you can find one from $10 and up at your local electronics or PC store.

> **CAUTION**
>
> If you've ever heard the echoey sound that happens when a speaker gets too close to a microphone, you've experienced what is called feedback. With voice communications systems on a home network, there is a good chance you will experience some feedback unless you use headphones. If you are using your home network for an intercom quite a bit (as you might with network gaming), you might want to consider investing in a headset for $15 to $25 to get the best quality sound (and to avoid those annoying echoes!).

Setting Up NetMeeting as a Home Network Intercom/Messenger

After you have equipped each PC with a speaker and microphone, you will be able to set up your network intercom. Setting up a network intercom is extremely easy because the software is included in many of today's PCs to do just that. Windows ME and Windows XP have a program called NetMeeting. NetMeeting allows users to communicate over a network, whether it is a home network or the Internet, using their voice, video, and instant messaging. NetMeeting is also designed to allow users to transfer files and share programs over a network. This section focuses on using NetMeeting as a home network intercom.

NetMeeting is installed by default on most ME and XP PCs. However, on some Windows ME PCs, you need to have the program installed as a Windows component. This is easy to do: Simply click Start, Settings, and then Control Panel, and then double-click Add/Remove Programs. From here, you go to the Communications tab and click the Details button, and if NetMeeting is not checked, check it and click OK. You should then have NetMeeting installed and ready to set up your intercom.

To set up your intercom, you simply need to launch NetMeeting and instruct it to begin a call session. To do so, follow these steps:

1. Click Start and then Programs (or All Programs in Windows XP), and then click Accessories.

2. From the Accessories menu, choose Communications.

3. From the Communications menu, click on NetMeeting.

4. You should see a pop-up screen that looks like that shown in Figure 17.4. This is the NetMeeting window. You need to have NetMeeting activated on each PC you want to communicate with.

FIGURE 17.4

The NetMeeting window.

5. To begin a voice Intercom session, click on the phone icon. This is the Place a Call command within NetMeeting.

6. A pop-up screen asks for the address of the person you want to call. To make a call within a home network, simply enter the name of the PC you want to call. As you know from setting up your home network, you assign each PC within a workgroup (usually you have only one workgroup for a home network), and this ID will now be used to dial up the other PC.

7. The person you are attempting to communicate with should hear a phone "ring." He is asked whether he wants to accept the call. After he clicks Accept, you should be able to talk over your home network.

NetMeeting is a convenient application for such things as home network intercoms. Because it was designed for use in business networks as well as home networks, it has many different functions you might want to take advantage of in addition to the voice capabilities. If you have a PC camera installed on each PC, you can use the video phone capabilities in NetMeeting to conduct a video call. Another neat feature is the white-board capabilities. If you want to draw a concept for someone using another PC on the network, simply click on Tools at the top and then click on Whiteboard, and you can draw your concept for the person on your virtual call. As with all things you do within NetMeeting, you need to initiate a call first before you can use some of the other handy features.

As I indicated earlier, NetMeeting also has messaging capabilities. These capabilities can be used over a home network without an Internet connection, unlike with the ICQ service we discussed earlier. Initiating a chat session in NetMeeting—*chat* is the term used for NetMeeting's messaging service—is simple. As with the other capabilities in NetMeeting, you simply click on Tools and then Chat, and you will be ready to start messaging with whomever is participating on the network.

What About Windows 95/98? Don't Worry, There's Roger Wilco

Users of Windows 98 and 95 should know that NetMeeting is not included as part of these operating systems. However, there are other voice communication systems you can use in lieu of NetMeeting. One of the most popular intercom systems is a shareware program called Roger Wilco. Roger Wilco is a nice chat/intercom program that is extremely popular among gamers, who like to yell things like "you stink" and "gotcha!" at their close friends during a multiplayer gaming session. And you can use Roger Wilco on Windows ME and XP PCs as well.

You can download Roger Wilco at `www.rogerwilco.com`. The program is easy to install, and after installation you should be able to instantly begin communicating with others on your home network. The program effectively allows you to pick a "channel," which is an IP address on your home network. In fact, it suggests a channel for you (so you don't have to type an IP address). You can also choose to join a channel on the wide area network by using Roger Wilco's channel page, which allows you to connect with gamers on the Internet for multiplayer gaming.

Figure 17.5 shows the Roger Wilco Channel tab. As you can see, Homer and Maggie have a channel over a LAN IP address, 192.168.1.102. As you learned in Chapter 10, "Getting Around the Home Network," this is an IP address within the range set aside by the Internet community for private communication on a local area network. When you choose to create a channel within Roger Wilco, it defaults to a private IP address on your home network where you can communicate with others. If you were to choose to use Roger Wilco's Channel page to choose a channel, the IP address would be a public address where you could converse with others on the Internet.

FIGURE 17.5
The Roger Wilco chat utility.

Voice Communication over the Internet

Just as you can communicate over a home network, your Internet-connected PC can also communicate over the Internet, as you have seen with Roger Wilco. In fact, many people today make their long-distance calls over the Internet or another IP-based network, whether they know it or not. Not only do hobbyists make use of PC-based systems to communicate with friends over the Internet, but phone companies are beginning to realize that putting voice traffic on the same network as much of the data traffic will allow them to save money in the long run. You have likely dialed a phone number and had a conversation with someone in which your voice was translated into an IP packet and then converted back to a voice signal on the other end.

Whether or not your phone company is investing in Voice Over IP technology today, you can begin to experiment with this technology if you have a PC connected to the Internet.

> **NOTE**
>
> *Voice Over IP*, or *VoIP*, is the industry term for sending voice communications over an Internet Protocol network. It is seen as the future of communications among many people in the telecommunications industry.

All you need to begin experimenting with VoIP with your PC is a program called Net2Phone. This program allows you to connect over the Internet for voice calls. Net2Phone the company is the manufacturer of the Net2Phone software and also the company that provides the service behind the voice communication.

The calls with Net2Phone are made from any Internet-connected PC equipped with a microphone and speakers. You can call directly to any phone number, meaning that people you call don't even need a PC. They can talk directly through their phone to you, at a sound quality that is surprisingly good (although nothing replaces direct phone-to-phone quality).

Although many voice calls with Net2Phone are free for a limited number of minutes, you will want to visit the Net2Phone Web site at `www.net2phone.com` to check out the rates (this is also where you go to download the free software). The company might ask you to begin paying rates for PC-to-phone calls after a certain number of minutes. Also, you will have to pay a per-minute charge for any international calls. But, as you will see if you compare with other phone-company rates, communicating through Net2Phone is much cheaper than communicating through a traditional phone-initiated call, even internationally.

Figure 17.6 shows you what the Net2Phone interface looks like. You can dial any phone number using the on-screen dial pad, and after you do you will soon hear a ring through your PC speakers. Make sure that your speakers and the microphone are not too close together, or you might get some feedback. I suggest that you experiment with Net2Phone and see whether you think the quality is good. Although long-distance communication is much cheaper today than it has ever been (thanks in large part to Internet Protocol technology), you can still save quite a bit of money by using Net2Phone if you are a college student, someone with a long-distance sweetheart, someone who calls internationally a lot, or just a real *talker*.

FIGURE 17.6

The Net2Phone interface for making Internet voice calls.

Also available are hardware options that allow you to talk directly into your own phone and communicate over your broadband connection. Linksys has a Voice Enabler device that attaches directly to your broadband modem that allows you to connect your phone directly into the device and then dial as if you were making a normal phone call. The product, called the EtherFast Cable/DSL Voice Enabler, uses Net2Phone as the voice-call service provider. The neat thing about this device is that it allows you to avoid using your PC as a phone and can allow you to add a second phone line without having to have the phone company come out and install one.

Wrap It Up

Communication using your home network and your Internet-connected PC is quickly becoming much more than simply sending data back and forth. Voice and instant-messaging communication over your home network is a reality today using the basic software included in Windows or through widely available software on the Internet.

Instant messaging is extremely popular on the Internet, and it can be done over your home network as well. Using ICQ or other instant-messaging utilities, you can communicate with other PCs on your network, as well as friends, family, or coworkers outside of the home network on the Internet. You can also use a program called LanTalk Pro (www.lantalk.net) to set up a home network–based messaging system.

Windows ME and XP PCs can use the many capabilities of NetMeeting to communicate. You can conduct real-time voice chat to create a home network "intercom" by simply beginning a NetMeeting call session. You can also take advantage of NetMeeting's instant messaging, white board, and video call capabilities.

Another neat intercom utility for use on any Windows (and Mac) PC is called Roger Wilco. Roger Wilco is easy to install and allows you to instantly set up a voice "channel," much like a CB radio, for conversation over your home network. You can also use Roger Wilco's Channel page to find others to communicate with on the Internet.

Voice communication over the Internet is extremely popular today. With an Internet-connected PC equipped with a microphone and a speaker, you can use Net2Phone software and service to communicate with any phone number for a limited number of free minutes, and then at much lower rates than are charged for traditional voice calls.

Running and Securing Your Network

IN THIS PART

Home Network Security Overview

IN THIS CHAPTER

It Can Happen to You!

Internet security, and network security in general, is one of the most important things to think about for your home network and PCs. The threats out there waiting to pounce on people connected in some way to a public network, such as the Internet, are numerous and all very scary. Here are just a few examples of possible security threats:

- A curious sort gets onto your private PC through your Internet connection, and peruses your diary and personal finance files.
- An e-mail is sent to your accountant with all your latest tax forms, and the file is intercepted and examined by a malicious person on the public Internet.
- A tainted e-mail corrupts your PC and other PCs on the network.
- Your child, or a neighbor's child, gets exposed to pornography while surfing the Web.

Although these scenarios might sound far-fetched to some, they are all very real possibilities today. In fact, as the number of Internet users multiplies, malicious users are licking their chops as their potential target list grows at an exponential rate.

What can you do about this? Well, the short answer is, plenty. But first you must have a basic understanding of what the threats are for an unprotected network. The following cautionary tale will walk you through a "bad security week" for one home network user named Homer, as he experiences various security breaches within just a few short days. Learning from Homer's experiences, we'll then take a look at the different threats that can rear their ugly head to anyone on the Internet. In Chapter 19, "Home Network Security Planner," we'll help you develop an action plan for network security and take an in-depth look at all options to protect your network and those who use it.

Meet Homer: Three Lessons in Broadband Security

Homer is basically a happy guy. He has a nice job and a wonderful family, and for the most part, he has no trouble negotiating the small twists and turns life shoots his way.

He, like many people, uses the Internet for getting news and sports information, as well as for downloading updates from his local bank for his savings and money market accounts. And not unlike many readers of this book, he is a new home network user.

Homer decided to install his home network six months ago, about the same time he had a cable modem installed. He figured that because he was going to be paying $40 a month for his new broadband Internet service, it would be good to share this with his wife and two children (his boy actually would say it was *he* who was sharing it with Homer). After buying a home network kit and setting up his network, Homer and family happily shared their resources and the snappy new cable modem service.

Homer Hates Mondays: The Start of a Bad Security Week

When Homer set up his network, he did not give much thought to Internet security. He figured that most people using the Internet are nice folks and that the chances of his being happened upon by one of those "hackers" he heard about in the movies and the news were pretty slim. And Homer certainly wasn't thinking too much about Internet security when he woke up this most recent Monday morning. He had other things on his mind, including the presentation he had to give to his boss about ways to save energy down at the plant.

Homer had been waiting for months to get time with his boss and show him his ideas, and finally the big guy had scratched some time on his calendar. To prepare for the big meeting this afternoon, Homer wanted to go online to do a little last-minute research. But when he went to get on his PC, he found his PC slow and unresponsive. After a while, he finally got his PC to start working, but he noticed words printed across the bottom of his screen that said, "CAN U BELIEVE IT? GOT U – SLINKY."

Slinky? Who is Slinky? Homer was perplexed, and most of all he was upset because his PC was not working properly and he had a big presentation to prepare for. He asked his wife, Mary, if she had heard of Slinky.

"I dated a guy named Slinky in college," she said, "but that was the last time."

Homer asked his children, Melissa and Billy, about Slinky, and they shrugged their shoulders. Billy did say that he had opened an e-mail yesterday that read, "Open to see something funny ;)" and that had a little program attached. Ever since then, the mark of SLINKY had been running across the screen.

Homer's Lesson in Security #1: Beware the Virus

Homer was finally able to get his PC to start working normally, but still couldn't get the words off the bottom of his monitor. After talking to his friend Steve at his work, Homer learned that what happened to him was one of the most common violations of Internet security.

The dreaded SLINKY virus is not unlike many of the other viruses or Trojans that have infected PCs in both work environments and the home. The virus was installed when Billy unknowingly executed a small program that was attached to an otherwise innocent-looking e-mail. Luckily, the virus was largely harmless, and other than printing a few words across the bottom of the screen and causing the PC to run a little slow until rebooted, it caused no permanent or disabling damage.

"You're lucky," said Steve. "Some of these things can erase your hard drives." Homer nodded and took a bite of his donut. He was lucky, and he knew it. That evening he went to his local computer store and looked at virus protection software, as Steve had told him to do.

Homer's Lesson in Security #2: Beware the Unwanted Intruder

The very next Wednesday, Homer was feeling pretty good about his presentation. He had gotten a raise and a promotion to Plant Level Operator Grade V, and he was now ready to play a little Solitaire on his PC to celebrate his newfound success ("I deserve to live a little!" he said to himself). But when he logged on and tried to access his games, he couldn't find any of them. Puzzled, he looked around and found that many of his programs were not available. In fact, it looked as though someone had erased many of his programs and data files.

Homer immediately called Steve. Although mildly annoyed at being pulled away from his microwave burrito dinner, Steve listened to Homer's explanation of the problem. He knew immediately what had happened: "You've been hacked, my friend."

Having noticed a large number of attempts to access his network over the past few weeks through the monitoring capabilities of his personal firewall, Steve had done some research. He soon found out through a discussion board on the Internet that a certain block of IP addresses assigned by SpeedyGuy Cable Internet service had been targeted by the notorious DELETE and CLEAT hacker group. As it turns out, the head of DELETE and CLEAT had been assessed a late fee for his cable Internet service and decided to wage a personal war against the corporate behemoth that is SpeedyGuy, leaving the Homers of the world in his destructive wake.

After consoling a shaky Homer for a half an hour, Steve told Homer to go buy a firewall and install it to eliminate these problems. Steve also told Homer he was going to be okay, because Homer had indicated to Steve (through his sobs) that he had backed up his hard drive Tuesday evening. "You can't underestimate the power of a backup," said Steve. Homer agreed as he dried his eyes.

Homer's Lesson in Security #3: Beware the Ugly Side of the Web

It was Friday and Homer was finally feeling as if he had conquered the problems he'd been experiencing over the past few days with his insecure network. He had installed a hardware firewall/router to enable sharing of his cable modem and, perhaps more important, to provide intrusion detection. He had also installed a self-updating virus-protection software package. He had created, as he told his wife, "Fortress Homer." Mary nodded politely and went back to her TV show.

That evening, after Homer had finished his usual after-dinner nap, he decided to go surf the Web a little and read e-mail on his den PC. When he got to his PC, he clicked on his e-mail program and downloaded the latest e-mails from his ISP's mail server. To Homer's surprise, a whole bunch of messages came through with words such as XXX, Sex, and Young Girls.

Homer was petrified. He had heard of the seedier side of the Web but had certainly never been there himself. Why had it suddenly decided to come to him?

You-know-who would tell him why. Homer dialed up his friend Steve—who was not very happy to be taken away from the video he was watching, *Perry Como: Behind the Muzak*—and started talking frantically. It only took Steve a minute to realize the source of Homer's ills.

Steve told Homer that it was possible that someone in his house had been visiting adult sites and had left enough information at those sites that they could now e-mail him. After Homer spent the next five minutes needlessly convincing Steve that it wasn't him, Steve told him that it could be that he or a family member had accidentally stumbled upon a site, or had been tricked into filling out a form requesting an e-mail address that later resulted in offensive material being sent. Steve informed Homer that he should put some content protection and parental-control software on his network. He also told Homer that many of these software packages also can restrict the flow of personal information—such as Social Security numbers and e-mail addresses—to Web sites without the approval of the user.

Are You a Homer: How Network Security Threats Can Affect Anyone

Believe it or not, anyone can be a Homer. And I'm not talking about Homer's sense of fashion or workplace savvy. What I am referring to is the security trouble he's experienced over the past week on his home network. The openness of the Internet and the lack of inherent security protection in many of the mainstream PC products such as Windows have created an open environment for many would-be evildoers. The next section looks in-depth at some of the problems Homer experienced to show you what you might be up against. It also looks at some methods of protection against these threats.

Internet Security Threats on a Home Network

Internet security can be divided into four main categories:

- Intrusion protection
- Virus protection
- Content protection
- Privacy protection

Each of these categories of threats is distinct and carries its own associated form of protection. Internet and network security, as shown by Homer's example, cannot be addressed by an all-in-one solution. Each form of Internet security threat has its own characteristics, and, consequently, its own form of guarding against the threat. Let's first take a look at the forms of intrusion against your PC or network and how to protect against them.

Intrusion Protection for Your Home Network

Most people do not realize how much they are at risk for unauthorized access to their private PC systems and networks. Believe it or not, if you have a cable modem or DSL modem, you might get a few curious types a day running scans on your IP address to see whether there is an "open door" into your network. Often these requests and activities are harmless, but once in a while you might get a person probing your system with not-so-friendly intentions.

Think of network intrusions as being like a burglar intruding into your home. A burglary can happen if there is little protection against such an invasion. If there is no real perimeter security, such as locked doors, as well as no real detection system, such as an alarm, to tell you that someone might be trying to access your home, you would be susceptible to attacks. Internet security is the same in that you need to protect yourself against attacks at the perimeter.

Why Would Someone Want to Access My PC?

You might be asking, "Why on earth would someone want to access my PC or home network?" You might not have any confidential financial or personal info, so there's really nothing a person could want to access your machine for, right?

Wrong. In fact, you'd be surprised to find out that a hacker (also called a cracker) might access a person's network or PC for reasons other than stealing private information. Some hackers access a machine in an attempt to essentially "kidnap" it. They see the person's machine as a launching pad for sending out profane material such as pornography, attacking other PCs, distributing your private information, and even storing stolen information from other PCs or networks. In short, after a person takes control of your system, they can hide behind your identification and perform all sorts of illegal activities.

This type of behavior is not always restricted to geniuses and computing wunderkinder. Accessing a person's unprotected machine over the Internet is made relatively easy through the availability of programs that scan a PC or network for vulnerabilities and then exploit them. It's like your tax software—you simply load the software and answer a few questions, and the software does the work for you. Hacker software can do the work for the most unsophisticated wannabe hacker.

Of course, this type of activity might not happen all the time, but the results of such behavior can be disastrous and worthy of protecting yourself against. This chapter, and the next, will educate you on what you need to be wary of and how to protect yourself.

How does one protect against such an intrusion? The best way to protect yourself against some form of intrusion to your home network is through the use of a firewall.

What Is a Firewall?

Firewall is the common term used in Internet security for the perimeter defense against unauthorized intrusions. Although firewalls have traditionally been used for protection of large business networks, people like Homer are realizing that a good perimeter defense is just as important to the home network.

The word *firewall* is taken from the real-world term for walls in buildings that are constructed to stop flames from spreading in the event of a fire. A network firewall is like a real firewall in that it helps stop the progression of a threat—except that the threat in this case is a network intruder.

How does a firewall work? Figure 18.1 is a simple graphical representation of what a firewall does to stop an intruder. This wall essentially is used to block vulnerabilities of different networks.

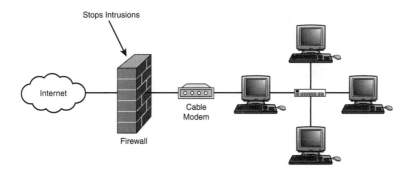

FIGURE 18.1

An Internet firewall protecting a home network.

How does a firewall determine whether a visitor is an unwanted intruder? The first thing it does is look at the IP address of a potential visitor. If the IP address is an accepted one, it might let the visitor in. But sophisticated hackers might try to trick the firewall into thinking that they are an accepted visitor with a friendly IP address (a technique called IP spoofing). Good firewalls will identify this technique and guard against it by also looking at what types of access the visitor is trying to get. To do so, the firewall examines which port the visitor is trying to access.

A hacker can scan your PC for active ports to infiltrate. If you do not have any sort of port-blocking software, such as a firewall, chances are that the hacker can walk through an open "port" and access your machine. We'll show you how to protect your PC using a variety of both software and hardware firewalls in Chapter 19.

> **NOTE**
>
> A *port* is a specific type of service or activity running on your PC that is a potential opening to the Internet. A port is a function of the world of TCP/IP in that when your PC is using IP as a communication tool, it will want to perform certain tasks or applications, and these tasks are identified by their port number. An example of an open port is a Web server or an e-mail program.

Virus Protection for Your Home Network

A virus, both the PC and human variety, is a sickness. Just as the human kind can be passed on from person to person through various forms of contact, so computer viruses can be passed on through a network through "contact." Usually a computer virus spreads by attaching itself to another file or document that is passed from one user to the next, and when this file or document is opened, often the virus is activated.

Viruses are sneaky things that like to attack without the knowledge of the user. Although some viruses might make themselves known immediately, some will often "hide out" on a PC somewhere in your hard drive or memory, waiting to strike.

Of course, viruses are not the only kind of PC sickness passed on from PC to PC with bad intentions. Techies and computer purists will point out other kinds of PC sicknesses that go by the titles of Trojan horses or worms. Table 18.1 explains how each of these works and the differences between the two. For the sake of simplicity, we will refer to all of these various sicknesses as viruses.

TABLE 18.1 Forms of Computer Viruses

Computer "Sickness"	Definition
Virus	A program that can spread from computer to computer, often with the help of a human who often spreads a virus by sharing a program or sending an e-mail. Usually requires a host program such as Word.
Trojan Horse	A program that infects a PC, often without any indication to the end user. These programs often will be disguised as a normal program, but have unintended consequences. Trojans can effectively "commandeer" your PC and allow a remote user to access and control your PC.
Worm	The self-spreading characteristic of a virus, but often more aggressive. It's spread via Internet applications such as e-mail and often can infect an entire network in a short time period. Does not require a host program.

How Do You Know If You've Been Attacked by a Virus?

As you can see, viruses come in many shapes and forms. Some are relatively harmless, which are referred to as *benign viruses*. More harmful or malicious viruses are called *malignant viruses*. Malignant viruses cause damage to a PC or network through various forms.

Here are some types of damage or activity you might see from a malignant virus attack:

- The virus can corrupt files or hard drives.
- The virus might act as a macro program that launches e-mails to those within your contact program.
- The virus can infect the key operating-system files that make your PC run.
- The virus might sit dormant somewhere on your PC waiting for a trigger date and then launch some harmful activity.

Most viruses are caught and contained before they do serious damage. There is a whole industry of dedicated folks who help to continuously protect against new viruses that pop up "in the wild."

NOTE

"In the wild" is a term for a new virus that is discovered in more than one organization's networks or systems. After the virus is discovered and a remedy is developed and widely distributed, these "in the wild" viruses are then seen as contained, or "in the zoo."

Viruses are examined, and cures and patches are worked on to help contain the viruses before they start to spread out of control. Even after a virus is spread, most of the time a cure can be discovered quickly for download for most businesses or home users. Still, viruses are costly, and some of the more well-known viruses, such as the LOVEBUG virus, can cause billions of dollars in damage.

Not So Loving: The LOVEBUG Virus Strikes

In May 2000, the world first came to know the infamous LOVEBUG virus. Unlike many viruses before it, the LOVEBUG spread fast and furious and actually was one of the first viruses to become known among nearly everyone who uses the Internet. News stories were written about the virus, which some estimated to cause damage in the billions of dollars worldwide.

How did the LOVEBUG virus move so far and so fast? Like one of its early predecessors known as the Melissa virus (probably the first well-known virus in popular culture), it took advantage of security weaknesses in Microsoft's e-mail program, Outlook. LOVEBUG was more malicious than Melissa in that it actually destroyed files, and it spread itself more aggressively.

Ironically, viruses such as LOVEBUG and Melissa have benefited society in that they have raised awareness among end users about what viruses are and how they can damage information systems. More people, both businesspeople and home users, are aware of the dangers of viruses and have taken steps to fight them.

Fighting Viruses on Your Home Network

As you read earlier, a whole industry has developed around fighting the spread of viruses. Companies such as Symantec and Mcafee.com have developed rapid response teams that look for viruses in the "wild" and develop remedies for them. Usually, the protection for a PC or a network comes in the form of software that is continuously updated by downloads of the latest security patches against new viruses that have been discovered.

Some of the newer models for virus protection are what are called managed solutions. A managed virus-protection solution is one in which you subscribe to a service and a service provider, such as your DSL company, automatically works with a virus protection company to get the latest updates that can be sent to your PC. An example of a company focused on this model of virus protection is McAfee.com.

We'll look at virus protection as part of a full home-network security plan in Chapter 19.

Note

A wise man once said, "Sometimes the best action is no action," and this can certainly apply to viruses activated through the opening of an e-mail attachment. Because many viruses are spread this way, often with a message urging you to action (such as "Check this out!"), you need to be conscious that any e-mail attachment could contain some form of virus. It is wise to scan e-mail attachments for potential viruses (as the virus protection packages reviewed in Chapter 19 will allow you to do) as well as be suspicious of any e-mail attachment from a sender—whether you know them or not—that you did not specifically ask for.

Content Protection for Your Home Network

Get used to this fact: The Internet, although it has a lot of wonderful information, has some very scary dark corners. The thought of yourself, or your children, accidentally happening across some of these dark corners can be very frightening to some people. As Homer found out, it is inevitable, if you or someone you know is using the Internet consistently, that you will at some point run across profane material in the form of pornography, hate messages, violent content, or even some form of predatory content targeting vulnerable user groups.

There are a few ways to protect yourself or someone in your home from such content:

- Throw away all your computers and move into a log cabin.
- Put a steel cage around the PCs in the home and unlock them only when you can watch whoever is going to traverse the Internet.
- Use filtering software to limit exposure to mature or private content to certain members of the network community, as well as establishing guidelines that are openly discussed with members of the household.

Now if this were a multiple-choice test, I would hope most of you would go for the third option. It is the least expensive and disruptive of the choices, and the one most likely to keep your family from thinking you're a couple cards short of a deck.

What Is Filtering Software?

Again, a good way to control the exposure of members of your network to certain types of content is through the use of filtering software. This software allows administrators to filter and monitor Web and chat content, as well as e-mail messages.

The filtering of certain Web sites and chats can be done by administering an objectionable word and Web-address list. Administrators can also view activity logs to see where a user has ventured in their Web travels, and can also set time limits on this software.

We'll take a look at types of filtering software, as well as how to install and administer such software, in Chapter 19.

Privacy Protection

The last form of security for the home network user is privacy protection. The fact that more and more personal information is going to be sent online, through either e-mail or online commerce, has created a need for protection measures.

Although you might feel secure when sending information over the Internet, you should be aware that there are potential dangers out there. Simply because you send an e-mail to someone with a specific address doesn't mean that they will get that information or that you are immune from someone taking a peek into your piece of "electronic correspondence." The practice of a hacker looking at e-mail traveling across the Internet is called "packet sniffing."

Something Smells Fishy: Packet Sniffers at Large

Do you hear that sniffing noise? Well, even if you don't, the information you send across the Internet might be subject to what is called packet sniffing. Packet sniffing occurs when a hacker uses a special tool called, what else, a *packet sniffer*. Packet sniffers monitor the packets of information (remember, all traffic on the Internet is separated into manageable chunks, called packets) and try to see into these packets.

What are they looking for? Chances are that whoever is doing some sniffing is looking for personal information such as a credit-card or Social Security number. Although this type of activity isn't likely to impact you on a daily basis, it is still a reality and something you should be aware of and protect against.

Packet sniffing is only one way personal information can be made available on the Internet. An activity as simple as Web surfing can leave traces of your behavior, as well as even your personal info, for Web site administrators to use and monitor. One of the great debates among privacy activists and the Internet community is the impact of what are called cookies. A cookie is a data file stored on your hard drive by a Web site you visit. The cookie contains information about your surfing habits on that particular site, as well as potentially personal information such as your account info, name, and password.

Are cookies harmful? If you are conscientious about what sites you visit or alert to the fact that these sites can place information on your hard drive without your knowing it, you might want to know when someone is storing a cookie on your system. You should know that cookies actually do serve a purpose. They provide a way for Web sites to recognize you and provide you with customized information. If you've ever visited a site and been greeted with a page that says Welcome Back and even gives you some personalized information, that's due to the existence of a cookie on your hard drive.

How to Protect Your Private Information on the Internet

There are a few ways to ensure that private information sent over the Internet stays private. One of the ways is to use different forms of cryptography, also called encryption. You might remember our discussion about encryption in Chapter 7, "The Wonderful World of Wireless Networking," when we looked at wireless networking. Much like in a wireless LAN, when information is sent from one PC to another using encryption, this information is concealed from unapproved sources via what are called encryption keys.

An encryption key is used to encode a message into a format that is readable only by someone who has the encryption key to decode the message. In the world of network encryption, the process of encrypting messages for travel over the Internet relies heavily on mathematical processing. How encryption actually works is a very complex subject that is beyond the scope of this particular book, but what we will do for you is look at how to use encryption to ensure that your private information remains safe.

In Chapter 19, we will also look at how to protect what information from your PC or network goes out on the Internet. Privacy protection software can be used to guard against the unknown sending of information over the Internet.

Wrap It Up

Home network security is a complex topic. When you are talking about security, you are talking about not one topic, but many subtopics. To make things easier to understand, we have divided home network and Internet security into four distinct categories:

- Intrusion protection
- Virus protection
- Content protection
- Privacy protection

Intrusion protection involves protecting your home network against unwanted visitors. When you are connected to a public network such as the Internet, there is the chance that people can pry and even take control of your PC for their own questionable means. This type of behavior can be guarded against using what is called a firewall, as well as with good authentication technology.

Viruses can infect PCs and networks with very little warning. Although some viruses—also known as Trojan horses or worms—might be harmless, others can damage or even erase your hard drive. Virus protection can be found in software that is installed on each PC in a home network. This software is constantly updated to protect against the latest viruses.

Content protection is the act of shielding yourself or others in your home network against mature or private content. You can protect children against seeing profane content using what is called filtering software.

The protection of your privacy is very important when you're connected to a public network such as the Internet. Information you send can be sniffed at by hackers, and even when you are surfing the Internet, some Web sites are recording your behavior and personal information. Software can help guard against invasions of your privacy, and a technology called cryptography can encode your communications so that others cannot read what is not intended for them.

If you are interested in implementing any of the technologies discussed in this chapter to ensure that your home network is secure, turn now to Chapter 19.

Home Network Security Planner

IN THIS CHAPTER

It's Easier Than You Think

After reading the preceding chapter, you probably think securing your home network against potential ills and malicious behavior by others is a full-time job. Don't go looking for a full-time security expert to hire just yet. There are some very basic things you can do to make your network, and the important information that resides on it, safe with very little time or cost. And, believe it or not, you might have some of the protection measures that we will recommend already working for you.

How do you begin to put security measures in place on your network? First of all, make sure you have a good assessment of the potential threats to your particular network. If you are a twenty-something who lives alone and you don't use your PC for much other than checking sports scores and playing multiplayer video games with your roommates, your security needs will differ from those of a father of four who manages his large stock portfolio through his high-speed Internet connection.

Just for a quick review, these are the basic security needs for someone using a PC or home network connected to the Internet:

- Intrusion detection—Detect and defend against unwanted intruders on your network
- Virus protection—Protect against files and programs that can infect your PC and your home network
- Content protection—Control the content that others on the network, including children, can access
- Privacy protection—Control who has access to your personal information, whether its on your own network or over a public network such as the Internet

The "bare essentials" of home network security include some form of intrusion detection, aka a firewall, and virus protection. Without these, you are exposing yourself to numerous risks, which you should know about after reading Chapter 18, "Home Network Security Overview."

The following sections cover the choices for implementing the different forms of network security. We will look at products you can use and how to install them. We will also look at combination products that are intended to give you all-in-one protection against most of the potential security threats on your network.

Choosing and Setting Up a Firewall on a Home Network

As you learned in Chapter 18, there might be folks out there trying to access your PC or home network. Whether it's for the sport of it or to obtain or destroy valuable files and information, chances are good that you don't want a total stranger perusing your home network.

The best way to guard against intrusions is to set up a firewall. A firewall can come in a piece of software that sits on each PC on a network, or a firewall can be its own piece of hardware. We'll look at both.

> **NOTE**
>
> It would be helpful at this point to make clear what a hardware firewall is. It is usually a device that can be bought at a low price in an electronics store or on the Internet that protects against unwanted intrusions, but it can also serve other functions. Often, a hardware firewall can be the same as a home router, which we discussed in depth in Chapter 14, "Internet Sharing on a Home Network." In fact, the basic function of a home router, called NAT, short for network address translation, provides some basic security protection against intrusion in that it doesn't allow an intruder to see behind the public IP address made available to the Internet from the home router. You can buy an all-in-one device, usually called a home router, that provides Internet sharing capabilities, some basic firewall protection, and a built-in switch for networking in your home.

Which Is for Me—Software or Hardware Firewall?

The choice for you to make is not whether you should have some form of firewall protection—you definitely should. The choice you should examine is whether you should have a software or a hardware firewall. There is an obvious difference in price between the two—home routers with basic firewall protection can be bought for about $100, whereas software firewalls can be purchased for $40, and some can be downloaded free—which is important.

Besides your ability or desire to pay extra for a hardware firewall, another important consideration is whether you are simply protecting one PC or many. Software firewalls must be installed on each PC you want to protect, whereas a hardware firewall usually resides behind a broadband modem and provides protection for all PCs on a network.

> **NOTE**
>
> One thing you should also know is that in the latest version of Windows, Windows XP, a basic firewall has been added. Because this firewall, called Internet Connection Firewall (ICF), is a basic one that does not include any level of configurability, I suggest using the Windows XP ICF only if you are not comfortable with at least downloading a free software firewall and installing it on each PC you want to protect.

You can use either a software or a hardware firewall on your home network, but you might want to go with this rule of thumb: If you are protecting many PCs on a home network, you should consider a hardware firewall because it will provide some basic protection for all PCs on your home network. If you have just one or two PCs connected to the Internet, a software firewall is usually sufficient.

In actuality, however, you don't just have to have one or the other. You can, in fact, have both. And some people would suggest that you have this double layer of protection, which would provide the most secure protection against unwanted intrusions on your home network.

Do I Need a Firewall with a Dial-Up Modem?

You might wonder whether you need a firewall if you are using only a dial-up modem on your home network or PC. You might, but realistically, the likelihood of some form of intrusion is much lower on a PC that is not accessing the Internet using an always-on connection. However, there is still a chance that while you are accessing the Internet someone could discover the IP address you are using and access your system. If you want to be 100% sure you are protected against unwanted intrusions, download one of the software firewalls we'll discuss later and install it on your PC. It couldn't hurt, and it certainly could help.

Now that you've given some thought to whether you'll be using a software or a hardware firewall (or both), let's look at finding each and how to go about the installation process.

Finding a Software Firewall

Software firewalls are easy to both find and install. The wide availability of free downloadable personal firewalls on the Internet should mean that you can install one without any out-of-pocket cost. There are also some very good software firewalls you can buy at a store or download over the Internet for a small cost. One advantage of a software firewall you pay for, is that you can get extra technical support, but really the need for such support is low.

In Table 19.1, you will find names of some manufacturers of software firewalls for pay or download.

TABLE 19.1 Software Firewall Manufacturers

Software Manufacturer/Product	Pay or Free?	Web Address
Network Ice/BlackICE Defender	Pay	www.networkice.com
McAfee/McaFee McAfee Personal Firewall	Pay	www.mcafee.com
Norton/Symantec Desktop Firewall	Pay	www.norton.com
Sygate/Sygate Personal Firewall	Free	www.sygate.com
Tiny Software/Tiny Personal Firewall	Free	www.tinysoftware.com
Zone Labs/Zone Alarm	Free	www.zonelabs.com

Which one should you choose? I would say that all offer adequate protection, but there are differences among them. Some Web sites give up-to-date reviews of the latest versions of the different products. If you want to do some research on software firewalls (or hardware firewalls, for that matter), visit the Home PC Firewall Guide at www.firewallguide.com. Another good resource on firewalls in general, and one that includes in-depth reviews of personal firewalls, is www.securityportal.com. A good location to download a software firewall (and many other kinds of free software) is CNET's download center at www.download.com.

I would say that the decision to at least try a software personal firewall is made easy by the fact that you can get some quality ones free. So even if you're a cheapskate like me, you still have no excuse!

Installing a Software Firewall

Installing a software firewall is simple. We will take a look at installing one of the most popular free firewalls available, Tiny Software's Personal Firewall. This firewall can be downloaded directly from the company's Web site. After downloading it, you can simply go to the folder to which it was saved and double-click the icon. From there it is a simple process.

CAUTION

After you install a personal firewall on a PC, you will immediately begin to see pop-up messages telling you that you have incoming or outgoing connections. These messages can be quite alarming and make you think that strangers are trying to access your PC or network at the same time. One of the drawbacks of many personal software firewalls is that the messages they give are still somewhat hard to interpret for a normal user. Most of the time, the pop-up messages are simply alerting you either about a PC within your own network or that some application on your PC is trying to access your PC. At first they're a little alarming, but most of these messages are harmless. More important to watch out for are the random messages that might pop up at any time after the firewall has been installed and in operation for a little time.

Follow these steps to get the firewall up and running:

1. After you double-click the icon, the Tiny Personal Firewall install program begins to guide you through the process. From the Setup screen that launches, choose where to install the firewall. You might want to install the firewall in the destination folder suggested to you. This will likely be C:/Tiny/Personal Firewall.

2. Click Next and the setup guide installs the program and the necessary drivers. This should take less than a minute. From there, you are asked whether you want to restart your PC. Choose Yes and then click Finish.

3. After restarting, you will begin to see pop-up messages about incoming or outgoing connections. This is because a firewall alerts you to any connections made on a home network or through the Internet—basically, any TCP/IP connection. Take a look at the type of connection; it is likely just another PC on your network or even a program operating, such as your Web browser trying to access the Internet. Choose to permit the connection and make a rule for allowing future connections. Figure 19.1 shows an example of a firewall pop-up message.

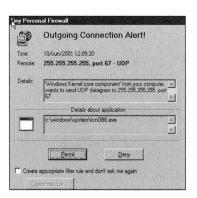

FIGURE 19.1

A firewall message for an incoming or outgoing message.

After you have installed your firewall and seen a few connection alerts, you will have a working firewall. As indicated earlier, you will likely have to create rules for a few of the normal connections that occur during operation of your PC to make sure that each PC can continue to communicate on a network.

> **CAUTION**
>
> The Internet Connection Firewall in Windows XP can prevent communication with other PCs on your network. One of the drawbacks of the ICF is that it does not allow you to create rules or permissions for acceptable connections, such as those within your home network. You might want to consider a third-party software firewall in order to have more flexibility in creating rules and less potential interference with your home network.

Most firewalls have toggles to adjust the level of security. These can be as simple as something like these:

- No security
- Medium security
- Maximum security

To check on the security-level toggle in the Tiny Personal Firewall, you can launch the program's administration window. To do so, simply carry out these steps:

1. Right-click on the system tray icon in the lower-right corner of your Windows desktop. Most firewalls have some type of icon in the lower-right corner to show you that they are activated

2. Choose the firewall administration option.

3. The Tiny Personal Firewall administration window looks like that shown in Figure 19.2. You can choose to toggle between low-level security, medium-level security, and high-level security. The general rule is that the higher the security, the more rules you will have to allow your firewall to make.

Most personal firewalls come with an uninstall program. You can try one, and if you do not like the user interface or the security it provides you (whether that's too much or not enough), you can choose to uninstall it and download one of the other free programs to try.

Remember, you will need to install the personal firewall on each PC you want to protect. If you are using a proxy server such as Windows Internet Connection Sharing that allows you to share one PC's modem, you will have some level of protection if you install the firewall only on the host PC. However, you will have greater levels of security if you put the personal firewall on each PC in your network.

19

HOME NETWORK SECURITY PLANNER

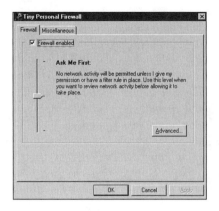

FIGURE 19.2
The administration window for the Tiny Personal Firewall.

Finding a Hardware Firewall

Hardware firewalls for home networks are widely available at PC and electronics stores, online or through catalogs. As you will recall from our earlier discussion, many of the basic home routers that are primarily targeted at sharing a broadband connection also position themselves as a firewall because of the basic protection through what is called Network Address Translation.

Some security experts would claim that you need to buy a product that provides additional protection in the form of something called stateful packet inspection.

> **NOTE**
>
> *Stateful packet inspection* is the intelligence to examine the packets that are sent onto and around your networks, not only to see their source destination (the IP address), but also to look at the type of content being sent. This can reduce certain types of attacks that are well known.

A firewall that has the extra intelligence to perform stateful packet inspection is certainly a requirement in a business. Whether you want to spend the extra money for a home firewall with these capabilities is up to you.

> **TIP**
>
> Generally, a home router with NAT working in conjunction with a software firewall is a perfectly good setup to prevent unwanted intrusions.

In Table 19.2, you will find a list of home router and firewall manufacturers. These vendors are similar to the ones listed in Chapter 14 for broadband sharing. However, because these products can also serve the purpose of providing intrusion protection, they are being listed here under hardware firewalls. All these products provide some level of protection using NAT, and many provide additional security such as stateful packet inspection. Those products with extra security features are noted. All products listed have four ports for sharing an Internet connection over an Ethernet network, unless otherwise noted.

TABLE 19.2 Home Hardware Firewalls

Manufacturer/Product	Web Address	Firewall Security
3Com/Home Ethernet Gateway	www.3com.com	NAT, stateful packet inspection
D-Link/DI-704	www.dlink.com	NAT, port blocking
Linksys/BEFSR41	www.linksys.com	NAT, port blocking
Netgear/FR314	www.netgear.com	NAT, stateful packet inspection
SOHOware/Broadguard	www.sohoware.com	NAT, stateful packet inspection
SMC/Barricade	www.smc.com	NAT

Installing a Hardware Firewall

Installing a hardware firewall is simple. In fact, it is the same process used to install a home router as shown in Chapter 14, with the exception that you now are more aware of the security capabilities of these products. Many have browser-based configuration utilities, such as the Linksys router we installed in Chapter 14.

In case you haven't read Chapter 14, a quick review of an Ethernet-based home router/firewall installation follows:

1. Shut off your PC and broadband modem.
2. Connect the cable running from your modem into the home router/firewall.
3. Connect the cable from your home router/firewall, usually a piece of category 5 twisted-pair wiring that will be included with your firewall at purchase, into the RJ-45 jack in the Ethernet card in the back of your PC.

4. Turn on the broadband modem and router/firewall. Turn on your PC.

5. You will likely have a Web-based configuration utility. Launch a browser and type the IP address given to you by your router/firewall manufacturer.

6. Configure the router/firewall with the necessary information provided by your service provider, including hostname and workgroup name.

7. You will likely have an Advanced tab that has a section called Filters. In the Linksys router/firewall configuration utility, the Filter tab has a feature that allows you to block WAN requests that attempt to access your network. This feature blocks ports, which are—as we discussed in the preceding chapter—services offered by your PC's TCP/IP protocol, and a way for others to access your PC or network. Figure 19.3 shows what the Filters page looks like in the Linksys configuration utility.

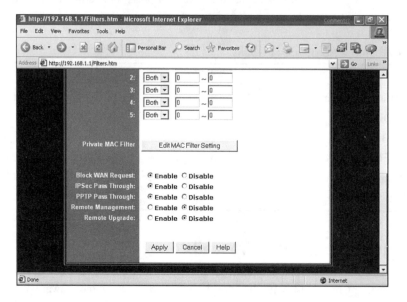

FIGURE 19.3

Configuring filters in a home router/firewall.

Testing the Security on Your Firewall

Whether you are using a software or a hardware firewall, you will want to test whether the firewall is actually giving you adequate protection. Luckily, a few good souls have created some test Web sites so you can see whether your network is accessible to others on the Internet.

As is to be expected, these sites are not perfect, and they themselves will tell you that even though they have checked your firewall and have or have not found some vulnerabilities, you cannot be 100% sure that you are getting adequate protection. But then, what in life is guaranteed (besides the knowledge you have gained from reading this fine book)?

Also, the free tests provided are generally somewhat limited, intended to show you that you might have some vulnerabilities in the form of open ports. However, you can often pay to have a more comprehensive test done. These sites also have a wealth of information about Internet security and how you can protect yourself against some of the threats we have discussed in Chapters 18 and 19.

Table 19.3 lists a few firewall test Web sites and what the charge (or lack thereof) is.

TABLE 19.3 Firewall Test Sites

Web Site Name/Web Address	Cost
Shields UP!—www.grc.com	Free
Hackerwacker—http://hackerwhacker.com/	First scan free, $5 for a scan thereafter, and monthly charge of $10
Security Space—https://secure1.securityspace.com/	Basic audit is free, standard audit is $33, and advanced audit is $66
Norton's Security Check—http://security2.norton.com/	Free

Virus Protection for Your Home Network

As you learned in Chapter 18, viruses can be very tricky in the way they move from PC to PC. Even when you think you are getting a program or file from a trusted source, there is a chance that a virus might be attached to the software that will infect your PC or multiple PCs on your network.

How do you protect yourself against viruses on your network? There are basically two things you can do to effectively eliminate the potential risk of infection:

1. Be careful about where and whom you receive PC files from—if you download files from complete strangers, you often do not have any idea of what that file might contain.

2. Use an antivirus software package that is consistently updated. These packages are widely available and can be updated continuously through your Internet connection.

The first method of protecting yourself against viruses is largely self-explanatory, and we will not go too in-depth into it. You should simply remember that when any PC or PCs are connected to the Internet and collect files, they are at risk. Even something as innocent as a downloaded music or video file could have a virus attached.

Antivirus Software for Your Home Network

The most mature area of Internet security for your home PC and network is virus protection. In fact, if you asked most people, they would believe that virus protection is the only Internet security protection they need, largely because most people who use the Internet are aware at some level of the threat of viruses. Although viruses are not the only security threat to your PC or network, virus protection is certainly one of the necessary components for a complete Internet security strategy.

Antivirus software is available from multiple vendors at affordable prices. In fact, some virus protection software comes in all-in-one packages that also includes a firewall and possibly even content and privacy protection features. Although these are separate types of protection, software companies looking to provide protection for Internet users realize that some will want to simply buy one piece of software rather than three or four pieces. Table 19.4 lists companies that offer virus protection software. Also noted are those that offer integrated security suites with other security features such as a personal firewall.

TABLE 19.4   Virus Protection Software

Manufacturer	Web Address	Products
Symantec	www.symantec.com	Standalone virus software, integrated security packages
McAfee.com	www.mcafee.com	Standalone virus software, integrated security packages, managed Web-based virus services
F-Secure	www.f-secure.com	Standalone virus protection
Kaspersky Lab	www.kaspersky.com	Standalone virus protection
Grisoft	www.grisoft.com	Free(!) Standalone virus protection

Is Antivirus Software Necessary for All My Networked PCs?

You might be wondering whether you need to install virus protection software on every PC on your home network. The simple answer is "YES! YES! YES!"

Why? Because even though one PC might be protected by a software package that captures and disables viruses before they can damage the system, this does not mean that a file cannot be passed on and activated on another PC on the network. Virus protection software is not network sensitive, but sensitive only to the individual PC on which it resides. It is important to maintain a secure home network to make sure that all PCs are equipped with virus protection.

CAUTION
Most software companies sell software assuming that you will install it on one PC. However, they also know that some individuals have more than one PC, and might have them networked. You need to check with the individual company to see what its policy is regarding multiple installations of a software package such as antivirus software. Most companies will understand if you install on more than one PC, if all these PCs belong to one person or family.

Content Protection

With the wild-west nature of the Internet, it is nearly impossible for anyone who is randomly surfing the Internet to not be exposed to some form of negative content, be it sexual, violent, hate, or criminal in nature. You certainly don't want just anyone being able to access this type of material on your PC or network.

The best way to eliminate exposure to such content is to use filtering software. As you learned in the preceding chapter, filtering software can help you choose which sites someone does or does not have access to.

With a home network, you need to install the filtering software on each PC on which you want to control content. Because filtering software is specific to a certain PC, a suggested strategy is to choose a specific PC that your children have access to. This makes it easier to monitor the kids' behavior (filtering software also has Web use monitoring capabilities) and control which sites they visit.

Table 19.5 lists content-filtering software manufacturers. These companies often manage a continually evolving approved (and unapproved) list of sites for browsing, which is automatically accessed using their software.

TABLE 19.5 Filtering Software

Company/Software	Web Address
CyberPatrol/CyberPatrol 5.0	www.cyberpatrol.com
Net Nanny/Net Nanny 4	www.netnanny.com
Norton/Norton Internet Security	www.norton.com
McAfee/Internet Guard Dog	www.mcafee.com

Privacy Protection

As with many of the other threats to your security on a home network connected to the Internet, some of the most basic ways to protect yourself are largely behavioral. Privacy protection is certainly no different. Here are some basic steps to privacy protection:

- Always be sure of whom you are sending personal information to over the Internet.
- Ensure that the connection you are using for any e-commerce is a secure one. You can determine how secure a vendor's transaction processing is by looking at their security policy. Generally, if the vendor has secure transaction technology, they will talk about it!
- Stay with larger and more trusted vendors.
- Keep good track of your passwords, and do not place them on your PC monitor with sticky notes or in plain view; access to your PC and network can be done from within the home network as well as from outside it.
- Use firewall and virus protection software. Unwanted intrusions and certain viruses can expose personal information to others.

Of course, in addition to some common-sense behavior, there are (as with most things) some technological solutions to help you protect your privacy. Theses are the two primary ways to protect privacy:

- Privacy protection software
- Encryption

Using Privacy Protection Software on a Home Network

Privacy protection software is installed on each PC and monitors how personal information is distributed over the Internet. Most privacy protection software asks you to enter a list of personal information, such as your name, Social Security number, credit-card numbers, and mother's maiden name. Then it will watch all traffic coming into, and going out of, your PC and send you an alert when this information is being sent to someone outside of your home network.

Privacy protection software also monitors the placement of cookies on your PC. You will remember that a cookie is a piece of information placed on your PC's hard drive by a Web site that wants to remember your personal surfing habits when you're on their site. Cookies are not necessarily bad and many people actually see them as helpful; but they can also be seen as somewhat intrusive by some people.

Table 19.6 lists privacy protection software manufacturers. If you want to install privacy protection software within your home network, such as content protection software, you need to install it on each PC on the network. The software monitors traffic in and out of a given PC, and it cannot monitor a PC it is not installed on.

Some privacy protection is not just software, but also a service offering. You can log in to a certain Web site and then be allowed to surf the Web and shop without risking exposing your personal information to others. Some of these "services" are also listed in Table 19.6.

TABLE 19.6   Privacy Protection Software

Company (Software/Service)	Web Address
Anonymizer.com (service)	www.anonymizer.com
Iprivacy (service)	www.iprivacy.com
PrivacyMaker (software)	www.privacymaker.com
Seigesoft (software)	www.seigesoft.com
Zero Knowledge (free software)	www.zeroknowledge.com

Some integrated solutions for Internet security, such as Norton Internet Security and McAfee Internet Guard Dog Pro, also contain privacy protection capabilities.

Using Encryption for Privacy Protection

Although you can control what personal information is sent out from your PC, it is harder to monitor and control its path (and who gets access to information) after it is sent over the Internet. You might think you are safe sending an e-mail with personal information to a close friend of yours, but, as we discussed in Chapter 18, there is always the chance that a curious hacker with a packet-sniffer program can intercept this e-mail and use the information in it for whatever purposes they want.

You learned in the preceding chapter that encryption allows you to send information securely over the Internet. This technology encodes your information so that it is unreadable without an approved decryption tool, often called a key.

Encryption is complicated and is usually the responsibility of IT managers within larger corporations. However, there are products and services that can enable encryption for someone sending information over a public network from home. Also, there is a concept called digital certificates, which enable secure, encrypted transactions.

> **NOTE**
>
> A *digital certificate* is a proof of identity of a particular sender of information. Digital certificates are often used in e-commerce transactions, in which a company giving a person information—such as when a person downloads a software program from a company's Web site—can identify themselves as who they say they are.

If you are working from home as a telecommuter and are connecting over the Internet to your employer, you might want to look at using a Virtual Private Network, or VPN. VPNs are private communication networks that utilize a public network, usually the Internet. VPNs are very popular for telecommuters because they allow the home user to send sensitive information over the Internet safely, using encryption technologies.

VPNs and encryption technologies, in general, are complicated, and mostly beyond the scope of this book. However, Table 19.7 gives links to some services and software providers that enhance the privacy of communications over the Internet, using some form of encryption technology, which you may be able to use with little previous education on the subject.

TABLE 19.7   Links for Encryption-Based Privacy

Company/Resource	Web Address	What Is It?
PrivacyX	www.privacyx.com	Free, encrypted emaile-mail accounts
GNU Privacy Guard	www.gnupg.org	Somewhat complicated, but free encryption program
McAfee/Internet Guard Dog	www.mcafee.com	Software program that encrypts private information
VPN Info	http://kubarb.phsx. ukans.edu/~tbird/ vpn.html	Good VPN info

Other Ways to Keep Your Home Network Secure

Although a major part of implementing a good home-network security plan is to use the software and hardware solutions mentioned previously, it is also a good idea to protect your home network against loss or corruption through constant backups. Backing up important data on your network onto removable media, such as a writable CD-ROM or ZIP drive, is a critical component of a good security plan.

Large removable storage drives, called network drives, are available for purchase. These products are like large hard drives, except that they aren't directly attached to your PC. These devices are somewhat expensive (beginning at around $500) but are great ways to create a network storage "tank" for storing large folders such as your MP3 music, or even video files such as movies. Potentially even more important, they can act as a backup drive. Some vendors of network storage drives are included in Table 19.8.

TABLE 19.8   Network Storage Devices

Company	Web Address
Linksys	www.linksys.com
Netgear	www.netgear.com
3Com	www.3com.com
Snap Appliances	www.snapserver.com

Wrap It Up

Having a secure Internet experience, whether you are a home network owner or just a single user on a dial-up modem, is something that should be given serious consideration. The best way to do so is to assess what your security needs are, and then implement the appropriate measures.

Intrusion protection can be guarded against by use of a software or hardware firewall. Hardware firewalls often double as Internet sharing devices and can be found for under $100. Software firewalls are low-cost, often free, software packages that are widely available on the Internet. Numerous sites are available on the Internet to test how secure your home network is from hackers.

Virus protection software is another critical component of a complete home-network security plan. Virus protection software is widely available from such companies as McAfee and Norton. Each PC on the home network should have some antivirus software installed on it that is regularly updated through the Internet.

Content protection software can be used as part of a home-network security plan to ensure that certain types of explicit content are not available to children or other users of the home network. Like virus protection software, content protection software must be installed on each PC and regularly updated over the Internet.

Privacy protection on an Internet-connected home network is done through privacy protection software, as well as encryption technologies to ensure safe delivery. There are software packages that enable both forms of protection, such as McAfee's Internet Guard Dog.

The other main security component in your home-network security strategy is a good backup plan. Use your home network for backing up important data on removable media such as a CD-ROM or ZIP drive. Networked hard drives can also provide a good storage facility, as well as an excellent way to securely back up important information on your home network.

Help Wanted: Home Network Manager

IN THIS CHAPTER

Hey, Someone's Gotta Do It

As much as we'd like to think networks run themselves, we're not quite to the age of talking computers and self-diagnosing robots. No, the one thing most home network users will tell you is that although networks have nearly limitless advantages, they also require a little oversight, or you can be up for possible problems.

That being said, it just takes a little organization and patience, and you will soon be able to call yourself a network manager (or All-Knowing-King-of-All-Things-Technology, whichever you prefer).

The network manager's job, should you choose to accept it, can be boiled down to a few important categories:

- Organization
- Preventative maintenance and diagnostics
- Network guru for other users

We'll look briefly at all of these categories and suggest how you (or someone else you nominate) can become a home network manager in very little time.

First Things First: Get Organized

The most important thing you can do as a network manager is keep your network—which means all related information about your network—well organized. Although this might seem like an easy concept and task (except for the perpetually messy people, such as me), you'll find that after you begin assembling a network, it's easy to let all the documents, passwords, and other associated items that come with a network get out of hand fast. This is where it pays to get things in place and structured from the very get-go.

You'll need three things in order to become a well-organized home network manager:

- A network book where you keep notes and pertinent information about your network and computer hardware, software, and users
- A list of all pertinent passwords and logons that you will keep separate and private
- A structured system of organization, including a well-kept shelf and storage space

Let's take a quick look at each of these individually.

The Network Book

The *network book* is the most important piece of your home network, because you'll keep all your critical information in it. What do you keep in your network book? Let's see:

- *A list of all your hardware and software components*—This includes a listing for each computer on the network detailing the latest operating system, the memory and processor specifications, and important components added, such as sound cards.
- *A list of network hardware information*—This includes all manufacturer support numbers and Web addresses, as well as model numbers and stores of purchase.
- *A network diagram and description*—This will help you to know what is connected where, which could come in handy when you're trying to troubleshoot problems.
- *All relevant information such as logon names, mapped drives, shared resources*—If you don't keep this information well tracked, it can easily get out of hand.

The network book will be an invaluable resource for you in the future, especially if you keep it up-to-date. You will want to keep some extra pages in the book for a journal of any important events such as troubleshooting. This might help you later when you're trying to resolve a problem (many times the same problem will happen again, or you might need to explain the problem to a support representative on the phone).

You might be tempted to keep all your passwords in this book, but resist this temptation! The network book is meant to be an available resource for you and others in the home who might have some questions about the network itself. You do not want to give away complete control of the network, and having the passwords around for all to see is just asking for problems. Not that those in your home would ever have dubious intentions—but all it takes is a curious user to go in and give himself or herself access to critical system resources, and you can be in serious trouble.

The Password List

To keep your network truly safe, you need to have some level of control over the network that others do not. Network managers have the ability to access critical files and drives, as well as set the security settings for a firewall and other important protective measures. To ensure that you are in firm control of these capabilities, you need to keep all these management options password protected.

An up-to-date list of important passwords is extremely important. You will want to keep all these passwords in one place, not necessarily on a computer. If you keep your passwords on a network on a computer, you are truly risking the possibility that someone, likely outside of your network coming in on the Internet, could get absolute control of all your important files, including personal data stored on any computers on the network.

A small notebook that you keep in a well-concealed place will do just fine. Remember to keep it up-to-date with any password changes (and you will want to change your passwords on a regular basis), and don't forget where it is (not an unusual happening in my house). Another option is what are called "lockbox" programs, which store important information, such as passwords, safely away from others.

The Structured Organization System

What does having a structured organization system mean? Well, it mainly means just keeping your network and its related information well tended, and setting aside some space for keeping this information, such as a network library.

Although you will likely keep all your important equipment information in your network book, you will also want to keep all the manufacturer literature in one place, because you might need to access it when there is a problem with the network. Also, any related books that you have (especially this one!) can go there. And along with your other books and manuals, you can place your network book smack dab in the middle, ready for use. You will also want to keep a file of important documents such as receipts and warranties for quick retrieval.

Preventive Home Network Maintenance

The best approach to solving home network problems is to get to them early. In fact, you can't do any better than to get to them before they happen. To do this, you need to establish a routine of preventive maintenance for your network. (Do I sound like the home network equivalent of a dentist yet?)

What are the key tasks for home network preventive maintenance? The key ones can be broken down as detailed next.

Keep Regular Backups of Important Files

By reading this book, you have learned a little about how to transfer files to other drives in order to have a backup. With network backups, you will want to take this a step further and regularly copy critical files to an extra drive to ensure that you have them backed up in case of a problem.

In fact, you might want to look into using tape or Jaz drives for entire system backups. Tape backups are expensive, but they allow you to store tens of gigabytes of data and more. Jaz drives, which are made by Iomega—the same company that makes Zip drives—are cheaper, and the Jaz disks offer up to two gigabytes of storage per disk.

Another option you might consider is using writable CD-ROMs for backing up your computer. Most new PCs come with a writable CD-ROM drive, and writable CD-ROMs allow you to record up to 675 megabytes of data. Although this won't back up an entire multigigabyte hard drive, you can certainly back up the most crucial files and folders using this media. And most

CD-ROM software comes with backup utilities to make things easier. With a home network, you can back up any PC on the network using a network connection.

A rapidly emerging option is the writable DVD drive. DVDs hold anywhere from 2 to 10 giga-bits of data, and drives are available today that allow you to write to DVD discs for under $500. Much like a writable CD-ROM drive, a writable DVD drive will allow you to back up important information, and with the larger amount of data you can store on a DVD, you can conceivably back up your entire PC disk drive.

Another option for backing up important files is to use an online storage service. With the arrival of high-speed links to the Internet, new service providers specializing in providing online storage have also popped up. Some providers of online storage are www.bigvault.com and www.storagevault.com.

Regularly Run Virus Checks on All Computers on the Network

If you read the preceding two chapters about network security (if you haven't, go back, you slacker!), you know how important it is to scan your PC regularly for viruses and other mali-cious code, such as worms and Trojan horses. With a basic virus-checker program, you can scan all your PCs over the network. You will also want to make sure that your program is kept up-to-date by regularly downloading all the latest virus information from the manufacturer.

Use Network Monitoring Tools

One of the neat things about networking in Windows is that the operating system has some built-in utilities to both monitor network activity and diagnose and correct problems with your PCs.

The built-in network monitoring tool for Windows 98 and ME systems is called Net Watcher. With Net Watcher, you can monitor the use of shared resources for any PC on the network. You can also choose to disconnect a user or add shared files from this utility.

Opening Net Watcher is very easy. To do so, simply click Start, Programs, Accessories, and then System Tools, and then click on Net Watcher. You then see a screen similar to that shown in Figure 20.1.

Windows XP PCs do not use Net Watcher, but instead use the Computer Management utility to monitor shared files, as well as other important system information. To access the Computer Management utility in Windows XP, click Start, Control Panel, Performance and Maintenance, and then Administrative Tools. From here, double-click on the Computer Management icon, which will launch the Computer Management screen.

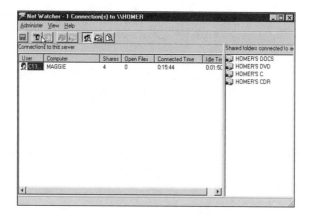

FIGURE 20.1

The Net Watcher screen in Windows.

The Computer Management utility has various capabilities, one of which is to monitor shared files as well as active network sessions. Network sessions are any occurrence of someone on the network accessing your PC through the network to access one of its resources.

Periodically Optimize the Computers on the Network

Some problems are related not to the network itself, but to individual PCs. You can use built-in diagnostic tools in Windows, such as the System Monitor utility in Windows 95/98/ME, and some of the system utilities available in Windows XP in the Performance and Monitoring section. You can get to System Monitor by clicking Start, Programs, Accessories, and then System Tools, and then clicking System Monitor. For the Performance and Maintenance screen in XP, click Start, Control Panel, and then Performance and Maintenance, and you will see such utilities that will help you clean up and organize your hard drive, as well as other administrative and performance tools.

Correct Network Problems When They Happen

Of course, you can't always correct a problem before it happens. If you could, you wouldn't be reading this book, but instead would simply be willing your network to happen by itself, without a word read or an ounce of energy spent. Unfortunately, it doesn't happen this way.

Although you might occasionally have trouble with your network and PCs, you won't need a PhD in computer science to figure out the problem. It usually can be boiled down to a hardware failure such as a bad NIC, a disconnection or loss of power to a network hub or connection, or a potential software problem. By simply physically inspecting the connections on your network and using some of the diagnostic tools mentioned previously, you might be able to figure out what is causing any problem on a network.

I would also suggest looking at third-party diagnostic and utility suites to help you figure out what might be the problem with your network or PC. You can find some of these packages from such vendors as McAfee (www.mcafee.com) and Norton (www.norton.com). These packages help you clean your system of clutter and reorganize your hard drives, and often can be combined in one package with an antivirus software package.

> **NOTE**
>
> One way to check whether your PCs are communicating properly on your network is to perform what is called the `net view` command from a DOS prompt on your Windows-based PC. This will allow you to see whether your PC is communicating with other PCs on the network (and if it isn't, check whether you have a disconnected cable or possibly a bad NIC).
>
> To perform a `net view` command, you need to access a DOS prompt (called a command prompt in Windows XP). To access a DOS prompt in Windows 95 and 98, simply click Start, Programs, and then MS-DOS prompt. To do so in Windows ME, click Start, Programs, Accessories, and MS-DOS Prompt. In Windows XP, you can access a control prompt by clicking Start, All Programs, Accessories, and then Command Prompt.
>
> After you have the MS-DOS or command prompt up—which will be in a black pop-up screen—type `net view \\computer name` where *computer name* is the name of the PC you are trying to access on the network. If all is working correctly, you will get a listing of the disks and printers that are designated as shared, as well as a message indicating that the command was completed successfully.

Being the Network Guru

Not only will you be asked to save the day in the event of any network problems, but your faithful network community will also look to you as their tour guide as they get to know more about the home network you've created. This is not necessarily a bad thing, and can, in fact, be very rewarding. And, as you will soon realize, a knowledgeable set of users will make your job as network manager much easier.

What can you do to help educate your home network users? The following sections cover just a few basic steps in creating a prepared and knowledgeable set of users.

Tell Them to Read This Book!

They should read, if not all of this book, at least the first section to help them understand what a network does and how it works. Also, you might want to have them read the sections that might be of interest to them. For example, if the music maniac in the house wants to stream digital music from the Internet or from one PC to another, have him or her check out the chapter on entertainment networks. You might even consider buying a copy of this book for the other users of the network (subliminal message from author: Buy lots of copies and make me rich!).

Create a Home Network Cheat Sheet

You will want to create a basic cheat sheet for them and tape it on the walls or on the computer stand, giving them all the crucial information about logons and sharing resources. This needs to be simple and short and understandable.

Keep Your Manuals and Other Resources Available to Others

In addition to this book, your users might want to check out any other computer or networking books you might have. Also, if you have any magazine articles that talk about technology or networking, be sure to share these with others.

Discuss the Home Network with Your Users

As my old college roommates used to say when I'd order a pizza, "Don't hide it, divide it!" The same goes for network knowledge. If someone has a question about your network, discuss it. Who knows, they might know a thing or two as well. You should strongly consider having a training session for each user when you first start using your network, because this will get some of the most basic questions out of the way and allow you to emphasize the important points (such as don't spill beer on the network hub).

Online Home Network Resources

Unlimited resources are available today on the Internet to learn about networks, technology, and anything else on your list. I'd be fibbing if I said I didn't use the Internet extensively to do research about my own home network, as well as for help in writing this book. Table 20.1 lists a few of the resources that you might find helpful in answering general home network and other technology questions. Some of these might include discussion forums so that you can ask questions you need answers to. For more detailed lists of Internet resources, see Appendix A, "Home Net Resources," which lists Web sites by category.

TABLE 20.1   Internet Resources for Home Networking

Web Address	Description
www.homenethelp.com	Good general home networking site with in-depth discussion boards
www.homepcnetwork.com	In-depth home networking site
www.threemacs.com	One of the best Mac networking sites on the Internet
www.securityportal.com	One of the best all-in-one sites for Internet security
www.techweb.com/encyclopedia	Great place to see what networking and computing terms mean
www.cnet.com	One of the best technology sites on the Web for news, downloads, product reviews, and product price comparisons

You'll also find that some of the best sites for networking information are the manufacturer sites themselves. If you are having a problem with a piece of hardware or just need general information about how a product works, check out the site of the manufacturer of the product, which is usually listed in the product literature.

Wrap It Up

Being a network manager is more than just setting up a home network and then letting everyone have at it. By organizing your information and making use of a few basic tools, you will soon find that you are the new hero in your home, because everyone loves the person who runs a tight ship.

The basic functions of a home network manager include organization, preventive maintenance, and being the network guru.

You can find numerous resources on the Internet for network information. In addition to the many networking sites available, you might find that the site of the manufacturer of your product has what you are looking for.

Lastly, if you are intrigued with finding out more about networking, you might want to consider taking a class at a local technical school or community college. Many schools today offer classes in networking and will even hand you a fancy certificate if you take enough of them.

20

HELP WANTED:
HOME NETWORK
MANAGER

Creating a True Digital Domicile

IN THIS PART

Smart Home: Home Automation Networks

IN THIS CHAPTER

So You Wanna Be George Jetson?

Home automation. You've probably heard a friend talk about it, read a magazine article or two, but always wondered if you could do it yourself. *Surely,* you think, *it has to be too expensive and technical, right?*

> **NOTE**
>
> *Home automation* is the control and (what else?) automation of lighting, appliances, and other home systems through controller and receiving devices. Most home automation networks allow you to control and automate your home systems through a PC.

Wrong. Home automation has been around for over 20 years and has become extremely affordable and accessible to everyone. In fact, with X-10, which is by far the most common type of home automation equipment, you can purchase a kit and have your home automated for around $50. And that's only the beginning, because with the inherent modularity of X-10, it doesn't take much knowledge to go from there and build your automation network.

Maybe you're not convinced, not because you think you can't afford it, but because you're not sure what home automation can do for you. Why the heck would anyone want to use it, you ask?

Quite simply, you can do some really impressive things with today's home automation. From basic things such as turning your lights on and off at a certain time to remotely controlling your home alarm or cooling system over the Internet, home automation and control has evolved to bring true life benefits to many people.

Here's just a sample of things you can do with home automation and control technology:

- Automate the lights in your home to go on and off at different times while you are away.
- Trigger your alarm system to turn off when you pull your car into your garage.
- Have a sensor alert you over the Internet when there is a leak in your basement.
- Control your lights and heating system using your voice from a seat in your living room.

Although some of these functions might seem exotic and out of reach for the basic hobbyist, they are not. A home automation sensor network that would allow you to sense changes in moisture in your basement and alert you over the Internet can be installed for under $200.

In this chapter, we will cover the landscape of home automation and control, looking at how it has evolved and how things will change in the future as new technologies become available. We will then examine what technology choices are available for you to buy. Lastly, we'll look at a couple of basic home automation installations to give you an example of how you can get started with this fascinating technology.

Home Automation History: It All Started with X-10

Back in the late 1970s, a technology with the strange name of X-10 made its way to the consumer. The technology, which was available at stores such as Radio Shack, enabled people to do things such as control their lighting or appliances so that they would turn on and off at a given time, all through a module that plugged into the wall and sent commands over the home's existing electrical wiring.

X-10 evolved and has since picked up a large following in the U.S. From humble beginnings at a small company that developed the technology in Scotland (for more info on the roots of X-10, see the following sidebar), X-10 products have proliferated and are now developed by hundreds of companies worldwide, including a company by the name of X-10.

Have a Drink on Me: X-10 Is Born

X-10 had its roots in the mid-1970s, developed by a company in Scotland by the name of Pico Electronics. Pico, which developed other technologies such as chips to go in calculators, came up with the idea to transmit signals over home AC power wiring. The actual idea for X-10 was hatched one night in a bar, after some of the Pico employees had had a few drinks. Soon after that fateful night, the company had its engineers working on the project, and over a three-year period, they fine-tuned the technology to the point to where it worked.

Over time, the technology was developed and many different X-10 products were introduced to the market. From basic controllers and modules, the technology has grown to include remote controls that use both infrared and radio signals, as well as computer control software. Now you can control nearly any type of electronic device using X-10 technology.

Pico Electronics struck gold with X-10 and ended up changing its name to—you guessed it—X-10, and built a worldwide business from there. Dave Rye, one of the original developers of X-10 technology, claims that more than 100 million X-10 units are installed around the world. The company had its patents run out on X-10 in the late 1990s, which opened the door for other people to manufacture the technology without paying a royalty to X-10.

Still, X-10, both the technology and the company, is continuing to enjoy the success of an idea hatched by a few engineers in the mid-1970s in a bar in Scotland. To read more about the history behind X-10, visit www.hometoys.com. To learn more about X-10 the company, visit www.X10.com.

Although other home automation technologies exist besides X-10, X-10 is by far the dominant automation technology today. Later in this chapter, we will take a look at some of these other technologies, but first let's examine how X-10 works. This should give you a good start on your way to building a smart home.

How X-10 Works

As you know by now, X-10 uses a home's existing power wiring to send signals to the lights or appliances you want to control. To enable the use of your power wiring for automation signaling, you need to employ two basic types of devices: receivers and controllers.

> **NOTE**
>
> A *receiver* in an X-10 network is any component that receives a control command from an X-10 controller. Receivers are also called modules. They can be simple plug-in modules for an appliance, such as a light switch that can turn a light on at a specific time.

> **NOTE**
>
> A *controller* in an X-10 network is a component that sends commands to a receiver to control a device. Some controllers can double as receivers as well.

The diagram in Figure 21.1 will give you an idea of how a basic X-10 network works.

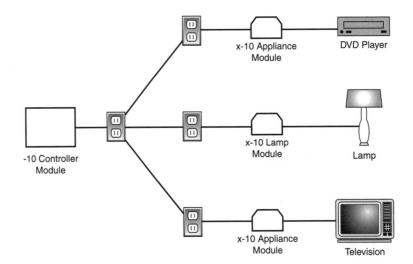

FIGURE 21.1

A basic X-10 network.

Smart Home: Home Automation Networks

CHAPTER 21

355

21

SMART HOME:
HOME AUTOMATION
NETWORKS

X-10 Signaling Basics

Now that you know about X-10 receivers and controllers, we will examine the signals these components send one another to control lights and appliances around your house. X-10 signaling and the X-10 addressing scheme are important topics for you to understand in getting up to speed on X-10 networks.

X-10 signals consist of a few variations, ranging from basic on/off or dim for certain lamp modules and light switches, to open/close for such home systems such as garage door openers. The complexity of the commands varies widely, including the capability to control gradations in performance of a device, such as increasing or decreasing the speed of a ceiling fan or controlling your heating or air conditioning to a certain temperature.

X-10 receivers and controllers also vary in whether they are one- or two-way signal components. Historically, X-10 receivers have been able only to receive signals, and controllers have been able only to send signals. In the past five years, new X-10 products have been developed that are able to both send and receive signals. This allows receivers to send a signal to a controller to let the controller know that it has performed the desired function.

Another important thing to understand about X-10 networks is the addressing scheme. Each module or controller houses two address codes, one being a house code, the other a unit code. There are a total of 16 house codes, identified with the letters A through P, and there are 16 unit codes, numbered 1 through 16. Each receiver unit gets its own address so that the controller can reach a particular device on an X-10 network. A lamp module/receiver plugged into a light in the living room might be coded A-3, so that from a controller you can tell device A-3 to shut off or turn on.

Now that you have an idea of the basics of how an X-10 network works, let's look a little more in-depth at the types of receivers and controllers.

The World of X-10 Receivers

Many kinds of receivers are available for X-10 networks. You can use a basic lamp module that does simple on/off commands, or more advanced receivers that enable devices to turn on when they detect a motion nearby or the sun rising or setting. Basically, the world of X-10 receivers is a big one. You can buy different receivers (as well as controllers) on a build-as-you-go basis, allowing your X-10 network to grow as fast (or as slowly) as you like.

Table 21.1 gives a sample of various receivers for an X-10 network. They differ by commands and types of devices that they control.

TABLE 21.1 Receivers for an X-10 Network

Receiver	Commands	Applications
Lamp module	On/Off/Dim	For lamps only; can dim and brighten
Appliance module	On/Off	For many electric appliances such as radios, TVs, hot tubs
Wall switch	On/Off/Dim	To replace existing switches; goes into wall and is a more subtle form of controlling lighting than modules
Universal module	Open/Close	For controlling garage doors, sprinklers, and other home systems

Receivers, because they vary in what type of device is controlled, also vary with respect to voltage. Because appliances can be either 110 volt or 220 volt—the bigger appliances, such as washers and heating/air conditioners, will generally be 220-volt appliances—you need to determine which device you want to control and choose the appropriate receiver.

Some receivers are also called switches. These allow you to replace an existing wall switch to control a light either directly by turning it on/off or indirectly through X-10 commands. In fact, some switches can be considered both a receiver device and a controller device, depending on whether you are using a three-way switch. A three-way switch controls more than one light, and can communicate with other three-way switches to share information on whether a particular light is turned on.

The World of X-10 Controllers

Controllers are what tell the X-10 receivers and switches to do what they do. Controllers, like receivers, come in all shapes and levels of functionality. From basic key-chain remotes to computer-software controllers to intelligent touch pads that allow you to control receivers all around your home, the world of controllers is as varied as that of receivers.

In addition to varying in the types of commands they can give, controllers also vary widely in the way the user can interface with them. There are very basic controllers that have on/off switches, such as key chains, and then there are more advanced controllers that allow devices to be controlled through a touch panel or even by voice control. There are also sensor controllers that allow devices to be automated by a particular environmental stimuli, such as motion or the amount of light in a given area.

Table 21.2 lists the types of controllers, with varying commands and user interfaces.

TABLE 21.2   Controllers for an X-10 Network

Controller	Interfaces/Applications
Basic plug-in controllers	Are basic on-off controllers that usually have a push-button interface.
Programmable controllers	Allow you to choose times and routines for lights and appliances to go on/off.
Wireless controllers	Can be anything from programmable remote controls to basic key chains that communicate via infrared or radio signals.
Telephone controllers	Allow you to control devices through voice commands. They plug into the X-10 network and allow you to control through any touch-tone dial pad.
PC controllers	Consist of software and a PC interface unit that combine to allow you to control any device, as well as to monitor the status of the device, such as whether it's on or off.
Voice controllers	Allow you to command devices through the home using voice commands. The software uses a microphone and its speech-recognition capability to understand commands and send appropriate signals to a receiver.
Sensor controllers	Can sense changes in environment, such as temperature or light changes, and sense whether a door or window is open or closed for security, as well sense motion.

The world of X-10 receivers, switches, and controllers seems practically endless. Because the technology has existed for so long and has so many users (5 million homes in the U.S. alone use some form of X-10 product), the technology has continued to advance. Installing a basic X-10 network does not cost much money and can be done with very little prior knowledge of home automation. We will show you how to get started using an X-10 network, but first let's take a look at other home automation technologies.

Other Home Automation Technologies

The world of home automation, although dominated by X-10 because of its long-standing presence and affordability, is not limited to just this one technology. In fact, several other technologies exist today, some of them more robust or just as affordable as X-10. Although most of these technologies are not widely adopted in the home, it helps to take a quick look at them in case you want to explore the different technologies in the home automation universe a little further.

> **CAUTION**
>
> The world of home automation, like that of home networking in general, is full of different standards, some that have found success, others that have not. Other than X-10, there is no real widely used home automation technology today. This situation will likely change, but before you go and purchase another home automation system that does not use X-10 technology, be aware that at least for the next few years these technologies may not be widely available.

The following sections explore different home automation technologies, some of which use an existing standard and some of which are proprietary.

> **NOTE**
>
> *Proprietary systems* are those which use a technology that is specifically supported by one company, but is not used widely in other systems by other companies.

Lonworks

Lonworks is a technology that was developed and is supported primarily by a company called Echelon. The technology can enable networks of non-PC devices to communicate over powerline, phoneline, or wireless links. Lonworks has been big for years in the industrial and business market, enabling communication with, believe it or not, things such as assembly-line machines or soda vending machines.

Although Lonworks does not exist in many home automation networks today, many companies have begun to develop Lonworks products that might someday be used in a home automation and control network. Merloni, an Italian manufacturer of appliances such as washing machines and dishwashers, has begun to incorporate Lonworks technology into its products, to allow for control from a centralized controller in the home or even by your utility company to enable your machine to run at off-peak times.

You will not likely be able to find any home automation equipment today at a store based on Lonworks technology, but it is certainly worth watching for potential products in future years.

Simple Control Protocol

Simple Control Protocol, or SCP, is a newer automation technology developed by Microsoft. SCP is planned to become a technology that allows control of non-PC devices, such as lighting, home systems, and appliances. Because this technology has been developed by Microsoft, there is a good chance that it will have some traction in the market in the future.

Xanboo

Xanboo is a company that has developed a proprietary technology to control different devices around your home using the Internet. Its products are available today and are similar in cost to X-10 products. The Xanboo system requires a monthly subscription to access and manage your account over the Internet. We will look at installing a Xanboo system later in the chapter.

Getting Started with Home Automation

Installing a home automation network in your home can be done with very little cost or knowledge. X-10 provides a cheap and widely available platform on which you can build a small automation network, and one that allows you to grow your system as your comfort and budget allow. Other technologies, such as that from Xanboo, allow you to install a home automation and control network in your home that allows for advanced monitoring of your home anywhere in your home or outside your home using the Internet.

We will look at buying and installing a home automation network using X-10. We will also take a look at a Xanboo network, for those who want to try one of the newer technologies that allows you to tie your broadband and PC home network together with your home automation network.

Buying an X-10 Network

One of the best ways to get started with X-10 is to purchase a kit that includes all the components necessary to build a basic home automation network. For around $50, you can buy a kit from X-10 that includes a lamp module, an appliance module, a wireless transceiver that acts as both a controller and a receiver, a wireless remote controller, and a PC interface to allow for control of your automation network using a home PC. The name of the X-10 starter kit with these components is called ActiveHome, and it is very popular. You can check out www.x10.com for this kit, as well as other kits and standalone products.

Table 21.3 lists some Web sites where you can go and purchase X-10 and other home automation equipment.

TABLE 21.3 Home Automation Web Sites

Web Site	Description
www.smarthome.com	One of the biggest home automation sites around
www.homecontrols.com	Lots and lots of home automation gear
www.x10.com	The company's Web site and probably the cheapest place for X-10 equipment
www.radioshack.com	The first retailer of X-10 still has a great selection
www.smarthome.ru	Russian home automation Web site!
www.bass-home.com	Good online catalog and good info about home automation

Next, we'll take a look at installing the ActiveHome starter kit. In particular, you'll want to see how to install the ActiveHome software that allows you to control your X-10 network from your PC.

Installing a Basic X-10 Network

Before we look at getting your basic X-10 network up and running, let's quickly review some particulars about using home powerlines that you should know before you install your network. Because AC powerlines in the home were not originally designed for communications purposes, there are specific characteristics you need to be mindful of that can have a direct impact on your home automation network.

The following sections list tips that are good to know before you begin your X-10 installation.

Split Phases

The powerline running into your home consists of a 220-volt powerline that is most likely split in two. This means that most devices getting power around your home are going off of one of the two 110-volt power phases. Because of this split, it is often difficult for X-10 modules and controllers to communicate if they are not on the same phase. To remedy this problem, you can have an electrician install a coupler that connects the two phases in your breaker box. If you do not install a coupler, the only downside is that each X-10 component might not be able to communicate directly with the others, and you will need to test each outlet individually.

Surge Protectors

Using a surge protector to protect your PC or other sensitive electronic equipment from a dramatic increase in electricity in your home—such as that from a lightning strike—makes good sense. But these same surge protectors can interfere with the operation of X-10 equipment. To get around this, you can use X-10 compatible surge protectors available on one of the X-10

Web sites listed in Table 21.3, or you can have an electrician install a surge suppressor that enables surge protection for the whole household.

Electrical Noise

One of the widely recognized characteristics about electrical wiring as a communications medium is that it is noisy. This doesn't mean that you will hear the hiss and crackle of electricity. Instead, it means that data packets being sent over the wiring can get lost or collide with noise on the wire, or your X-10 equipment can confuse normal electrical traffic with that of an X-10 signal and execute a command such as turning on your lights (this is a bummer in the middle of the night). There's not much you can do about this other than prevent electrical noise coming from outside your home by having an electrician install a noise block in your breaker box.

Plugging It In

With an ActiveHome kit, the first thing you will want to install is the transceiver module, which acts as both a controller and a receiver. It can receive commands from the wireless keychain remote and then send signals to the lamp module to turn a light on or off. The transceiver module, as well as all modules on the X-10 network, needs to have its X-10 address assigned. With the ActiveHome kit, you will go with the first available address for the transceiver module, A-1. This is house code A and unit code 1. To set an address on a module, you simply tune the address dials on the module itself.

The lamp module will also need to have its X-10 address fixed to communicate with the transceiver module. Figure 21.2 shows a lamp module and the dials for both the house code and the unit code. With the lamp module, you will likely want to set the address to A-2.

FIGURE 21.2
House and unit codes on an X-10 module.

After you set the address on your transceiver and lamp module, you simply plug each into an electrical socket near the device you want to control. You will want to have the transceiver unit somewhat centrally located in the home, because it will be controlling the other modules, such as the lamp module.

If the modules cannot communicate after they are installed, there is a chance that the outlets you've chosen are on different phases, meaning that they cannot communicate, unless an electrician has installed a phase coupler in your breaker box. You can also try to move your controller or module to a different outlet.

After both the transceiver and the lamp module are installed, you will want to see whether you can make the lamp and the device plugged into the transceiver module (which can be a light or an appliance such as a radio or coffee pot) work by using your wireless key-chain remote. This remote is a small control unit that can talk to your transceiver module from a distance of 75 feet.

The key-chain remote looks as shown in Figure 21.3. The remote can control either the device plugged into the transceiver or the lamp module.

Figure 21.3
A wireless key-chain remote.

As with the other modules, with the key-chain remote, you will first need to set the house and unit code. The choices of house code include the normal A through O, and unit codes are limited to a selection of two ranges: 1–2 and 5–6. Choose 1–2 and house code A and then put in the batteries. You should then be able to control the two devices plugged into the transceiver and the lamp module.

Using Active Home Software to Control an X-10 Network

One of the neat things about the ActiveHome kit is that it includes software to control your home automation network. You can turn devices on or off through the software and the PC interface unit, as well as set macros that can control the different modules at whatever predetermined schedule you decide.

> **Note**
>
> *Macros* are specified routines that you set to run on your X-10 system. You can create macros in your ActiveHome software to set a certain time for any receiver-connected device to go on or off.

Smart Home: Home Automation Networks

CHAPTER 21

363

21

SMART HOME:
HOME AUTOMATION
NETWORKS

To use your ActiveHome software, you must first install the PC interface unit included in your ActiveHome kit. This involves plugging the PC interface unit into the wall and connecting your PC to the interface unit with an interface cable that connects into your PC's serial port. The serial port on your PC is one of the basic ports included in each PC.

The ActiveHome software is very easy to install. The instructions for installation will be included with your ActiveHome kit. After you install the software from the CD-ROM and have your PC interface unit hooked up, you will be able to send commands to the modules on the X-10 network. The ActiveHome software will be able to control not only the transceiver and the lamp module, but also the appliance module and other X-10 components that you purchase. In fact, you can control hundreds of modules (now that's George Jetson!) through your software.

As you can see in Figure 21.4, a nice graphical user interface allows you to control your X-10 network by simply clicking on or off, as well as by creating macros. The ActiveHome software also can divide your modules by the area of the home they are in, as you can see by the tabs located at the bottom of the screen.

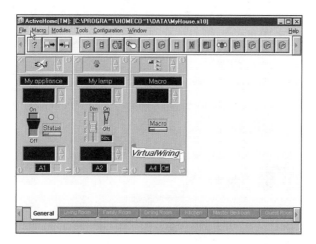

FIGURE 21.4
ActiveHome software for an X-10 network.

The ActiveHome software, and the kit it comes with, are just one way to get started with X-10. After you start to experiment with the technology and see how X-10 can both be quite fun and make your life more convenient, don't be surprised if you start wanting to add new modules and controllers into your X-10 network.

A Look at a Xanboo Control Network

Although X-10 is a great way to get started in home automation, other technologies, such as that by Xanboo, offer new ways to automate and control your home. As described earlier, Xanboo offers a technology that allows you to control your home through the Internet, using a browser to do things such as monitor your home's temperature, check pictures through Web-cams, and notify you if your basement has flooded. We'll take a quick look at how a Xanboo network works.

A Xanboo network operates using a system controller that attaches to a PC using a standard USB connection. This controller then acts as the centralized point of contact for the different Xanboo sensors that communicate with the controller using wireless communications. An example would be a temperature sensor that you locate in your small greenhouse in the back of the house, communicating to your controller and then to you from anywhere you desire over the Internet. Figure 21.5 shows how this Xanboo network would work.

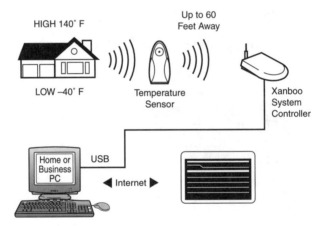

FIGURE 21.5

A Xanboo control network.

As you can see, control of your Xanboo network is done through a standard Web browser. This means that if you are on a trip, and you want to take certain actions—check a live camera to see what is happening outside your front window, check whether a door or window has been opened, check the temperature in a room, check the moisture in a room—you simply get on a PC and go to your Web account.

The downside to using the Xanboo network is that you do need to use a PC as part of your network. This means that if you are on a limited budget or do not have a PC to spare, for example, for a vacant home you want to monitor, you will not be able to use Xanboo.

Smart Home: Home Automation Networks

CHAPTER 21

365

21

SMART HOME:
HOME AUTOMATION
NETWORKS

You also need to subscribe to the company's monthly Web service, which starts at $10 a month for monitoring sensor events as well as storage of video-captured events. Overall, you can begin with a Xanboo network for about $150, which is the cost of the starter kit, and includes the centralized system controller and a motion-sensor camera. Additional sensors can be purchased for about $20 each.

Wrap It Up

The world of home automation is an exciting one. From the established technology of X-10 to newer technologies such as Xanboo's Web-based control system, you can begin to experiment with home automation for a small investment and over time build your network as you see fit.

X-10 is the most established and widely used home automation technology by a large margin. The technology was developed in the mid-1970s and since then has developed a huge following, being adopted in five million U.S. homes.

X-10 automation networks use a few basic components:

- *Controllers*—These components send commands to the devices you want to automate.
- *Receivers*—These components plug into whatever devices you want to control; they receive commands from the controllers.

You can automate nearly anything electrical using X-10, from something as basic as a lamp or coffeepot, to your heating or cooling system. You can also create routines called macros to make your connected devices go on or off according to a predetermined routine.

You can use your PC to control an X-10 network. X-10's ActiveHome software allows you to monitor your X-10 network, control devices, and create macros.

Other home automation technologies are also available. From newer ones such as Xanboo to technologies such as LonWorks that have been in use for some time in industrial settings, you can experiment and see whether some of these technologies are right for you in creating your "smart home."

The Coming Digital Domicile

IN THIS CHAPTER

Move Over, George Jetson

Now that you've read most of this book, you probably know a fair bit about home networking. If you're like me, you're amazed at the technologies that have emerged over the past few years to allow you to communicate more easily within and outside your home. But I truly believe that, as someone famous once said, "We ain't seen nothin' yet."

To realize how quickly things change, it's instructive to look at how far we've come in a short time. Just take a quick look at how things have changed in the past few decades:

- Just 35 years ago, no one owned a personal computer. Today, nearly 60% of homes in the U.S. have a PC.
- Twenty years ago, cell phones had just emerged and were owned only by the wealthy. Today, it seems practically everyone is walking around with one of those things on their hip.
- In the early 1980s, a 1200 baud modem was considered a pretty fast communication tool. Today's DSL lines and cable modem lines communicate at thousands of times this speed.
- In 1990, Internet usage was restricted to mostly educational and research users. Today, more than half of U.S. households have Internet access, and usage continues to grow at breathtaking speed.

The Next 10 Years

One advantage of being involved in this industry and getting to talk to a lot of companies is that I get a good picture of where all this technology is going. The advances in the electronic chips that are at the center of all these devices continue to accelerate, and the intelligence that ordinary products in our homes will have in the future is mind-boggling.

And don't think that these advances will come 50 or even 20 years from now. Things are changing quickly, and I expect that within the next 10 years we will all see major changes in our lifestyles due to new networking and communications technologies coming into our homes.

What are some of the biggest changes I expect over the next 10 years? The following sections cover just a few.

Your Kitchen Will Talk to You and Your Grocer

Many companies today, such as Whirlpool, Sunbeam, and GE, are concentrating on building networked appliances such as refrigerators, dishwashers, and microwave ovens. Why in the world, you ask, would you ever want to do that?

Well, believe it or not, there are real benefits to having this technology, including these:

- You will be able to monitor your usage and inventory of products, and when you need a certain product in your weekly delivery of groceries, you'll simply use the built-in scanner in your refrigerator to scan in that product.

- With rising energy costs, there are considerable energy savings to be had by using your dishwasher and other devices at certain times of the day. With a networked device, your dishwasher, or other device, could get a signal to let it know when is the most energy-efficient time to wash a load.

- You might be at work and need to preheat your oven for dinner tonight. With your networked oven, you can access it over the Internet and turn it on so that it's ready to go when you get home.

Your Car Will Talk to You and Your Home

Soon, your car will become part of your networked home. Communication technology will be available to enable your car to communicate with both a PDA and your PC through some access point or bridge device. This way, you can load any music you might want onto your personal car music server, and also have those driving directions you got off the Web stored on your car PC. Your car will also have connections to the Internet allowing you to get Internet radio, maps, and other information you may want or need.

Your Web Connection Will Become the All-in-One Communication and Entertainment Link

Within 10 years, some (not all, but quite a bit) of your communication and entertainment will be channeled through a high-speed Internet link. Much of your entertainment, such as audio, gaming, and even some video links, will be accessed at any time over the Internet, and your home network will be the platform for this content to be distributed through the home.

Think about it: Your phone company is trying to become your cable TV and Internet company. Your cable company is trying to become your phone company. And they are all trying to do it over one line such as the copper pair that traditional voice communication runs over, or the coaxial cable that your cable TV signal travels on. With the advances in communications and compression technologies, it is not inconceivable to think that more and more you will see convergence of different communications technologies coming into and out of your home.

Someday, Everything Will Be Networked

Today, if you have a home network, chances are that it's for computers. For those geeks out there, you might have some home automation equipment installed. In the future, everything will be networked. Every major manufacturer of consumer electronics, appliances, and any other electronic home system, is looking at how to "network enable" their product. Robert Metcalfe, the inventor of Ethernet and founder of 3Com, once said that the value of a network grows with the square of the number of its users. What does this mean? It means things are much more valuable if they can talk to each other, all those things in your home included. And someday, they will.

Technologies to Watch

If you've read this book from beginning to end (if you haven't, go back, you cheater!), you've heard me talk about many of the technologies that are, or will be, available for the home. Following is a list of technologies, some of which I've already mentioned, that I think are important to watch in the coming years as part of the networked home.

Wireless

If you've tried wireless networking, you'll find that the convenience of being able to communicate across your home without stringing any cable really can't be beat. The wireless networking world is full of emerging technologies, including higher-speed standards such as 802.11a and technologies that will be embedded in everyday devices such as Bluetooth. I expect the world of wireless networking to continue to be one of the most interesting over the coming years and that someday, nearly everyone will have some form of wireless networking technology at their fingertips.

High-Speed Internet Access: New and Faster Ways to Get Connected

Companies have poured billions of dollars into bringing you high-speed Internet connections. Technologies such as DSL and cable modems are always improving, and other technologies are always being advanced as a better way to do things. Today, many companies are looking at using Ethernet technology not only as a way to communicate in the home, but also as a way to communicate over the Internet. Don't be surprised one day if your PC is equipped with a gigabit Ethernet network interface card that is your direct connection to the Internet. Also, keep an eye on your power company, especially if you live in Europe, to see whether it will one day begin to offer you Internet access over your powerline.

Interactive TV and More

For a long time, interactive TV has been a dream of executives in Hollywood and at the top of the list of many companies trying to sell you goods or services.

Think about it: Imagine watching TV and seeing your favorite actor stroll onto the set with a nice jacket or a cool new gadget that you feel you must have. Although some of you might simply resist the temptation (my wife is not one of these people), others might want to click on their TV monitor through a mouse or a pointer device and be able to get information about the product. Now that's an advertiser's dream!

And it isn't all going to be advertising. Interactive TV can be used to do instant polling of audiences or to communicate with others with similar interests (imagine: "Wow, I can't believe you like to watch 300-pound wrestlers in G-strings pound each other into oblivion as much as I do! Want to go on a date?").

Home Servers Will Be Everywhere

Only the most advanced home network users today have a home server, a PC that sits somewhere and controls their home network. In the future, you will likely see quite a few homes with some form of home server, and it likely will not be PCs doing the dirty work. A home server can really be any device that has a lot of storage, such as cable set-top box or a video player such as a DVD with a hard drive (or a personal video recorder from a company such as TiVo). In fact, in the future, it is likely you will have more than one device that acts as a storage device, as well as handles communication among devices in the home.

Above All, Enjoy Yourself

One problem most people who are involved in the technology industry have (whether they'll admit it or not) is that we sometimes get carried away with all the neat gadgets and gizmos we see and hear about everyday. We spout off about how everyone needs one of these things to make their life better, often without serious regard for whether these devices are really serving a purpose, delivering a real benefit.

I am a believer that home networks can and do deliver real benefits to anyone who has one. I also believe that often, however, a home network might just be nothing more than a way to play a game or send a file from one PC to the other—real benefits, but not exactly saving lives.

What a home network means to you should be exactly what you want it to, meaning you should tailor the home network to deliver what it is you feel will make your life better. We've discussed a lot of neat, new technologies in this book, and many of these technologies will make a big difference in people's lives in coming years. However, you should never buy technology just for technology's sake; you should focus on what is right for you. If that is a simple two-PC Ethernet network to share files, then do it. If you want to tie together multiple PCs, home systems, and your entertainment center into one big smart home network, then I think this book is a great way to learn how to do so.

Above all, enjoy your home network and let me know how it's going. If you have any feedback or questions, send it to me at homenetmike@yahoo.com.

Good luck and enjoy!

Appendixes

IN THIS PART

Table of Internet Resources on Home Networking

www.homenethelp.com—Good overall site with instructions on how to set up a home network.

www.hometoys.com—News and information site for home networking.

www.cnet.com—Technology information portal with good how-to's on home networking and other topics, and a price-comparison tool for networking gear.

www.threemacs.com—One of the most comprehensive sites for information on home networking for Macs.

www.practicallynetworked.com—Good overall resource for info on home networking, Internet security, and products for home networking.

www.howstuffworks.com—Wonderful site that explains technologies and other wonders of the world in a language everyone can understand.

www.homepcnetwork.com—Good general info about networking your home.

www.firewallguide.com—Great site to get info on home network security and to learn about basic home routers and gateways for Internet sharing.

www.sohointer.net—Good site to learn about small-office and home-office networking.

www.download.com—Excellent place to get free software, including personal firewall protection software for your home network.

Table of Internet Resources on Home Automation

www.automationfaq.com—A good place to learn about home automation.

www.homeautomationforum.com—A place to ask for and get answers regarding home automation.

www.homeautomationmag.com—A portal site for *Popular Home Automation* magazine and its related sites. A good place to spend some time if you plan on becoming a true home automation hobbyist.

www.x10.com—A company that sells all sorts of home automation equipment and is, after all, the company that started it all.

www.smarthome.com—A portal for all sorts of home networking and automation information, as well as a great place to go to purchase home automation gear.

www.beathome.com—A manufacturer of cool remote home automation and control products.

www.home-automation.org—A directory of tons of home automation sites.

www.caba.org—An association that promotes smart home and networking technology.

INDEX

SYMBOLS

A